Global
Competitiveness

THE AMERICAN ASSEMBLY was established by Dwight D. Eisenhower at Columbia University in 1950. Each year it holds at least two nonpartisan meetings which give rise to authoritative books that illuminate issues of United States policy.

An affiliate of Columbia, with offices at Barnard College, the Assembly is a national, educational institution incorporated in the state of New York.

The Assembly seeks to provide information, stimulate discussion, and evoke independent conclusions on matters of vital public interest.

CONTRIBUTORS

KRISTOPHER J. BROWN, International Services Institute

JOSEPH DUFFEY, University of Massachusetts

DOUGLAS A. FRASER, Wayne State University

A. BLANTON GODFREY, Juran Institute

MAREK P. HESSEL, Fordham University

PETER J. KOLESAR, Columbia University

RICHARD D. LAMM, University of Denver

ARTHUR LEVITT, JR., American Stock Exchange

MARTA MOONEY, Fordham University

DOROTHY I. RIDDLE, International Services Institute

MARTIN K. STARR, Columbia University

GORDON C. STEWART, American Stock Exchange

JAMES A. F. STONER, Fordham University

ARTHUR TAYLOR, Fordham University

LAURA D'ANDREA TYSON, University of California, Berkeley

JOHN E. ULLMANN, Hofstra University

CHARLES WANKEL, University of New Haven

B. J. WIDICK

MILAN ZELENY, Fordham University

THE AMERICAN ASSEMBLY
Columbia University

Global Competitiveness

Getting the U.S. Back on Track

MARTIN K. STARR
Editor

W·W·NORTON & COMPANY
New York   London

Published simultaneously in Canada by Penguin Books Canada Ltd.
2801 John Street, Markham, Ontario L3R 1B4.
Printed in the United States of America.

The text of this book is composed in Baskerville.
Composition and manufacturing by The Haddon Craftsmen, Inc.

First Edition

Library of Congress Cataloging-in-Publication Data

Global competitiveness: getting the U.S. back on track / Martin K.
    Starr, editor.
        p. cm.
    Bibliography: p.
    Includes index.
        1. Competition—United States. 2. Competition, International.
    3. Industrial management—United States. 4. Industry and state—
    United States.
    HD41.G58 1988
    338.6'048'0973—dc19   87-35047

ISBN 0-393-02566-7

ISBN 0-393-95770-5 PPK.

W. W. Norton & Company, Inc.
500 Fifth Avenue, New York, N. Y. 10110
W. W. Norton & Company Ltd.
37 Great Russell Street, London WC1B 3NU

1 2 3 4 5 6 7 8 9 0

Contents

Global
Competitiveness

Preface

The United States is "gambling recklessly with its destiny" unless it takes immediate steps to change its spending habits and increase its global competitiveness. Details on this and other "findings" are included in a report prepared by sixty-five leaders of business, labor, academia, and government who met under the auspices of The American Assembly, November 19–22, 1987. This book includes the background papers prepared for that November Assembly, as well as its hard-hitting, self-sacrificing report of specific recommendations for the government and the private sector.

The report sets the stage for this book. While the full report can be found as an appendix to this volume, let me set out some portions of its preamble here, because it expresses better than I can what this book is all about and why it was written:

America's economy is growing more slowly than it used to, more slowly than we need it to, and more slowly than our competitors' economies. We are consuming far more than we produce and earn—and we are having growing difficulty paying the bills. Our prosperity is threatened, as is our capacity to provide world leadership and to achieve a more just and competitive society.

The evidence is unmistakable. We have the largest budget deficit, trade deficit, and foreign debt in our history. Individual debt, corporate debt, and government debt are all perilously high, while our savings rate is among the lowest in the industrial world.

We cannot long continue on this path without profound consequences. Economically, we risk a continued slide of the dollar, higher real interest rates, accelerating inflation, still slower growth, and prolonged recession at home and abroad. Socially, we are staring at the possibility of even deeper domestic inequities than those we have allowed to fester in recent years. Insufficient attention to the problems of the growing American underclass will erode the capacity of the United States to be a more competitive international society. Politically, we may well suffer increased polarization and paralysis. Globally, as economic competition grows in importance relative to military confrontation, we face a possibly irreversible U.S. decline, with an attendant erosion of our ability to protect vital national interests. This would be accompanied by growing threats to Western values, influence, and prosperity, and to democratic interests throughout the world.

In short, we are gambling recklessly with our destiny. That we are not alone in this judgment is evidenced by the October 19th stock market crash, the ensuing turmoil in the world's financial markets, and the broad urging by world leaders that the United States put its house in order.

Because of these deeply troubling realities, the American Assembly examined the governmental, private sector, and individual and societal dimensions of America's declining competitiveness. We also examined the complex connections among these different sectors because of their importance in getting America back on track.

Our sense of urgency results from the fading opportunities to make the necessary changes before grave, perhaps irreparable, consequences are upon us. . . .

Building on the nation's formidable strengths, this Assembly report offers a vision of what we must do, including concrete first steps to control an uncertain future and move the United States toward sustained competitiveness at home and abroad.

By this we mean that the average annual growth of the U.S. economy and of each American's standard of living must be both as fast as practical and at least as rapid as the other major industrial economies. Only then can we hope to achieve our economic, political, social, and geopolitical aims.

Our economic troubles, it should be emphasized, were primarily made in America, and the solutions must primarily be made in America as well. We should begin by enhancing the will and capacity of individuals and businesses to compete more successfully, bringing our trade and current account back into balance, and restoring our economic vitality. But the need to accomplish the foregoing does not stop at individual firms and other institutions or at our own borders. International cooperation to achieve faster and more balanced world trade and growth are also essential to improve the prospects for increasing our global competitiveness as well as producing potential gains for all nations.

The entire project, including the November Assembly, its report, and this book, was funded by The Ford Foundation, the Xerox Foundation, and AT&T. We are grateful for their support. The opinions expressed in this volume are those of the individual authors and not necessarily those of the sponsors nor of The American Assembly, which takes no position on the issues it presents for public discussion.

Daniel A. Sharp
President
The American Assembly

Introduction

MARTIN K. STARR

The purpose of this volume is to bring together the main ideas relating to the U.S. achievement of global competitiveness. These ideas fit into three categories.

First, there is the effectiveness of the national economic system. This involves the use of macroeconomic controls for achieving competitiveness. A partial list of issues includes trade and budget deficits, tariffs and quotas, currency exchange rates, saving and consumption rates, tax rules for both domestic and international activities, and antitrust laws.

Second, there is industrial competitiveness, which involves microeconomic firm and union policies. A partial list of issues includes quality and costs of production, innovation, market share, union and management negotiations, supplier relations, export sales, and import content.

Third, there is societal competitiveness, which includes such

It is with total gratitude that Judith L. Dumas is acknowledged. As program manager of the American Assembly meeting on competitiveness, she was faced with a constant overload of truly significant matters, which she handled with consistent professionalism and grace.

factors as family structure, education, health care, litigation, savings and consumption, personal freedoms, crime, and individual happiness.

The book has been designed to facilitate change by adhering to a model developed by David B. Gleicher, which requires that three factors be as large as possible. Change is impossible if any one of the three factors is zero. The three factors are:

• Dissatisfaction with the present situation
• Vision of what the future can become
• Practical first steps to achieve the vision

This book has contributions from leaders and innovators concerning dissatisfaction, vision, and practical first steps to enhance competitiveness. The chapters are intended to raise the levels of intensity of each component. For example, great dissatisfaction is required to overwhelm resistance to change.

How dissatisfied are we? Americans have an optimistic attitude of a cup half-filled. The rest of the world tends to perceive a cup half-empty. Governor Richard D. Lamm, in his chapter entitled "Crisis: The Uncompetitive Society," raises our individual dissatisfaction by pointing to the numerous social issues that absorb the energies of society in a nonproductive fashion. He writes, "The United States is not structured for long-term success. It is structured for long-term decline. Our economy, our major institutions, and perhaps even our political system will not keep this country strong without major reform."

Professor John Ullmann and I highlight dissatisfaction at the industrial level in our chapter, entitled "The Myth of U.S. Industrial Supremacy." The performance of foreign competitors in the 1980s surpasses the highest standards that existed in the earlier decades when the United States was the world leader. At the same time, the abilities of the United States declined with respect to product and process innovation, commercial application, engineering education, the age of equipment, overreliance on economies of scale, and military preemption of both capital and technical talent. A comparison with Great Britain provides further insight.

Visions of what the future can be like are introduced by

Chancellor Joseph Duffey in his chapter, "United States Competitiveness: Looking Back and Looking Ahead." He emphasizes the "social dimension" of productivity and that "rebuilding the U.S. economy will require a new sense of collaboration and trust among business, labor, and government." He points out that "the existence of a dependable set of rules facilitated the growth of the world economy as a whole." A vision of future prosperity must include the fact that "the economies of the free world have become increasingly interconnected." We must recognize that the United States has shifted "from a manufacturing- to a service-based economy," and we must heed the importance of stability.

Professor Laura D'Andrea Tyson supplies vision by providing insight into the use of rational government policies. In her chapter, "Competitiveness: An Analysis of the Problem and a Perspective on Future Policy," she examines government policy with respect to the technologies of the manufacturing sector, R&D spending, and education to generate commercial innovations. One of her major points is that "the United States must fashion a new set of economic policies if it is to retain its position as a major economic power, perhaps no longer ahead of the pack as it was earlier, but as first among equals." Major sections of her chapter are devoted to "creating advantage by macroeconomic policy" and "creating advantage at the microeconomic level."

Professors Marek Hessel, Marta Mooney, and Milan Zeleny have pioneered the development of new materials for M.B.A. education. The vision that they propose in their chapter, "Integrated Process Management: A Management Technology for the New Competitive Era," is of a revision of the traditional management model. It emphasizes the importance of microeconomic changes at the firm level. The authors state:

We view the erosion of U.S. competitiveness to be above all a problem of management. Problems of management require managerial solutions. Traditional remedies, such as trade protectionism, tax incentives, and governmental regulation, are inadequate and misplaced tools; they simply will not do. We submit that the problem stems from the inability of traditional management systems . . . to keep pace and fit with the new competitive environment it helped to create. The system has lost proper coupling with its own niche; it has become obsolete.

The propositions of Dr. W. Edwards Deming are very important with respect to integrated process management.

The concluding chapter in the vision section was written by Douglas A. Fraser and B. J. Widick. It provides critically important vision concerning the relations of union and management to the achievement of global competitiveness. Their chapter is entitled "Challenges of Competitiveness: A Labor View." They state:

At long last, the high cost of uncompetitive U.S. business practices has come into question. Among them are excessive management compensation, the negative impact of authoritarian managements hostile to labor, short-term horizons that exclude long-range strategies, and excessive preoccupation with mergers and acquisitions.

This chapter, which states the need for a managed trade policy, is related in many ways to Dr. Tyson's chapter.

The final section of the book is dedicated to practical first steps for achieving the visions and removing the elements of dissatisfaction. After reading the chapter by Professor James A. F. Stoner, Dean Arthur R. Taylor, and Professor Charles B. Wankel, we should ask: who else, beyond the individuals already named in the paper, can take what specific actions to increase the speed at which American companies and managers move toward world class management practices—such as those described in the Hessel, Mooney, and Zeleny chapter? Empowering is the major focus of this chapter. Leadership is the complex issue.

Dr. A. Blanton Godfrey and Professor Peter J. Kolesar have written the chapter entitled "Role of Quality in Achieving World Class Competitiveness." They deal with quality as it is created on the plant floor. To those who deal with global aspects of interactive macroeconomic systems, the plant floor may seem mundane and too far down in the hierarchy of what counts. But by both analysis and empiricism, this is not the case. The problem solution is as much from the bottom up as it is from the top down. As the authors state, "The failure of American competitiveness is largely a failure to manage for quality. . . . The only long- and short-term remedy for the United States is to recapture quality dominance or at least quality parity in key industries."

Dorothy I. Riddle and Kristopher J. Brown have written their chapter, "From Complacency to Strategy: Retaining World Class Competitiveness in Services," to provide insight about the dominant and growing portion of GNP derived from the service sector. The authors define services in the broadest terms and develop perspectives about the role of services in the economy. Their section on "complacency as the root cause of diminished U.S. services competitiveness" explains how "many U.S. industry leaders and policy makers have assumed rather arrogantly that we will always be 'the leader.' " Further, they state:

. . . unless the United States acts immediately to reverse complacent attitudes and the domestic neglect of proper incentives for services quality in the face of foreign competition, the United States will lose its competitive position to countries such as the Republic of Ireland, Japan, and Sweden, which are implementing programs to promote their service industries.

Arthur Levitt, Jr., and Gordon C. Stewart provide important empirical information in their chapter entitled "Can American Business Compete?—A Perspective from Midrange Growth Companies." This study of globally successful American Stock Exchange companies and American Business Conference firms sheds important light on what practical first steps growing midsize firms have taken. The authors state:

Before abandoning the competitive field totally to macroeconomics, . . . it is worth considering that many businesses are actually competing very well right now, regardless of foreign trade barriers. Despite the real and exaggerated problems, there are U.S. companies that have been winners in foreign as well as domestic markets for some time. A substantial number of them come from what might be called the 'midrange growth sector' of the American economy.

While this volume represents an attempt to cover the major aspects of this complex subject, it probably is not possible to cover all aspects or all points of view. The topics have been selected to provide background for examining the current U.S. condition in the global community and to stimulate informed discussion of the issues involved in carving out a competitive future for Americans.

1

Crisis: The Uncompetitive Society

RICHARD D. LAMM

L et me start off with a parable. A Navy ship was on the high seas and all of a sudden a little blip showed up on the radar screen. The admiral told the ensign, "Tell that ship to change its course fifteen degrees." The word came back on the radio, "You change your course fifteen degrees." The admiral said, "Tell that ship that we're the U.S. Navy and to change its course fifteen degrees." The word came back on the radio, "You change your course fifteen degrees." The admiral himself got on the radio and said, "I am an admiral in the U.S. Navy—change your course fifteen degrees." The word came back, "You change your course fifteen degrees—I am a lighthouse."

RICHARD D. LAMM was governor of Colorado from 1975 to 1987 and a member of the Colorado House of Representatives from 1966 to 1974. He is currently with the law firm O'Connor and Hannan in Denver and holds the position of university professor at the University of Denver. Governor Lamm, who has also held an academic appointment at the University of Colorado at Denver, is the author or coauthor of several books and articles dealing with challenges facing contemporary America.

It's a perfect parable for my views. I believe the United States is heading for shoals. It can be corrected. We can change our course. But if we do not change our course, we are heading for shoals.

The United States is not structured for long-term success. It is structured for long-term decline. Our economy, our major institutions, and perhaps even our governmental system will not keep this country economically strong without major reform. Problems are outrunning solutions. The United States is not at the cutting edge of competition any more, and while the problem has many roots, to a large extent the United States is a victim of its own institutions.

Much has been written about America's industrial competitiveness. There is a consensus that we must dramatically revise many industrial practices to remain competitive in the international marketplace. With this proposition few disagree.

But that alone will not be enough. The United States must make all of its *institutions* more competitive or else lose its place in the new international marketplace. We need more than new industrial plants; we need new thinking about our basic institutions.

I should like to tell you a tale of two high school graduations. I graduated from high school in 1953. I inherited from my parents the richest, most productive economy that history had ever seen. In every year of my grandfather's life and every year of my father's business career, America ran up trade surpluses. We had 44 percent of the world's economic product when I graduated from high school, and our economy was eight times larger than Japan's. When I graduated from high school, "made in Japan" meant junk. We made 80 percent of the world's automobiles, 90 percent of the world's color television sets, and our students' educational testing scores were the highest in the world. I took the generational baton from my parents, then I looked over my shoulder, and there was no one in sight.

My son Scott graduated from high school in June of 1986. He inherited a country where my generation has run up a $2.5 trillion deficit, where the interest on the federal debt amounts to $458 million a day, and where in 1987 we had to take an amount equivalent to the total individual income tax collections from everybody living west of the Mississippi River just to pay the interest on the national debt. The 1987 federal deficit was greater than the gross national product (GNP) of 158 of the world's 167 countries.

In 1983 we ran up the largest trade deficit that history has ever seen, and in the following year we doubled it. Two weeks after my son graduated from high school we became a debtor nation with the lowest rate of productivity growth of any country in the industrialized world. Our productivity growth is 50 percent of the German rate, 33 percent of the French rate, and 25 percent of the Japanese rate. We have the lowest rate of savings of any country in the industrialized world, and our students are in the bottom third in all comparisons of international educational levels. We now make less than 30 percent of the world's automobiles and color television sets, and the percentage is falling fast. "Made in America" now often means poor quality. Hewlett-Packard recently found that its poorest Japanese supplier was six times more reliable than its best American supplier.

In short, I suggest to you, not only is it not a "morning in America," but it is high noon. History's kaleidoscope has turned—we were hardly noticing—but the pattern that has emerged is a whole new world. Our destiny is no longer manifest. The United States must learn what it takes to live in the new international marketplace. We must not only have competitive industries, but we must have competitive institutions. We must revitalize all American institutions to make them competitive.

No society can ever see itself objectively in the stream of time. There is an "uncertainty principle" in public policy just as in physics. Historian Arnold Toynbee describes it this way:

The position of our western society in our age cannot become known with any certainty of knowledge 'til the voyage comes to an end; and so long as the ship is under way the crew will have no notion whether she is going to flounder in mid-ocean through springing a leak or be sent to the bottom by colliding with another vessel, or run ashore on the rocks, or glide smoothly into a port of which the crew will never have heard before they wake up one fine day to find their ship at rest in dock there. A sailor at sea cannot tell for which, if for any, of these ends the ship is heading as he watches her making headway during the brief period of his own spell of duty. To plot out her course and to write up her log from start to finish is a task that can be performed only by observers who are able to wait until the voyage is over.

However, Toynbee warns that all great nations eventually fall and that the verdict of history is always *suicide*. He argues that the lesson of history is that all greatness is ephemeral. All great nations develop great problems.

Civilizations, unlike airplanes, do not have mechanical voices which warn "pull-up, pull-up" when they come close to crashing. They tend to go on their indolent ways until a crash occurs. Yet, I suggest, the warning lights of an economy in trouble and a civilization at risk are all around us. Consider for instance:

- The U.S. productivity rate, that key indicator to the ultimate wealth of a nation, has been gradually but continuously dropping. It averaged an anemic 0.6 percent in the 1970s and then fell to an average of .04 percent yearly during the 1980s.
- The United States at the end of 1981 was a creditor nation with a net balance of $140 billion, and at the end of 1986 we were the world's largest debtor nation with a net debt of $220 billion. That is a swing of $360 billion in five years. Manufactured goods, long one of America's great assets, went from an $18.1 billion surplus to a $150 billion deficit from 1980 to 1986.
- Our consumption per worker has grown during the 1980s at a rate three times that of our net output per worker. We are dramatically consuming more than we produce.
- Of the 77,251 U.S. patents issued in 1985, 43.8 percent went to applicants from other countries. In 1986 that number rose to 45 percent.
- A recent study concluded that the United States had

dropped from second to seventh place among the industrialized nations in the skill level of its workers.

- The average American family made *less* money in 1987, adjusted for inflation, than it made in 1969.
- President Ronald Reagan's Commission on Industrial Competitiveness found that over the twenty years from 1967 to 1987, seven out of ten technologically oriented industries lost ground in the world market. In 1967 only 8 percent of our industries faced foreign competition.

Americans are great at self-delusion. We continue to view these economic challenges as ephemeral footnotes in an otherwise uninterrupted story of prosperity. Alas, I suggest they are the title page to a whole new chapter of American history.

The purpose of this chapter is to argue that, while soluble, these problems are not going to be solved by "business as usual" remedies. The United States is faced with one of the major challenges of its history. We have not begun to appreciate the demands of living in an international marketplace. Our institutional and national memories are of a time when we had a continental economy and a growing pie, and we shall have to dramatically readjust our thinking to the new realities of a competitive international economy when our economic pie is not growing at historic rates. It is not growing nearly fast enough to satisfy all the expectations, debts, and demands that we have placed against it.

I believe that we cannot have a competitive economy unless we address the dysfunctional nature of some of our systems. The ultimate test of a civilization is to keep its institutions efficient and functional. Technology alone will not save a civilization whose basic problem-solving machinery has become dysfunctional. The ultimate test of a civilization is not the number of Nobel Prize winners it produces, nor how much gold it has stored in its treasury, nor even how many natural resources it has, but whether it is and can continue to be a wealth-producing country. Thus, to keep America great and its economy productive, I suggest we must reform and revitalize the following basic institutions.

Legal System

U.S. international competitiveness is affected by its litigiousness—the greatest on earth. Japan trains 1,000 engineers for every 100 lawyers; the United States trains 1,000 lawyers for every 100 engineers. Japan, with a population half that of the United States, produces about 50 percent more engineers each year than does the United States. Our nation boasts 700,-000 lawyers, 100,000 of them having graduated in the five years from 1981 to 1986. Every year the United States graduates as many lawyers as exist in *all* of Japan. Two-thirds of all the lawyers in the world practice in the United States. Our rate of litigation far exceeds that of any other industrial society. In 1966, 70,906 cases were filed in the federal courts, but by 1986 this had exploded to 254,828 cases. Lloyds of London estimates that 12 percent of its business is in the United States, yet 90 percent of its insurance claims are here.

This litigiousness adds to the cost of American goods as assuredly as does our inefficient management and inefficient labor. The U.S. Chamber of Commerce reports that because of the litigation crisis "business in every region of the country has experienced extreme hardship. Each day, we learn first-hand of another segment of our economy which has been affected by this crisis. There seems to be no boundaries."

Our U.S. airlines, for instance, are in a competitive race for international passengers. Price is a major competitive factor. However, our method of litigating airplane accidents is the most expensive, most complicated in the world. When Japan Airlines had a crash in the mountains of Honshu the matter was quickly settled. But U.S. airline accidents are long and expensive, and lawyers usually get far more money than the victims. U.S. airlines had to pay $600 million for passenger liability in the early 1980s. By 1987 it was over $1 billion and rising fast. This factor alone can make U.S. airlines uncompetitive. Lawyers and litigation have become a serious drag on U.S. competitiveness. We have, over many decades, slowly increased the risk of liability and decreased the defenses available until almost any loss has a good chance of being compensated, regardless of fault. We assume if there is a loss, someone must be found to pay.

This system dampens entrepreneurship. It clearly discourages American business from taking risks, and it retards innovation and imagination. Excessive litigiousness goes to the heart of a society's creative mainspring. A risk-free society will not maximize its creative potential. Litigation not only increases the inefficiency of the economy, it also drains off brains and talent desperately needed elsewhere. Forty percent of Rhodes Scholars go to law school. This deprives our society of considerable talent needed elsewhere. You cannot "sue" a nation to greatness.

While the United States is first in training lawyers, other important skills are suffering. The United States, for instance, now ranks eighteenth among countries graduating engineers with postdoctoral degrees.

Other societies run governments, resolve disputes between citizens, and dispense justice using far fewer lawyers. It is not only possible, it is imperative. If the United States is to regain its former international competitiveness it must do something about the "legaliflation" that is dramatically pulling down its international competitiveness.

Health Care

Health care is as much a component of American goods and products and services as are raw materials. The United States spends eight times more than many of its international competitors on health care. In 1950 the United States was spending approximately $1 billion a month for health care; in 1987 it spent well over $1 billion a day. Health care costs are growing at a rate over twice the rate of inflation. This is causing American goods to be at a competitive disadvantage. For example, Chrysler spends $317 per automobile on health care costs, a sum that far exceeds its Japanese competitors. Chrysler must produce 82,000 automobiles a year just to pay its health care costs.

What does all this spending get us? It does not buy us even that much health. American health outcomes are no better than other nations that spend only a fraction of what we spend. Many nations spend far less than we do on health care and yet are healthier. The United States, despite spending more per capita for health care, still ranks fifteenth in male life expectancy at birth and eighth for females. A male baby born today in the United States has a shorter life expectancy at birth than a male baby born in Cuba, Greece, or Spain. A healthy society is not the one with the most doctors or hospitals. Interestingly, there is almost an inverse correlation between the number of doctors in a society and how healthy the people are. West Germany has the largest number of doctors per capita and has the worst health statistics. Japan has the least number of doctors per capita and has the best health statistics. A healthy nation has a healthy life style, not the largest number of doctors or hospitals.

Many factors affect a nation's health—many more important than how much money is spent on doctors, hospitals, and nursing homes. The habits of a nation—its diet, alcohol consumption, and smoking patterns—all have a tremendous influence on a society's health.

We have allowed the term "health care" to become synonymous with doctors and hospitals, and this was a serious mistake. We assumed that because it was called "health care" it had to be good. But a nation's health has little relationship to the number of its doctors or hospitals. The leading causes of premature death in the United States are not lack of health care, but smoking too much, drinking too much alcohol, not wearing seat belts, and not eating the right foods. We would bring far better health to America by seriously addressing these social problems than we would by pouring endless resources into doctors and hospitals.

But even within the health care industry we are not beginning to get our money's worth. The United States has one of the most inefficient health care systems in the world, as well as one of the most expensive. It has 200,000 excess hospital beds. Many people in hospital beds do not need to be there.

They are there for the convenience of their doctors or their insurance policies. In the mid-1980s the Rand Corporation analyzed U.S. hospitals and, using criteria that erred on the side of hospitalizing people, concluded that 40 percent of the admissions were unjustified.

We train far too many doctors; it is estimated that by the year 2000 we will have 145,000 surplus doctors. Lawsuits hang over American medicine like a guillotine, requiring doctors to overtest, over x-ray, and overtreat. Like the man who carries a first aid kit, the weight of which gives him blisters (which is why he is carrying the first aid kit), our health care system in America has become part solution, part problem.

Health care costs are rising over two times the rate of inflation and now consume eleven cents of every dollar we spend. If this rate of increase were to continue, in less than seventy years the United States would be devoting 100 percent of its GNP to health care. These rates would be unsustainable even in a continental economy, but are totally unacceptable in an international marketplace. Our health care spending is making our nation economically sick. If the future belongs to the efficient, the United States must dramatically increase the effectiveness of its health care system.

This is the first, but by no means the last, example of where America outspends all its economic competitors yet does not get anywhere near the output achieved by our competitors. No nation spends more on health care and education than we do; yet our results are mediocre. We spend massive resources on research and development and yet fall behind on commercializing the results. There is an institutional entropy at work in America where we do not get efficient and effective use out of the money we spend. We no longer have a blank check to hand to the various sectors of our economy, and we must focus much more on *how* we are spending the money we do spend.

I am reminded of a story that came out of World War II when we rationed many of our commodities. A man went into a restaurant and ordered a cup of coffee and then asked for more sugar. The waitress cast a cynical eye at him and said, "Stir what you have, stir what you have." That is what I propose America do with the money it spends on many of these inefficient institutions—stir better the money we already spend.

Tax System

A country's tax system is a de facto industrial policy. Reacting to the growing criticism of our tax system, Congress in 1986 reformed the crazy quilt pattern of taxation. The full implications of this reform are yet to be observed, but even under the most hopeful scenario, America's tax system still creates a drag on our international competitiveness in several ways. While arguably better, it is still a crazy quilt. First, our tax system depends on direct taxes that give an advantage to imports and penalize exports. Our international competitors have a value-added tax, or its practical equivalent. These taxes are rebated to exporters, but not to importers. For instance, Japan has a commodity tax that acts much the same as a value-added tax. The U.S. tax system encourages consumption and further puts our goods at an economic disadvantage.

The complexity of our tax system also bedevils us. The jury is still out on whether "tax simplification" has made our system any better: it may well have made it more complex. Senator Bill Bradley of New Jersey noted that under the old system the number of tax shelter cases had risen from 11,000 in 1975 to 263,000 in 1985. Approximately 300,000 of our best and brightest young men and women are employed advising Americans on tax shelters. U.S. taxpayers spent more than 541 million hours in 1987 filling out forms, and more than 45 percent of our 95 million taxpayers sought help from our nation's 80,000 tax lawyers and accountants. Those who did their own taxes spent an average of 8.12 hours each on preparing their tax returns. Tax shelters were a $20 billion a year industry, and there is reason to believe this will continue at approximately the same level under the new legislation. Tax avoidance and evasion have become a part of American mores. While we can decry this attitude, one has to admit our tax system breeds contempt; it is unfair and economically inefficient. Newspapers report daily examples of large corporations and large income producers who pay little or no taxes. Massive amounts of income go into the underground economy and escape taxation altogether. A societal ethic fosters an attitude that it is foolish and naive to pay one's full tax bill.

Our international competitors do not stand still. Since 1985 Britain, France, West Germany, Denmark, Belgium, Australia, New Zealand, and Sweden have reformed their tax laws by cutting rates and simplifying their tax systems. In many instances these reforms were more comprehensive than our own.

We have, even under the new tax legislation, a system that encourages consumption and discourages investment. It still gives preferred treatment, in the form of hundreds of billions of dollars of tax expenditures, to the interests with the strongest lobbyists. Our system still encourages the overconsumption of housing (including vacation homes) by allowing a deduction for mortgage interest and real estate taxes, while our international competitors often discourage all housing in favor of wealth-producing assets. Tax reform is often thought of as a domestic issue, but its ramifications go to the heart of our international competitiveness.

Costs of Capital

Our national savings rate is shrinking and now stands at an all-time low. Because we save so little per capita compared to our industrial competitors, it costs American industry an average of three times more than our competitors for access to capital. America's savings rate has been falling for a number of years and was projected to fall to 3.6 percent in 1987, which would be the lowest savings rate since 1947. Many of our international competitors save five to ten times the U.S. rate. The lack of savings raises American interest rates and brings in massive foreign capital, but the net result is that American businesses pay much higher rates for their capital.

The spread between U.S. net domestic investment rates and net national savings rates and those of our international competitors is dramatic and growing. A productive economy and industrial machine are built on savings. With a population only half the size of ours, Japan's new investment in 1986 was $270 billion, compared to $220 billion for the United States. To compound this problem, approximately one-half of our 1986 investment was imported from abroad.

A nation of savers, by definition, allows its businesses to borrow at lower interest rates. A nation of consumers inevitably drives up the cost of capital. Consumer debt essentially borrows from tomorrow's standard of living for today's gratification. We are neither saving nor investing enough to meet our international competition.

The Debt Bomb

At the same time that we are saving less, we are borrowing more. A tidal wave of red ink is sweeping across all U.S. spending patterns. Between 1977 and 1987 consumer indebtedness rose 211.9 percent, from $3,906 to $11,003. Business debt rose 192.3 percent during the same period, and governmental debt (federal, state, and local) rose 190 percent. Since 1980 household liabilities have risen faster than household assets, and now merely servicing this burden absorbs about one-third of after-tax income. Two and a half million U.S. farmers borrowed more money than Mexico, Argentina, and Brazil combined. Most dangerously, this tidal wave of red ink has occurred mostly in times of economic expansion.

However bad the published debt figures are, they are not complete. The $2.5 trillion federal debt is itself an inadequate accounting of the nation's governmental debt. If we take the unfunded liabilities of the government, which are promises made by our generation but payable by another generation, we find that we must add $1 trillion to the national debt for unfunded military pensions and federal civil service pensions, and then add between $5 trillion and $6 trillion for the unfunded liability of the Social Security system. These are inescapable "costs of the future," which we are handing down to the next generation.

The United States is borrowing from abroad to maintain temporarily our consumption pattern, but this clearly cannot last. Our nation has gone from a net credit on the international marketplace of $140 billion in 1981 to a negative $220 billion at the end of 1986. Over a very short term a nation can borrow from abroad, but ultimately we cannot consume what we do not produce. We cannot continue this fiscal madness very long. Bank failures already are at a postdepression high, and the stage is set in both businesses and households for chain reaction bankruptcies in the next recession.

A nation can borrow money to fight a war or a depression, but it cannot become a constant habit. There is still wisdom in the words of Dickens's Wilkins Micawber: "Annual income twenty pounds, annual expenditure nineteen nineteen six, result happiness. Annual income twenty pounds, annual expenditure twenty pounds ought and six, result misery."

We cannot continue the current level of fiscal irresponsibility. In 1987 the United States consumed at least $150 billion more than it produced, much of this by borrowing from abroad. After 1990 it will cost the United States over 1 percent of its GNP a year just to service its international debt. This number will undoubtedly grow. For an economy that has only been growing about 2.5 percent a year, this is a terrible price to pay for deferring our problems. Borrowing money to fund current consumption will postpone the pain, but it will not keep a country competitive.

Education

The United States clearly is not educating its children as well as its industrial competitors are educating theirs. A twelve-nation study of seven subjects (mathematics, science, reading comprehension, literature, English, French, and civic education) found our national average comprehensive scores in the lower third. In mathematics, American students were lowest among all the nations tested. In civic education, our students tied with Ireland for the lowest average score among industrialized nations.

An average eighth grader in Japan knows more mathematics than a graduate of a master of business administration program in the United States. An average seventeen-year-old American knows half as much math as an average Swedish seventeen-year-old. Homework in Japan is about two hours a day, compared to approximately half an hour in the United States. Japanese students go to school 240 days a year while U.S. students go 180 days a year. By the time a Japanese student graduates from high school, he or she has as much classroom time as an American college graduate. The net effect: average students graduating from Japanese high schools have significantly more IQ points than average American students. On top of that, Japan graduates 95 percent of its students from high school while the United States graduates 75 percent.

There are more *teachers* of English in Japan than there are *students* of Japanese in America. Noting that only 4 percent of Japan's important technical literature is translated into English, Professor David J. Teece states, "The lack of Japanese language skills outside Japan affords the Japanese an important degree of national protection on issues of technology and strategy."

Yet even where excellent education is available, there is often a lack of motivation to take advantage of it. American students take our prosperity for granted. They seem to believe that a high standard of living is an American birthright. This is part of a broader problem. Studies show that while the Asian school systems outproduce our system dramatically, Asian mothers are *more* concerned about the education their children are getting. A nation's motivation and aspirations to excellence are also components of its competitiveness.

Approximately 23 million American adults are functionally illiterate, and as many as one of five American workers is functionally illiterate. The United States has the largest number of functional illiterates of any industrial country. Between 40 and 50 percent of all urban students are estimated to have serious reading problems. Former Labor Secretary William Brock estimated that 700,000 U.S. high school students graduated in 1987 and were not able to read the words on their diplomas. The Educational Testing Service has found that only 39.2 percent of seventeen-year-olds in 1984 were classified as competent enough to understand and explain relatively complicated reading. The National Commission on Excellence, in its report "A Nation at Risk," said that by letting our educational system deteriorate, the United States has committed "acts of unilateral education disarmament."

We are also falling behind in higher education. The National Science Board reports that academic programs in college-level science, mathematics, and engineering have severely declined, posing a grave long-term threat to the nation. They found that "the deterioration of collegiate science, mathematics and engineering education is a grave long-term threat to the nation's scientific and technical capacity, its industrial and economic competitiveness, and the strength of its national defense."

We are not maintaining that critical mass education essential to a strong industrial base. The Joint Policy Board for Mathematics found:

American mathematics is in a state of crisis in an age of high technology and supercomputers; we face a dangerous shortfall of trained minds to advance our frontiers. American students are achieving less in mathematics than their counterparts in other countries. The number of Americans earning Ph.D.s in mathematics has been cut in half between 1973 and 1983.

As a percentage of the GNP, the federal government is now spending on basic science one-half of what it was spending twenty years ago. In addition, in the physical sciences, we are graduating half as many Ph.D.s as we did in the 1970s—with 50 percent of that decreased number being foreign students (compared to 10 percent in the 1970s). As has been previously noted, Japan produces twice as many engineers per capita as does the United States.

In a competitive international world, an educated citizenry is our most valuable resource. This point was made by John

Wilson, chief economist of the Bank of America, who, in his book *The Power Economy,* observed:

What has happened is that comparative economic advantage has taken on new meaning. The classical or static notion of comparative advantage referred to geographical differences and various natural endowments among economies that are supposed to produce a global division of labor. The newer concept replaces traditional criteria with such elements as human creative power, highly educated work force, organizational talent, and the ability to adapt. Moreover, these attributes are not conceived of as natural endowments but as qualities achieved through public policies such as education, organized research and investment in social overhead capital.

Our advantage in a newly emerging world economy and our ability to achieve equal economic opportunity for all are directly related to the ability to provide education for all our citizens. But we must insure that education is of a high quality. The nation that is second best educationally today will be second best economically tomorrow.

We must think deeply about what it takes for our kids to succeed. We are a nation that is replacing itself with a generation where one out of four children live in poverty; 14 percent are children of teenage mothers; 14 percent are children of unmarried parents; 40 percent will live in broken homes before they are eighteen; 30 percent will never finish high school; 30 percent are minorities, many unintegrated and unassimilated; and where up to 15 percent do not speak English.

Such a nation sails into uncharted demographic waters. It is against all human experience to expect smooth sailing. The only realistic question is "how big will the storm be?"

Societal Benefits

Let us look at a partial list of those benefits that American companies must or generally do provide:

minimum wage
Occupational Safety and Health Administration (O.S.H.A.)

environmental protection
pollution control
workers' compensation
unions
Social Security
vacations
national holidays
affirmative action
health benefits
day care
pension policies
paid sick leave
compliance with patent laws
compliance with copyright laws

We can ask what would happen if one company had to comply with the above list and its competitor did not. The company that had to comply would soon be out of business. It is little solace for a company to brag to the bankruptcy court that it has the best benefit package in the industry. We can similarly ask what would happen if one state required these and the other states did not. Clearly, the state that would require companies to provide these benefits would soon lose most of its industry to competitors in other states.

Now, the dilemma that the United States faces is that we have, out of compassion and justice, built up a series of benefits to American workers which our international competitors do not require and seldom have. In addition to having higher labor costs and higher management costs, the haunting question is whether we can carry all these historic benefits and still stay competitive in the Darwinian jungle of the new international marketplace. It will benefit the United States little to brag about the social justice of its institutions if it cannot produce quality goods at competitive world prices.

Crime

The United States is the most violent and crime-ridden society in the industrialized world, and this also affects its international competitiveness. We have five times more homicides, ten times more rapes, and seventeen times more robberies than Japan. New York City alone has twice as many homicides as Japan. There are 218.2 robberies per 1,000 people a year in the United States, compared to 33.4 in West Germany and 2.1 in Japan. The U.S. rate of all violent crimes increased 156.4 percent between 1960 and 1975 and then grew another 15.9 percent between 1976 and 1985. No other society requires its citizens and business people to spend as much on burglar alarms, security officers, and internal security. American businesses in one recent five-year period had to hire 602,000 security officers, an expense that must be added to the overhead of American goods. American business spent $51 billion in 1986 for private anticrime measures such as alarms, iron bars, video cameras, and security guards. Crime is costly both to citizens and to the efficiency of the economy.

The societal costs of this crime wave are enormous. Japan's taxpayers support 50,000 inmates (including pretrial detention inmates) while the U.S. taxpayers support 546,000 adult prisoners. One and a half percent of the entire adult population of the United States is under "correctional supervision."

Related to crime is the problem of drugs. A recent study in Washington, D.C. showed that 67 percent of the people arrested for crimes had used drugs recently. Drugs also relate indirectly to the quality of our work force. Studies show that as many as 10 to 20 percent of U.S. workers use drugs at the workplace. Some one-half million Americans use heroin, some 20 million smoke marijuana fairly regularly, and 5 to 6 million people use cocaine. Such figures can hardly be inductive to quality products.

The financial and psychic strain of a society that increasingly lives behind bars to protect itself from an increasingly violent and crime-infected society will find it harder and harder to

marshal the skills and dedication necessary to compete in the international marketplace.

Defense Expenditures

The United States spends 7 percent of its GNP on defense. Japan spends less than 1 percent. A nation that has minimal defense spending can afford to concentrate its public and private capital on its international competitiveness. Conversely, those nations with large defense expenditures find their goods increasingly uncompetitive.

Seventy percent of U.S. research and development and testing and evaluation programs now go to the defense industry. While this spending does have some spillover effect on the civilian economy, it is marginal. Military spending ultimately comes at the expense of the civilian economy. About 40 percent of all our engineers and scientists are involved in military projects while virtually all of Japan's and Taiwan's scientists and engineers are engaged in bolstering their domestic economies. While we place an increasing effort into researching weapons, the Japanese are placing their efforts in designing and producing innovative goods and processes further to weaken our economy.

The United States is spending proportionately less for its economic size on nonmilitary research and development. In 1984 America spent 66 percent of its governmental research and development (R&D) on the military, while West Germany spent only 9.8 percent, and Japan spent only 2.8 percent. In 1983 our nation spent 1.9 percent of its GNP on nonmilitary R&D while West Germany spent 2.47 percent, and Japan spent 2.6 percent. In 1984 the Department of Defense spent $26.9 billion on R&D, compared to $49 billion spent by all private industry combined. The United States spent more on R&D of the B1 bomber than our steel industry did on all R&D.

Now a nation must spend what is necessary to keep itself free. Defense spending must be sufficient to protect the nation's interests. But that notwithstanding, military power is purchased at the expense of economic power. A nation's "national security" must include not only the strength of its military, but the competitiveness of its economy and the strength of its basic institutions. The innovative founder of TRW Company, Simon Ramo, has put it this way:

> In the past 30 years, had the total dollars we spent on military R&D been expended in those areas of science and technology promising the most economic progress, we probably would be today where we are now going to find ourselves arriving technologically in the year 2000.

By skewing spending toward the military and away from the domestic economy, we weaken our ability to compete internationally. To the extent money is not needed or is inefficiently spent, we ultimately weaken that which we seek to protect.

Political System

No industrialized society spends as much to elect its politicians to office as ours. The average candidate for the U.S. Senate in 1984 raised and spent $3 million in an election bid. The average cost for the candidates to the House of Representatives was more than $500,000 and has been increasing at a dramatic rate. The number of political action committees (PACs) has risen sevenfold in the past ten years, and contributions to candidates have grown more than ten times. In an average campaign, over a third of all those elected to office receive more than half their total campaign funds from PACs. U.S. politics has become a bidding process, with voters electing the candidates who have the largest amount of special interest money raised from the approximately 8,800 registered lobbyists in our nation. Less and less do local funding sources elect people to office; more and more, special interest money elects our politicians. In 1986 PACs gave well over $6 million to candidates who were running *unopposed*. It is estimated that well over $1.5 billion a year is spent trying to influence Congress and the bureaucracy. Most of this money is a business expense, and it all adds to the inefficiency of America's political system.

Meanwhile, the voter turnout in 1986 was a mere 37.3 percent, the lowest rate of participation since 1942. Over 112 million eligible Americans failed to vote in the November 1986 elections. A sense of alienation increasingly separates the American voter from the American politician.

America's political system finds it increasingly hard to act. It is increasingly hard to reach a national consensus. One of the reasons for the success of the Japanese is their extraordinary ability to reach a national consensus and then to call on the discipline and self-sacrifice of their people to achieve those national goals. Americans stress rights and privileges, and our competitors stress duties and responsibilities. The concept we remember best from our founding fathers is "the pursuit of happiness." We forget that freedom has reciprocal responsibilities.

"England expects every man to do his duty," signaled Horatio Nelson immediately before Trafalgar in 1805. Those words fall on uncomprehending ears. The social contract today involves entitlements but not civic responsibilities. Men who risked their lives during World War II, Korea, and Vietnam do not walk to the local schoolhouse to vote.

A number of thoughtful people—Lloyd Cutler, James McGregor Burns, and Douglas Dillon, among others—have raised the question of our nation's structural ability to solve its problems. While their solutions differ, they all ask whether or not America's political system is adequate to sustain itself. The American political system seems to have lost its ability to make hard choices.

Infrastructure

The inability of the political system to make hard choices is clearly seen in our deteriorating infrastructure. America is almost deliberately letting bridges, roads, subways, water systems, railroads, ports, public buildings, and other public facilities decay. It is estimated that maintaining the interstate highway system alone would cost $10 billion a year. Approximately

56 percent of the interstate system needs major repair work. One author has called our neglect of the infrastructure "structural euthanasia." An overstatement, certainly, but clearly in the long run a deteriorating infrastructure will cause a deteriorating economy. Our infrastructure is our economic lifeline. These are the structures of our economic viability; yet they also are among the first things that a politician can cut from the budget, because the effects are not immediately apparent. If America is going to revitalize itself, it must dramatically increase spending on its infrastructure.

Culture

Winston Churchill once said, "We build our buildings and then they build us." It was a wise statement. We build our institutions and then we reap the products of those institutions. A society whose institutions build productivity, hard work, education, and scientific research will build a monument of wealth. A society that encourages hedonism, sloppy work, poor worker motivation, and illiteracy is one that builds on sand. A nation whose culture encourages resolving differences quickly without strikes or litigation will prevail over one whose national motto is "sue the bastards."

A society's work culture also has much to do with its international competitiveness. Americans already work far fewer hours than their international competitors. The average Korean worker averages 54.4 hours per week at work, while the average Japanese works 44.8 hours per week, and the average American 35.3 hours per week.

In addition, however, the United States loses 813 days per 1,000 workers to industrial unrest, while Japan loses 31 days per 1,000 workers, and West Germany loses 6 days per 1,000 workers. On an international motivation index of 100, U.S. employee motivation stands at 61, West Germany at 65.3, and Japan at 85.3. U.S. workers have over twice the absenteeism rate as the Japanese. In Japan, if workers take sick leave, they feel that they are letting their fellow workers down; in the

United States, sick days have become additional vacation days, and employees are considered patsies if they do not use all they are entitled to, whether or not they are even vaguely ill.

A nation's success is built on the bedrock of its worker motivation. The fact that the United States has twice the absenteeism rate and twenty-five times the industrial unrest as Japan is also evidence of increasing uncompetitiveness.

Studies have shown that less than 25 percent of U.S. workers believe they are working at their full potential. One reason for this is that 75 percent of U.S. employees believe that there is little connection between their levels of pay and the quality of their performance. Only 9 percent of U.S. employees believe they would benefit from increased productivity. Compare this to the 93 percent of Japanese workers who believe that they would personally benefit from improvement in productivity in their firms.

Demographic Diversity

America is an immensely diverse nation, and we are proud of that diversity. Clearly, diversity has been good for America. Yet the nation must make sure that all its subgroups share in the nation's prosperity, lest we open up social fissures in our body politic. Daniel Patrick Moynihan tried to warn us in 1965:

From the wild Irish slums of the 19th century Eastern seaboard to the riot torn suburbs of Los Angeles, there is one unmistakable lesson in American history; a community that allows a large number of young men (and women) to grow up in broken families, dominated by women, never acquiring any stable relationship to male authority, never acquiring any set of rational expectations about the future . . . that community asks for and gets chaos.

Twenty-five to 30 percent of all four-year-olds in America are black or Hispanic. These children are our future. If they succeed, we succeed as a nation; if they fail, we shall have a social and economic burden of nation-threatening proportions.

While the status of blacks has in many ways improved over

the past thirty years, the social pathology is still staggering—and in many cases, growing. Spanish-speaking immigrants make up a majority of all immigrants; they often live in Spanish-speaking ghettos where they fail to learn English or assimilate into the culture. We ignore the problems of these communities at our peril.

There has been a general breakdown of public and private morality in the United States. Scandal, lawbreaking, and unethical behavior become daily news. America's divorce and illegitimacy rates have skyrocketed in recent decades. Yet this breakdown has been especially pronounced in the minority community. The illegitimacy rate among blacks now stands at more than 50 percent and is increasing. Almost 80 percent of all births in Harlem are to single mothers.

The free fall in American educational standards has hit the minority community especially hard. Seventy percent of all black and Hispanic ninth graders in New York City will not finish high school. Approximately 44 percent of black teens and 56 percent of Hispanic teens are illiterate. Nearly 50 percent of all Hispanic youth in America never finish high school. Black and Hispanic joblessness is hard to accurately pin down, but it clearly is substantially more than Labor Department statistics show. One foundation study estimated that 46 percent of this nation's black males over sixteen are essentially jobless.

A child without an education is a child without a future. Today's undereducated or neglected child is too often tomorrow's unemployable adult. One social pathology usually leads to another. Blacks account for 12 percent of the U.S. population, but 46 percent of arrests for violent crimes. The victims are usually themselves minorities. A black male has a 1 in 21 chance of being murdered in his lifetime and a white male a 1 in 131 chance of being murdered, while a white female has a 1 in 369 chance of being murdered. Poverty and crime seem to be Siamese twins. Hispanics account for 6 percent of the U.S. population, but account for 12 percent of all arrests for violent crime. What we neglect to invest in children too often comes back to haunt us as neglected children turn into antisocial adults. A Chinese proverb reminds us: "He who goes to bed to save candles, begets twins." Today's budget cut too often presents us with a much larger future bill.

These statistics are a social time bomb. If we do not act, we will see an America that has two angry, underutilized, undereducated, frustrated, resentful, jealous, and volatile minority groups existing unassimilated and unintegrated within our borders. Large numbers of these groups will be largely outside the mainstream economy and world of jobs. One educational expert observed:

> In a very real sense, an underdeveloped country of some 40 million people has grown in our midst. The majority of its inhabitants are poor, nonwhite, uneducated if not illiterate, unemployed and often unemployable, and largely dependent on government for their survival.

America's future requires that this problem be solved. This nation will not remain economically competitive if our crime, welfare, adolescent parenthood, high school dropout, and illiteracy rates remain so much higher than other industrialized nations.

Immigration

Interrelated with the question of demographic diversity is the question of immigration. Immigration has largely been good for America and can continue to be an asset. But it also could turn into a liability, and the chances of this happening are growing. The dangers are twofold, involving the sheer numbers of immigrants as well as the issue of assimilation.

First is the concern of runaway immigration pouring into our borders more people than we can incorporate into our economy or assimilate into our society. America is a powerful magnet for the rest of the world. We already take twice as many immigrants and refugees for permanent settlement than all the rest of the world combined. We already have from 5 to 12 million illegal immigrants living within our borders, and 400,000 more people fly into the United States every year than fly out. Yet the real pressures lie in the future. Latin America's population is now approximately 400 million, but it will be 800 million by 2025. Mexico's population has tripled since the Second World War, and considerable growth is built in and inevitable. The average age in Mexico is sixteen, and 33 percent of the population is under ten years old. In 1986 Mexico had more babies born with 76 million people than the United States did with 240 million people. For Latin America to maintain its present unemployment rate (which is already a staggering 40 percent), it must provide 4 million new jobs every year and create these jobs from an industrial base one-fifth the size of the United States. Many of these people seek to come north. The *New York Times* did a poll in Mexico and found that 40 percent of the Mexicans want to come to the United States. There are thus 32 million people who are a bus ride away from the Texas border.

Similarly, a poll done in South Korea found that 70 percent of those polled in South Korea wanted to come to the United States. The pressures on the United States to find jobs for its own people, let alone all those who dream of coming to America, will be staggering.

The second immigration related issue is the question of assimilation. The United States has been a true melting pot. We have succeeded as a nation largely because we have found a social glue that has held us together as one nation. Nations without this social glue experience grave problems. The scholar Seymour Martin Lipset put it this way:

The history of bilingual and bicultural societies that do not assimilate are histories of turmoil, tension and tragedy. Canada, Belgium, Malaysia, Lebanon—all face crises of national existence in which minorities press for autonomy, if not independence. Pakistan and Cyprus have divided. Nigeria suppressed an ethnic rebellion. France faces difficulties with its Basques, Bretons, and Corsicans. In Spain, Basques and Catalins demand linguistic rights and greater autonomy.

In the United States the question of assimilation is not a simple one. Large "linguistic ghettos" have developed in most of our major cities, particularly in the Southwest. While these have always been some part of the American immigration story, the size and number are growing rapidly. California and Texas will become America's first "Third World states" shortly after the year 2000, with a majority of minorities. People can now live their whole lives in America and never learn to speak English. A number of studies show that because approximately 50 percent of U.S. immigrants are Spanish speaking, people do not have the same desire or impetus to learn English. Demands for bilingual and bicultural education grow daily, and increasingly immigrants are demanding "linguistic rights." The melting pot has become a salad bowl, and the historic social glue that holds us together as Americans is in danger of becoming unstuck.

That diversity is growing. The reform of our immigration laws in the 1960s, confirmed by the 1986 reform, was intended to promote diversity and pluralism among legal arrivals. It has succeeded. The United States receives more immigrants from India than it does from Italy and Greece combined. It receives fewer from West Germany than it does from Thailand, and fewer immigrants from Ireland than it does from Egypt. It takes in more legal immigrants from Mexico with 76 million people than it does from all of Europe with some 450 million people. It takes more legal immigrants from Haiti than it does from Italy, France, Ireland, and Norway altogether.

The ten top sources of immigration into the United States in 1985 and 1986 were Mexico, the Philippines, Korea, Cuba, Vietnam, India, Dominican Republic, Mainland China, Jamaica, and Iran. Immigrants from Latin America, the Philippines, and the Caribbean make up well over half of the immigration into the United States. Yet these cultures on the average have the poorest economic success rates and have the poorest educational records even for those who have been in the United States for years. This, of course, could and hopefully will change. But, as Professor James Lee of Ohio University has pointed out, most of innovative-creative yield in science and technology has come from Western European countries. The number of patents issued to citizens of our principal sources of immigration (Latin America, the Philippines, and the Caribbean) is very small, amounting to only about 120 out of the 30,000 issued to non-Americans. We are taking a substantial demographic gamble that we can make these new immigrants as productive as we did our historic immigrants.

Only 6 percent of our immigrants are chosen because of their skills; 94 percent are allowed entry under the category of "family reunification or refugees." A majority of these are unskilled workers. Unlike Canada and Australia, which choose their immigrants for their skills, the United States accepts primarily low-skilled immigrants, over 95 percent of whom are chosen because they qualify as refugees or under the family reunification sections of our immigration laws. The United States is maximizing its low-skill immigration flow just at a time when millions of low-skilled jobs are moving offshore and domestic unemployment hovers around 7 percent. For a nation that already has 33 percent of its children born in any given year on the welfare rolls at some point before their eighteenth birthday, continuing this policy is demographic stupidity.

We have succeeded brilliantly in reversing the "national origins" concept of immigration, but our ability to assimilate these new immigrants and integrate them into a high-technology economy remains an open question.

Hubris

I believe lastly that America is lulled into complacency by an almost blind optimism. We believe as part of our national subconscious that God is an American and will keep us from harm. But no civilization in history was ever permanent: all great civilizations develop great problems. We can reassure ourselves endlessly that "the sun is rising" on America, but the facts, while mixed, do not support mindless optimism. We are whistling past history's graveyard wherein lies the wreckage of every other once great economy. I am haunted about what a crew member of the *Titanic* told a reporter as that doomed ship set sail: "Mister, even God Almighty couldn't sink this ship."

We are surrounded in America by that same kind of hubris. We do not need new cheerleaders, we need a new sense of reality by the American people. Arthur M. Schlesinger, Jr., makes a similar point in his book, *The Cycles of American History* (1986), where he warns of a similar list of challenges facing America:

There are enormous potentialities for disintegration in contemporary America—the widening disparities in income and opportunity; the multiplication of the poor and underclass; the slow down on racial justice; the structural propensity to inflation; the decline of heavy industry before competition abroad and the microchip at home; the deterioration of education; the pollution of the environment and the decay of our infrastructure; the rotting away of the great cities; the farm crisis; the mounting burden of public and private debt and the spread of crime and violence.

Schlesinger is much more optimistic than the author of this chapter, but even so ends his litany of woes with a haunting warning: "Should private and public solutions fail—what rough beast, its hour come round at last, may be slouching toward Washington—to be born?"

I believe that many of America's solutions lie in a political no man's land where both parties fear to tread. We, as the Roman historian Livy said of Rome, "can neither bear our ills or their cures." But a problem ignored is a problem made worse. I believe that America has to take on some of its own sacred cows. I believe that we must reform military pensions, veterans benefits, and civil service benefits. I believe that we have to drastically streamline the health care system to make it more efficient and cover more people more effectively. I believe that we have to look at our whole legal system to find ways that we can delawyer our society, to enact things like no-fault automobile insurance, tort reform, and mediation. I believe that we must look at the Social Security system, at least raise the retirement age, and start taxing Social Security benefits for the middle class and the wealthy. I believe we must start a national dialogue about what we want from our medical technology. We must be wise enough to use the machines we were wise enough to invent.

I suggest that America must rediscover some of the old values of hard work, thrift, discipline, and sacrifice. A French philosopher once observed that "freedom is the luxury of self-discipline." Americans are no longer a very disciplined people. We no longer have many of the stern virtues that made us great, and this is more than an inconsequential loss. Historians tell us unequivocally that "the essential qualities of national greatness are moral, not material."

In short, I believe that America must reform all of its institutions and spend at least a generation restarting America's economic engines.

Summary

The United States is rapidly losing its industrial competitiveness and its societal competitiveness. We have not met the challenge required by history to keep our institutions effective and efficient. We have the illusion of prosperity, but in many desperately important areas we are losing our ability to compete. Our institutions have lost much of their problem-solving capacity. They have grown too incestuous, bureaucratic, unresponsive, risk averse, noncreative, and complacent. The assets we have as a nation, like our ingenuity and creativity, are too easily transferred offshore; our liabilities are buried deep in the national character and grow like a cancer. A societal hubris infects America and prevents us from coming to grips with our substantial problems.

We as a people are consuming more than we produce and borrowing more than we save. We are importing far more than we are exporting, and as a nation we are spending far more government money than we are willing to raise in taxes. None of these trends can go on much longer.

The wealth of nations is not found in its Dow Jones average; it is in the productivity of its workers, cost of its capital, excellence of its education, cost of its health care, efficiency of its institutions, patterns of its investment, and the viability of its political system. America is becoming increasingly uncompetitive by these standards. The solutions do not lie in quality control circles or "just-in-time" inventory systems, but in a major sustained reform of all its institutions.

2

The Myth of U.S. Industrial Supremacy

MARTIN K. STARR
JOHN E. ULLMANN

Once I built a railroad, made it run,
Made it race against time.
Once I built a railroad, now it's done,
Brother, can you spare a dime?*

Unwillingness to Recognize Trouble

Steeped in affluence, proud to a point verging on arrogance,
American industry and commerce looked forward to entering the 1960s with the secure feeling of a sure winner. U.S.

MARTIN K. STARR is a professor in the Graduate School of Business at Columbia University and director of the Center for Operations there. He has a long history of affiliation with Columbia University, having served in various capacities on the faculty since 1952. Dr.
Starr has consulted with or lectured at many corporations, government organizations, and educational institutions, and has published
extensively on management, productivity, and operations.

JOHN E. ULLMANN is professor of management and quantitative
methods at Hofstra University and is a registered professional engi-

leaders designed the Marshall Plan to help restore the European economy at a point when the United States had never lost a war and was dominant in world trade. With a strong dollar, Americans toured Europe, earning envious condemnation as "ugly Americans." In France, Jean Jacques Servan-Schreiber wrote with passion about the threat of American managerial supremacy dominating the world, and how the "brain-drain" was siphoning scientific and technological talent from Europe into the United States. In the Far East, General Douglas MacArthur was given the mission of rebuilding Japanese industry. He called upon American engineers, manufacturing planners, and quality control experts (such as W. Edwards Deming) to create a successful program for reconstruction. Business publications in the United States hailed the coming "golden era," and the pundits told the stock market to expect the "soaring sixties."

The flawed prognostication helped hide the truth that a variety of new factors was operating. Probably, the soaring sixties would have occurred in the United States if nothing had changed. The forecast would have been right if U.S. plants and machines did not age; if U.S. managers had remained conscious of the joy of having loyal customers rather than hordes of faceless consumers; if managers and workers had seen themselves as still working together to win a war; if the U.S. government remained committed to bipartisan success; and, above all, if the rest of the world's nations had continued to be satisfied with their low standards of living and with having the United States supply their needs forever.

As suggested above, many factors are responsible for changing the situation. With early warning systems, change might

---

neer in New York state. Prior to his teaching career, Dr. Ullmann was in engineering practice for fourteen years, mainly in factory design and planning. He served as chairman of Hofstra's Department of Management, Marketing, and Quantitative Methods from 1961 to 1973, and has taught at the Stevens Institute of Technology, New York University, and Columbia University. Dr. Ullmann has written numerous books, monographs, and articles in professional journals.

have been anticipated. There were no early warning systems to recognize change and no preparation for taking appropriate actions. The fact is that there was massive unwillingness to recognize competitive troubles. The warning system was not even turned on abroad. U.S. companies considered only domestic competition worthy of note.

A paper written in 1969 entitled "Productivity is the U.S.A.'s Problem" reflected the deteriorating productivity and trade statistics of the United States in the 1960s. It was rejected by the *Columbia Journal of World Business* and the *Sloan Management Review* because the referees agreed all too unanimously that the topic was a "red herring." In 1973 the paper was published by the *California Management Review*. Although its findings were brought to the attention of all the major U.S. business publications, nothing was ever reported in their publications. The unwillingness to recognize trouble, even by those whose business it is to look for trouble, was blatant.

With the focus on competition being primarily domestic, companies accepted relaxed rules for product innovation and quality. They divided up the market turf, without consciously violating the antitrust laws. By being less aggressive than they could have been, there was unconscious violation of the spirit of these laws. The definition of competition was widely accepted as convenient accommodation without collusion. Domestic competition was a comfortable situation for all of the managerial participants. The Justice Department's antitrust threats were used as much to keep foreign competition away from the U.S. shores as to keep domestic companies comfortable about not competing too fiercely. At least as far as U.S. supremacy was concerned, legal regulations backfired.

One form of nonaggressive behavior emerged which befuddles the mind. It was the ability to spend enormous sums of money on research and development (R&D) without creating viable new ideas that could upset existing markets with their unspoken territorial agreements. U.S. auto manufacturers spent billions of dollars annually on R&D over many years. In spite of this, they studied and emulated Japanese manufacturing process innovations. The results of enormous U.S. R&D

expenditures remain unclear. Studies of product innovations, new process technology, and patents granted in these areas confirm the fact that small and medium-size firms with minimal R&D budgets unequivocally led and continue to lead the way in implementable industrial creativity. Another important statistic to consider is that in 1986, of all patents granted by the U.S. Patent Office, 45 percent were received by non–U.S. citizens.

The responsibility for the unwillingness to change can be traced to many causes and individuals at all levels of societal activity, including government, industry, labor, and the universities. But for one group, the buck stops at its door. This group consists of the managers entrusted with the mission to achieve and maintain global competitive status. An editorial about Malcolm Baldrige in the *New York Times* dated July 28, 1987, stated, "For failing to develop the technology themselves, he said, 'There is no one to blame but American management—not labor, not the Government, but management.'"

Had management changed over the years? Was the change so subtle as to go unnoticed, and yet so significant that it was responsible for the U.S. inability to keep up with the times? Perhaps U.S. management was marching to a different drummer than the managers of nondomestic competitors. According to a well-known saying, the more things change, the more they stay the same. It would not be surprising for U.S. managers to tackle new problems with the same values that had been successful for them with old problems.

Anxiety reduction is a major factor that causes a person (including a future manager) to choose a career. A person tends to move toward an occupation that will increase his or her comfort level. According to Stanley Segal in *Metropolitan College Mental Health Association* (April 1979), "Insofar as he has freedom of choice an individual tends to gravitate toward those occupations whose activities permit him to express his preferred ways of seeking gratification and of protecting himself from anxiety." When the job of management is viewed as making "lots of money" as quickly as possible and not making the highest quality goods (or providing the best possible services), existing managers and the people they hire must be comfortable with that idea in order to succeed and stay. This type of manager derives comfort from financial transactions and is likely to experience discomfort from handling product and process innovations. When management increases its comfort by avoiding the risk of product and process innovation, neither its workers nor its customers are likely to prosper.

Managers who are not comfortable with the short-term financial drum beat will move to other firms in search of a more equitable environment. Managerial shifting between firms is so much greater in the United States than anywhere else in the world that it is worthy of analysis. It could be pointed to as our secret of success—if we had captured some of the trophies for industrial supremacy. As it is, it can be faulted as a probable cause of failure.

Only when management comfort is linked to being competitive by understanding production on the plant floor will managers return to the applicant pool that can compete with the global players. The profile of managers in the 1940s and 1950s clearly indicates a plant floor orientation no matter what the functional area of the manager. Controllers, marketing managers, and financial executives in that era were expected to be able to play the piano if they were selling the music. It is hard to imagine a major league coach who had never played the game.

The analogy of competitive sports partially fits the industrial situation. Joseph Duffey states in chapter 3 that too much rhetoric about competitiveness relies on sports metaphors. We agree that sports relationships capture only some aspects of competition, but guidelines for prospering in global competition that can grab the attention of managers are not likely to be couched in terms of economic theory.

We can try to explain what happened to U.S. competitiveness by considering a tennis tournament among (domestic) buddies. All of them are out of shape, and no one is playing too hard. Then new players arrive (from abroad) to compete at the games. Their standards are higher. The new competitors are always in training and they continuously strive to play a better game.

Imagine what would happen if the American teams started playing against other teams on a global league basis. Assume that the American teams are all about on a par with each other, but consistently lose to the teams from abroad. The sports reporters for the *New York Times* and the *Washington Post* would quickly assess team competence and spirit as sadly lacking. Performance would produce the score equivalent of a huge trade deficit.

The manager's role and responsibility are clear to all. Losing games in competitive sports is never rewarded by bonuses. The only question is how long will they lose before the manager is bounced. Why are the standards so different for industrial competition?

As the competitors from abroad continuously win, some of the domestic teams begin to import foreign players. Others call for foreign player handicaps or drop out of the league. The supremacy title has passed from the original winners to the current crop of winners. In sports, it is hard to sustain the myth of supremacy based on past history.

Team play and training are critical in basketball, football, and baseball competition. In all of these sports, it is fair to say that the players must keep their eyes on the ball. U.S. industry began to resign from the league when it gave up looking at the ball and concentrated instead on manipulating the scoreboard. Curiously, the stock market became indifferent to the quality and even the nature of what was being produced. Managers stopped caring about the players on the team, except for a few bosses who were given bonuses whether or not the team won or lost. The players became confused and lost heart.

You can count on hearing some managers say, "American players don't want to work hard. All they want is money. They don't care about the game." That is what has been said about American workers. But studies performed at the Columbia University Graduate School of Business Center for Operations in 1985 and 1987 show that Japanese owned firms in the

United States, while employing American workers, perform almost as well as their parent companies in Japan. Americans working for Japanese owned firms exhibit a high degree of team spirit. In terms of our sports model, this means that good coaching can transcend national boundaries. Poor coaches blame the players.

The record books show which teams had supremacy and when they had the right to that claim. The effects of time on such claims are not obscure. Assessments are clear in the sports world because the performance measures are entirely unambiguous. A team cannot claim to be great when it is not. The myth of supremacy does not befuddle the manager's mind. Winning and losing are a matter of team performance with everyone playing a part.

Trouble Defining Competition

Competitive problems in sports are quickly recognized, but the manager may not be able to define the trouble immediately. Yet the definition of competition is far simpler with sports than with industry. There is difficulty in recognizing trouble when the definition of competitiveness is too abstract, too vague, too macroeconomic, too legal and not tied in to the actual realities of the system of competition (the game).

We need to discuss the definition of competitiveness for the industrial situation. What first comes to mind is the concept (as in sports) of zero-sum games, where what one team wins the other loses. Competition for markets is not zero-sum, even though market share does fit the zero-sum concept. This is because many competitors can be happy at the same time as they share an expanding sales volume from which they all profit. Such market growth can occur because the competition improves quality, lowers prices, and makes more people aware of the attractions of buying the product or the service. So, being able to win a zero-sum game is not what we mean by achieving world class competitiveness.

In fact, it has become increasingly evident that in global relations, countries, industries, and companies must be mutually prosperous. Major trade imbalances lead to constraints on trade that penalize customers, increase unemployment, and create volatile shifts in the performance of companies. As the number of countries involved in international trade has grown, the need to have balanced equations of imports and exports has increased. Many of the countries have subsidized industries, and the effect of such national interests must be accounted for in the definition of competitiveness. This is an important change in the consideration of competitive supremacy.

The definition of competitiveness frequently centers on the issue of trade deficits. At the macro level, it is often said that the global competitiveness of the United States requires the ability to restore trade balance so that, over a reasonable period of time, the net of exports minus imports would be zero (or, as it used to be, strongly positive). There are a number of problems with this definition. First, the method of accounting for net trade balance ignores many factors that would shift the balance, e.g., the income of multinationals. It may be easy to sustain the myth of supremacy by juggling the books.

Second, macro measures lead to macro solutions, which ignore the micro factors of competitiveness that exist on the plant floor. The quality of the players' performance is washed out if the macro solutions do not address the managerial imperative to raise standards, improve training, and destroy bureaucracies that sustain the myth that situational change is illusory.

Third, the kind of trade advantage that the United States once enjoyed was based upon a unique situation. Competitive supremacy in the world market was based upon quantity and not quality. The ability to deliver high volumes of goods of satisfactory quality at a reasonable price in an acceptable time was the mark of the winner. As the number of global suppliers increased, the delivery of volume in an acceptable time became a nonissue. World market elasticities emphasized quality and price. The prime factor for decreasing substitutability became value (qualities obtained per unit of currency).

In the 1950s only the United States had what it took to win

the accolades of competitive supremacy. By 1980 many countries had in place the technological infrastructure to support their companies' bids for global market share. Many of these countries were too small to provide a sufficient domestic market to sustain a competitive industry. They had no choice but to go for the global market using the current competitive imperative, which is top quality and low price. As U.S. companies adjust to the new rules for play, they will join a crowded field of competitors.

A working definition of competitiveness is needed. It will combine macro and micro issues in a systems framework, i.e., they both have to be considered together. A competitive country is able to sell its products and services in the global marketplace, including its own domestic marketplace. Its companies are able to deliver the highest possible quality (including innovations) at the lowest possible cost. As a result of the performance of its many companies, the country improves its overall standard of living and its global influence.

To understand what is required to be competitive, we now look at the way in which the U.S. myth of supremacy was developed and lost, and the way in which it can be regained again.

Reacting to Trouble

The level of a country's industrial skills and development must be measured against the achievements—past, present, and in prospect—of its international competitors. It consists of a combination of abilities, resources, and activities in commercial development, scientific and technical innovation, and the organization of production. That the United States has lost a great deal of ground in these fields is no longer in dispute; beginning with a few identifiable trouble spots in the early 1960s, the decline has continued without letup ever since, accelerating after the early 1970s. The way it was long ignored is itself a study in national self-deception; for many years one had to make a considerable effort to persuade one's readers or audiences that it existed at all. Now the miseries it has engendered are so plain and so general that such persuasion is no longer needed, but there are still far too many illusions and rationalizations for what has happened to lead to any consensus on what to do next.

In 1936 Winston Churchill said in a speech in the House of Commons, "The use of recriminating about the past is to enforce effective action at the present." It is a useful point of departure in that it defines rather clearly the utility of what are sometimes called "the lessons of history." In this spirit, we can note that if there is one lesson to be learned from this grim century of ours, it is that there is no institution, enterprise, society, or human achievement of any sort, no matter how strongly established and esteemed, that cannot be ruined. When disasters occur, the reaction of those afflicted can take one of three forms, aside from the simple denial noted above.

The first of these is the view that it was bound to happen anyway. This is essentially fatalistic, but is inherent in the writings of such questionable historical sages as Arnold Toynbee and the even more questionable Oswald Spengler, as well as of those economists who see grand cycles against which we are essentially helpless. The trouble is thus viewed as irreversible except maybe in the long run, and in the long run we are all dead.

The second reaction is to demonstrate that the good thing that has fallen on bad times was never there in the first place. Debunking the good old days is something of a staple in much historical writing, though one must concede a point to Franklin P. Adams who once said that nothing was more responsible for the good old days than a bad memory. The problem is, of course, that this view too tends to absolve us from analysis and action to help ourselves in our current situation. The reason is that if something never existed, there is no point in trying to restore it or anything like it.

The third reaction is to look at the problem without self-serving illusions and try to see what can be done to produce or accelerate a proper set of remedies. It is not an easy thing to do, in part because whatever has gone into a decline has probably acquired a cocoon of illusions, especially during its waning years, or because its characteristics have been inadequately described.

American industrial decline is eminently one of these subjects, and the first two reactions cited above are alive and well. As we will show later, there is an abundance of excuses, the bottom lines of which are acceptance of what has happened and a refusal to "enforce effective action at the present." As to the second reaction, there really was a very high level of U.S. industrial skill at one time, and we do ourselves no favor in ignoring the extent of our fall. On the other hand, it is necessary to look at the structure and specific strengths and weaknesses, rather than to coast along on generalized memories of past glory or, worse still, on illusions and unwarranted self-esteem.

A useful first point in arriving at a realistic view is to note that the troubles of our times are often perceived as essentially intractable; hence a growing sense of the helplessness of individuals, and even government leaders, is a central characteristic of modern societies. Indicative of this is the description of our political environment after the oil shock: the "politics of falling expectations." This sense of helplessness now shows itself in the ever lower rate of voter participation in the governance of a so-called free society and, as it has done for a long time, in the morale and motivation problems encountered in business. These include not only the familiar problems affecting employees, but also those of managements that count it as the best part of valor to get out of operations and instead sit back and engage in what amounts to coupon clipping. In short, if everything is the fault of higher powers, then what can an individual or individual business enterprise do except, so to speak, to open the last of the good stuff in the *Titanic*'s cellars?

The answer surely must be that few disasters are ever so complete that everyone is more or less fatally affected. Even in bad economic times, some usually prosper, which is not to say that not having the troubles would not be better all around. It may be that, as Shakespeare says, "sweet are the uses of adversity," but getting rid of the adversity is even sweeter. In a business context it means taking such microeconomic remedies as offer themselves but also pushing for the necessary changes in macroeconomic policies. To remedy U.S. industrial decline, it is thus necessary to look at the assets and liabilities of better times, both individual and societal, and what these suggest for current and future actions.

The Structure of Technical Competence

The first requirements of this analysis are definitions of the objectives of technology and the nature of technical progress, noting that industry, in general, consists to a crucial extent of the implementation of technology. In turn, we can take technology as the body of knowledge that translates the findings of the natural sciences and its own discoveries into practical applications. In a sense, there is a continuum of increasing knowledge that stretches from theoretical studies without any applied objective (whose practitioners are, indeed, often proud of that fact) to direct commercial development. The latter may be defined as taking a technical or scientific discovery and turning it into a product—a commercially viable one, if the exercise is successful. Commercial development goes beyond technology itself in that it must also make use of economics, finance, other branches of technology (as, for instance, in the construction of production facilities or the ancillary development of special machines), and applied social sciences in general, as in the marketing phase.

It follows that to judge a country's status in technology one must take into account its strengths and weaknesses along this spectrum from science to commercial applications. Here one must note that, for much of their history, the very considerable achievements of U.S. scientists and engineers have tended to be at the commercial development end rather than the purely scientific one. This is not meant to put them down in any way, but it serves to make the point that, as we will show, it was the decline of the erstwhile American skill in commercial development that triggered the much broader technological retreat now experienced.

A second element was the fact that U.S. technological progress took place against a background of relative opulence, of ample capital and natural resources, and in an open society. But these, it should be emphasized, are not necessary conditions for technological competence. (In a wartime speech, Winston Churchill once described the consequences of a Nazi victory as "a new dark age, made darker and more protracted by the lights of perverted science.") Nor are the above sociopolitical characteristics shared by the most successful countries in technology today, most notably by Japan, which lacks most raw materials and has a much more authoritarian society. Even the West European countries are, in various degrees, more authoritarian than the United States and have larger public sectors. There is, in fact, so much variety in their political atmospheres that modest differences in these national arrangements probably have little effect on the technological pecking order.

What, then, was it that has shaped American technology, its rise and its decline? The first part of the answer is to note that a large part of American industrial success consisted of taking discoveries made elsewhere and turning them into viable products and production systems. In other words, the United States devised the kinds of applications that have long been called "imitations" when practiced by others, notably by Japan. Again, just as is happening with Japan today, a period of successful application of the work of others then served as a basis for extending American efforts back toward more basic discoveries. Invention and application thus became closely linked, but the linkage worked both ways as problems encountered in applications prompted more basic work on the problem at hand, which, in turn, precipitated further exploration of the technical areas involved.

The evidence for this process of change and feedback goes back to the beginnings of the industrial revolution, and specifically to the development of machine tools. As the British historian K. R. Gilbert puts it:

The invention and development of machine tools was an essential part of the industrial revolution. The steam engine, the railway and

textile and other manufacturing machinery required machine tools
for their progress; and it was this demand that stimulated the great
progress in the invention of machine tools that took place.... In 1775
the machine tools at the disposal of industry had scarcely advanced
beyond those of the Middle Ages: by 1850 the majority of modern
machine tools had been invented.

The credit for this remarkable progress belongs largely to a group
of British engineers, though towards the end of the period the leadership moved to the United States. ("Machine Tools," in *A History of
Technology*, V.4. ed. C. Singer et al. Oxford University Press, 1958).

Gilbert goes on to note that there was a British "school" of
inventors that was mainly responsible for this remarkable
progress and that its members were linked to each other in
that the later ones had been employees or partners of the
earlier ones and then struck out on their own. As he says, "One
inventive mind was stimulated by contact with another, and
experience became cumulative." In fact, similar linkages can
be observed in the early development of other industrial products, notably steam engines, railroad locomotives, and textile
machinery, and in the simultaneous development of scientific
instruments, which took place mainly in France.

It is remarkable that these very early developments already
show the important ingredients of industrial success. First,
there is the evident growth of a "technological culture," i.e.,
the emergence of entrepreneurial interest in a specific field
and the growth of a work force at all levels, from professionals
to factory workers. People become used to given technologies
and their products and attain a certain skill or "handiness" in
dealing with them. Continued scientific and technical progress
at the "frontier" is clearly required, but it cannot live by itself
without percolating into other parts of industry and society.

Second, in a given country, there is a certain critical mass in
such developments. Unless there is an opportunity for interaction at close range—and even modern communications do not
make up for its lack—technically oriented enterprises find it
extremely difficult to exist in isolation, unless they are content
to serve only very restricted local needs. The interdependent

relationships among technically oriented enterprises are common in all industrial regions (or, for that matter, in any specialized business district). While their interdependence is not irreversible, the strength of the linkage is such that problems within one enterprise affect the others. Once the rot starts and a major player goes, the cohesion and effectiveness of an entire industrial region are quickly impaired. The well-publicized troubles of Silicon Valley, as its progress faltered in the face of competition from high-quality imports, are a case in point.

The third element of success is attention to production and marketing. It is here that American strength showed itself at an early stage. Until the 1860s mass production of mechanical piece parts was primarily concentrated in the manufacture of military items. Sir Samuel Bentham's mass production of naval pulley blocks in the 1790s was the first example, but it was soon followed in the United States in 1798 by Eli Whitney's musket factory which used fixtures to machine tools of unprecedented high accuracy and consistency. The 1853 factory of Samuel Colt, for which Elisha K. Root designed the tooling, was the most extensive of its kind in the world. The method was quickly adapted to the manufacture of sewing machines, typewriters, and other products as these were invented later in the nineteenth century. These and many others were consumer durables, and their commercial development was closely linked to the beginning of a closely integrated marketing effort, most notably perhaps in the case of the Singer sewing machine.

Such combined deployment of technical and commercial resources became the essence of commercial development and the true embodiment of American industrial success. In no other country had the use of technical products by consumers become more universal. This in turn shaped the whole atmosphere of work. As American labor grew more productive, the sharing of productivity gains gave rise to a steadily rising real income and thus to the relative well being of American wage earners in comparison with the low-wage producers of the time. It is a particular characteristic of the contemporary de-

cline that a failure to keep products and equipment up to date
ended this process of improvement, leading to grave losses in
real income. Added costs could no longer be absorbed by
improving the productivity of the system and so had to be
passed along in the form of higher prices, leading in turn to
the ruinous impact of foreign competition.

One of the unhappier features of this trend is that it is
regarded in some quarters as a good thing, because it reduces
the power of trade unions, which had been concentrated in the
manufacturing sector, and takes the pressure off some environmental concerns in the name of "saving jobs." However,
"givebacks" that workers successfully demanded in many
cases are anything but a symbol of responsible action in the
face of competition. Measured against the successful past, they
are the ultimate confession of weakness and of rising misery.

The glory days did, however, leave us with two lessons that
emphasize the indivisibility of industrial strength and progress, because the pattern of these successful examples has
been followed almost universally ever since. The first point is
that technical innovation was closely linked to production
methods; in other words, there was a total system. Secondly,
the design of the production system itself prompted more
technical progress. The best example is the invention of the
milling machine and turret lathe by engineers with close ties
to the mass production systems of the time. This exemplifies
the kind of feedback between innovation and application described earlier.

The Nature of Industrial Decay

It is hard to exaggerate the extent of the decline in the
industries that had the remarkable origins described in the last
section. Both the British and American machine tool industries (increasingly the latter) had achieved a global supremacy
of a most remarkable sort. Until about 1960 it was difficult to
find a large machine shop anywhere where the famous nameplates of the British and American makers could not be found;

for certain major machines, American and British manufacturers were virtually the only game in town. Now the British
industry is almost gone, and the American one survives only
in vestigial form.

The departures of the once famous major companies continue. For instance, the sturdy factory building of the bankrupt
Bullard Machine Company in Bridgeport, Connecticut, where
the vertical lathe was invented long ago, was turned into high-
priced condominiums. Two contenders were fighting over the
remains of the Morse Cutting Tool Company of New Bedford,
Massachusetts, which had been founded in 1864 by Samuel A.
Morse, the inventor of the twist drill. One possible buyer
hoped to keep things going, but the other wanted to salvage
the name, while describing the machines as obsolete—as
"greasy antiques."

In the once great machine tool center of Springfield, Massachusetts, the large companies are mostly defunct, having been
turned into agents for imported machine tools and occasion-
ally making extra-specialized tools for military contractors
where costs and quick delivery are secondary. Small shops
have been more successful, doing high-quality precision work
for customers around the United States, but surviving only as
job shops in the interstices of an industry whose core is gone.

In the last section, we defined several major characteristics
of industrial competence. They also show what has happened
in the course of the industrial decay in our time. A prominent
rationalization (perhaps better described as cold comfort) for
the American situation has been that we could still hang on to
the high end of technology but let the rest go elsewhere. The
indivisibility of invention and application described earlier not
only demolishes that argument, it also shows why it is so hard
to keep the rest of the competition in its place: as its skills
grow, it too receives the kind of feedback that prompts technical innovation of its own, and before long it has an independent capability that competes vigorously and sometimes fatally
with the source of original inspiration. This is what happened
in the United States in relation to its adaptation of British

inventions; it is happening now in the industrial challenges to U.S. industries by Japan and other countries of the Pacific Rim and by Western Europe.

The feedback between applications and innovations is, in fact, at the center of some major specific cases. For example, the traditional allegations of cheap foreign labor become absurd when, as in the case of electronic chips, the manufacturing processes are necessarily automatic, with only very little— seconds per unit sometimes—direct labor. What then becomes crucial is the price and running cost of capital equipment. When an industrial society neglects that part of its resources, it quickly loses its ability to respond to competitive pressures. What we lack, in other words, is the kind of effort that once created the first milling machines and turret lathes in response to the perceived needs of a production system.

The issues in industrial decay go much further than this, however, and to do them justice in a historical context, it is useful to look in more detail at the case of Great Britain, where it all began, but which in our time has served as a most appalling paradigm and forerunner of U.S. industrial troubles. The troubles of American industries were experienced first by their British colleagues. It happened with steel, automobiles, machine tools, other capital equipment, and a host of other products.

Britain is now close to being a net importer of manufactured products; as an opposition member of Parliament once put it, its people have been reduced to "shoddy, greedy and . . . second rate gobblers of discounted goods from overseas" (*New Statesman,* January 6, 1984). For the United States, such a description might be a trifle hyperbolic, but a trade deficit of some $160 billion a year has its own dynamic that should discourage smugness. In what follows, we will discuss the ingredients of decay and how they manifested themselves in both countries.

The basic premise here must be that high skill in commercial development is crucial to industrial success, and thus its loss in the United States and its failure to develop adequately in Britain were central to the decline. Why this happened in

Britain has several answers. First, until after World War II, there was much less of a desire to create a mass consumption society, comparable to the United States. That was in part a matter of resources, of course, but it also had other reasons. The middle class in Britain was relatively smaller than that in the United States, and members of the working class, in their desire to do better, have long run up against class prejudices which, in fact, appear to have had something of a rebirth in the age of Prime Minister Margaret Thatcher.

The difference in technical-economic objectives was also related to Britain's role as the center of a global empire that set different priorities for its governments and for its business establishments. Though perhaps more inward looking than such export oriented industrial countries as Germany and Switzerland, British businesses nevertheless were very internationally minded compared to their American counterparts. For one thing, Great Britain was used to regarding the Empire markets as something of a private preserve for durables of all kinds, and this was indeed fostered by various forms of "empire preference."

A third factor, in part related to the first, involved the professional and educational requirements of successful commercial development. The ability to integrate science, engineering, and business, which is the kind of skill needed, is not easy to create, but the task becomes impossible when the educational system is stacked against it. The issue of professional skills and education is in fact so important that it deserves a section of its own.

The Role of Education

An examination of educational factors is relevant both for the British and American cases. A key reason for Britain's problems was the class stratification of its educational system and the problems that created for technically oriented industries.

Britain came to universal public education later than any other west or central European country, some 160 years after

Prussia, which was the first. Its education system was extremely elitist, and this has created many problems in the governance of the country and, particularly, in the operation of technically oriented industries. It certainly was no help to these industries that university degrees in engineering only became common after World War II, when many new universities were built. Before then, even bachelor's degrees in engineering were uncommon. Training was primarily the result of apprenticeships of sorts; apprentices destined for better things—those who had come with some sort of high school diploma, which was uncommon among industrial workers—were sometimes called "gentlemen apprentices." This was followed by studies at technical institutes or even by correspondence, followed by examinations administered by the main professional societies. In a status conscious society that sort of second-class citizenship discouraged talented young people from technical vocations in favor of finance and other professions where "a good classics honours degree" was still an acceptable entry ticket, especially if it was from Oxbridge rather than the Red Brick schools. All this led to what C.P. Snow eventually called the "two cultures"; even the "hard sciences" were somewhat déclassé in this environment. There is a temptation for Americans to dismiss conditions such as these as foreign aberrations; we order things better. However, the American engineering profession has long been severely criticized for the poor pay; insecure employment; failure to provide a route to top management, which tends to be reserved for accountants, lawyers, M.B.A.s, and others; and a multitude of problems in professional ethics, as in product and environmental safety. For a long time, engineering schools were among the most unfashionable domains of academe, second only to schools of education. For the brightest young people, law, medicine, and business schools gave greater promise.

One result has been that, by now, about half of all engineering graduate students are foreign, including the doctoral candidates who, eventually, could be expected to provide the faculties of the schools. Real and imagined issues of "national security" have handicapped their studies even further. Nor should we ignore the class aspect of engineering in the United States; it may be less crass than in England, but engineering students still tend to come from the lower middle class and first generation college group. We also have observed that the children of engineers who did manage to climb the corporate ladders to top management rarely, if ever, become engineers themselves.

Matters are likely to become worse as the result of current pressures on the public schools. These are, in part, financial, but of late they have mainly taken the form of a resurgence of political and religious obscurantism that rules ever greater areas of intellectual endeavor out of bounds. How much scientific originality can one expect to come from the ever growing part of the population emerging from the more benighted systems? Studies of the lives of the better American scientists have already shown that they come from a narrow societal layer; at present, there is no prospect that the base will be significantly broadened.

Of particular interest in our present context is the effect of these educational dysfunctions on skills in commercial development. Specifically, engineering education has been subjected to pressures for substantial additional material which, while not objectionable in general, produced some unfortunate side effects. There were three main areas that were to be added: pure science, especially more physics, chemistry, and mathematics; computers; and liberal arts. Since the time when environmental concerns first grew, ethics has been yet another factor for engineering students, just as adding "values" and ethics is now advocated for business schools.

When such additions must be shoehorned into an essentially finite total curriculum, something has to give. In engineering schools, this has meant the eclipse of the teaching of production skills. The workshop courses (indeed, the often splendid workshops themselves) have gone. Industrial engineering, an academic specialization that originated in the United States, has been cut severely and several renowned departments have been eliminated or are moribund, waiting for the last tenured members to depart from the scene. The skills involved have been replaced, in part, by the study of computer-based production systems and of operations research, which applies mathematical models to production operations and is itself a prodigious user of computers. These subjects are unexceptionable in themselves, but they only amount to control techniques and, if applied to unoriginal, junky products, they only assure that increasingly unsalable junk will be produced. The way technical innovation itself has been handled must therefore be examined.

Innovation and Its Discontents

We noted earlier that there exists a continuum of effort from pure science to commercial introduction and that its nature defines the industrial competence of a society. Considering the long decades of American industrial success, one would suppose that innovations had been its particular strength. However, it is necessary to look at this belief rather carefully. Several factors then emerge, the first of which is that American industry has relied rather more on outside sources for its development than might at first be supposed.

The first element is the treatment of pure science. For a long time, it was possible to take for granted a steady supply of new scientific knowledge that would emerge virtually gratis from the universities. Indeed, much of it came from abroad and its use in the United States benefited a great deal from the fact that the countries of origin failed to develop the discoveries themselves. We noted the central role played by prior British work in the early development of the American machine tool industry; one could make similar comments with respect to the chemical industry. Fluorocarbons and organic silicates, for instance, were both first described by British scientists, but the commercial development was done predominantly in the United States and, to some degree, in Germany, which had been the leader in industrial chemistry since the 1880s.

In contrast to its enormously inventive and prolific engineers, formally trained and otherwise, the United States did not play a commensurate role in pure science until the 1920s, when an influx of European scientists first started, in response to the economic and political dislocations of World War I. The immigration of European scientists greatly accelerated in the 1930s, especially in response to the Nazi persecutions, although, despite the most desperate need, it was progressively restricted by immigration policies that eventually failed to fill even the quotas provided by the sharply discriminatory Johnson Immigration Act of 1924. After World War II, it resumed and became in part a "brain drain" relative to the Third World, but also to Western Europe. The facilities for research were unequalled here, and the large number of universities provided employment opportunities. The United States has by far the largest single share of the post–World War II Nobel Prize winners, and a very large proportion of them had immigrant backgrounds.

The progress that emanated from the many creative scientists and engineers did percolate down into industrial use and applications but the effect was countered by certain managerial habits that had become ingrained and had been kept far beyond their logical usefulness.

The first of these is the excessively long survival of the mode of organization in production originally devised by Frederick W. Taylor in the 1890s. Taylorism was to rationalize production methods and help increase productivity and the earnings of factory workers. Though successful at first, it led eventually to ever greater fragmentation of the work process; the job was chopped into ever smaller repetitive pieces, each capable, as Taylor himself put it, of being done by workers "of the type of the ox." Since workers are becoming progressively more educated, Taylor's oxen are no longer plentiful. The fragmentation of work inevitably became combined with a fragmentation of responsibility, and these two factors became a leading cause of the eventual quality collapse of American products. More seriously still, the consequences of division of labor were speed-ups as well as monotony for the workers, with attendant added danger. In a 1987 *New York Times* report on the present condition of the meat packing industry, for example, it was noted that conditions had not improved a great deal since Upton Sinclair wrote *The Jungle* in 1906; workers were "sliced and crushed by machines that were not even invented" in Sinclair's time. Yet these machines were to help improve safety and create better conditions. Speed-ups, and a failure to make further improvements or even to install long-familiar safety devices, did the rest.

A second problem concerned the ample resources available to American industry. It showed itself especially in excessively and inefficiently applied energy, which would prove to be a very expensive problem when energy costs soared in the 1970s. It was a problem compounded by the wrong kinds of capital investment as well as failure to keep up with the energy-saving technology that was second nature to the international competitors of the United States.

A third overindulged habit, which is less often recognized, was the overreliance on economy of scale for purposes of productivity improvement. If economy of scale is present, large production units cost less per unit of output capacity than small ones, so that, in that sense, business expansion brings its own reward. Unfortunately, as simple analysis shows, this cannot go on forever, and eventually, as markets reach their saturation, this avenue to progress is closed. Yet, as a study directed by one of the authors showed, manufacturing industry and some others, such as agriculture, mining, and power plants, kept relying on that mechanism (Ullmann, *The Improvement of Productivity*, 1980).

The utilization of economy of scale requires that products be standardized, but the question is then whether one's customers can use such products and do not have special needs that they cannot fill. A failure to realize this was a key element in the technical end runs around a once dominant American textile machine industry by West Germany which, by dint of good research organization, managed to satisfy the new technical requirements. The cry of "low wages" clearly cannot be applied to West Germany.

In fact, technological end runs are the best way around this and other dead ends, and it is no answer to assert that such a view is nothing but naive faith in a "tech fix." At least two other major American industries are in their present miserable state largely because they left others, including their foreign competitors, to develop the new ideas of their industries. The worst of them is steel: as the Congressional Office of Technology Assessment (OTA) put it in a quite devastating report in 1980, the industry believes that "the costs and risks of innovation outweigh its benefits and that it is cheaper in the long run to buy proven technology than to create it."

The situation has not improved; much of the industry is still obsolescent, and what little is left of it introduces essential innovations, like continuous casting and the basic oxygen furnace, more slowly, if at all, than its many foreign competitors. The third major innovation is direct reduction, i.e., the elimination of the blast furnace. Here, major work is being done by U.S. makers of the new equipment, but it is the foreign competitors who have bought it so far. The American industry is not interested.

It is true that there is great global overcapacity in steel and that, because of substitution and, sometimes, because of better design practices, modern industrial output requires relatively much less steel than formerly. Even so, the American practice of picking up what somebody else is already using is not a viable way to the future.

Nor is steel the only culprit. The automobile industry has always relied on outside sources for its best new ideas, as, for instance, in the case of the automatic transmission. Product development essentially meant restyling.

Finally, what about "high tech," that often touted prospective salvation? According to a 1986 report for the Joint Economic Committee of Congress, the U.S. trade position in high-tech products has shown a steadily declining surplus since 1980 and moved into deficit, beginning in 1986. Observers of new major concepts like genetic engineering, superconductivity, optical fibers, and robots regularly worry that others will quickly take the lead; considering what has happened in all the sophisticated new consumer electronics products or in computer chips, it is a justifiable concern. Perhaps the saddest cases of this kind are the ones where, as in the case of chips, the basic discoveries were made in the United States.

Another such example, especially poignant in view of our epigraph, is electric traction, which also was invented largely in the United States, but where there is no longer any significant American effort. Thus, the rail transit systems that are being expensively built or painfully resuscitated in a few cities must rely on imported equipment, the attempts of once famous American manufacturers to buy foreign technology having ended in expensive and ignominious failure.

All this has not deterred many American manufacturers from surrounding their output with an ever-rising volume of hoopla, of image creation and other substitutes for substance. One wonders, for example, why one should be pressured to buy "service contracts" for products that should last a long time or should be covered by more adequate warranties and why this should be a steady theme at a time when American products are struggling with a bad quality reputation. One recalls the old and not exactly reputable advertising motto "don't sell the steak, sell the sizzle," but now there is yet another variant of these messages, i.e., the elaborate campaigns by industries in which it is argued that new ideas don't work. Energy companies especially sound that theme when it comes to any novel concepts other than nuclear power, as does the auto industry with respect to safety devices or new propulsion systems, both of which are sorely needed. In short, "first sell the sizzle, then the fizzle."

What is breaking down, therefore, as implementation lags, is the supply of new ideas as well. This shows up objectively in the so-called patent balance—foreign patents granted to U.S. entities minus U.S. patents granted to foreigners. After decades of often substantial surplus, that too has now moved into deficit. The patent statistic cited at the outset of this chapter is thus the end point of a long process of decline.

The issue of poor quality and mishandling of innovation finally raises a point of central importance in the management of a modern economy. Over the last few years, the so-called control of inflation has been the source of almost deafening self-congratulation. However, inflation statistics are based on price indexes and thus on some sort of market basket of products that is held constant. If product design or quality changes significantly, costs or manufacturing effort are affected, positively or negatively. For instance, in productivity statistics, if less effort is required to make a brilliantly designed new product instead of an old one, productivity (meaning output per labor hour) rises, but it also rises when manufacturers make the users assemble their stuff, as they often do these days. Their assembly labor is saved and not counted as input if it is somebody else's.

Similarly with quality, if something much better costs the same or less, we have an advantage in constant dollars. Suppose, however, we have the all too pervasive current quality decline: when one could once buy a reasonably priced product that fulfilled its purpose, and its quality has declined to the point where only what had once been a high-priced brand will do the same job, the effect is the same as inflation; when a decent pair of trousers once cost $17.99 and now can be had only for $29.99, there is a price relative there of 166.7, i.e., a dollar is worth only about sixty cents. Yet trousers at $17.99 are still available; the problem is that they don't fit properly or that the material takes on a dazzling shine after a week or so. Such information, however, is not and probably cannot be taken into account in the Consumer Price Index (CPI). Inflation is thus felt more strongly than the comforting single digits of the CPI would indicate. Product markets become not merely segmented but bipolar; this may well have been a major contributing factor to the eclipse or demise of several retail chains that had catered successfully for many years to the middle and low end of the market.

Finally, a potent reason for U.S. industrial decline is undoubtedly the enormous role played by the military sector in relation to the technically oriented industries. This preempts both capital and technical talent and, perhaps worst of all, makes respectable a degree of waste and mismanagement that would not be tolerated elsewhere. Increasingly in the United States, the "frontier" of technical progress is redefined in military terms. Japan and Germany, which do not share these industrial priorities, owe much of their competitive strength to this factor. On the other hand, Great Britain's military sector in relation to GNP is second only, among Western countries, to that of the United States, and shares the same industrial decline.

The frequent assertion that there would be a significant spin-off from the excessive military involvement is hardly tenable. Products with military ancestry have to be practically reinvented in order to make them commercially viable, and the fact that most of this has been done by Japan effectively counters the spin-off argument. There are really only two major technical areas that can claim predominantly military ancestry— radar and jet aircraft. The former, however, has not so far "spun off" to the extent of providing us with a good air traffic control system or an alarm system for clear air turbulence, both of which are vitally necessary and would have been logical extensions of radar technology.

Moreover, the United States and Britain are not alone in such troubles. Rather, technical or industrial decline has become a problem of some generality in that other countries have also experienced it to varying degrees. It is, in fact, so pervasive a danger to developed countries that it cannot be ignored by business planners or their governmental counterparts. One of the best examples is the Soviet Union; many more of its industries run along military-industrial lines, so the country is increasingly unable to fend for itself technically. Judging from the reports of visitors to Soviet industrial facilities—indeed just from news programs that show factories— and from the endemic shortages of even simple products, the country is in serious trouble. At the very least, its current reliance on imported capital equipment is a far cry from the autarchy that had once been an article of faith of its political system. Reversing its industrial decay is clearly a priority objective of the present leadership, with serious efforts being made in the face of obvious political obstacles and dangers. It would be useful if such efforts on the part of the Soviet Union would spur comparable ones in the United States; for one thing, both would benefit, and it would be a welcome change from their usual negative-sum games.

Our analysis of industrial self-image, however, shows that many diverse elements and aspects of national life go into its making and into its decline. If there is a capsule prescription for improvement it is surely "stop doing what you are doing." Applying this simple precept to the defects we have described will not be easy and will call forth resistance from all the interest groups that can still prosper under the present circumstances, and from those who, rightly or wrongly, see themselves as bearing an excessive share of the costs of change. However, the time for incantation and complacency is well past. The United States has been fortunate in having been able to avoid the kind of sociopolitical turmoil and violence that has destroyed other countries. It was able, in the 1930s, to weather even its most severe economic depression with its political institutions intact at a time when many other countries resorted to dictatorships.

The kinds of therapeutic efforts that are now required to restore industrial strength, international solvency, and a general sense of renewed progress will have to be as serious and extensive as those in earlier times of grave trouble.

3

U.S. Competitiveness: Looking Back and Looking Ahead

JOSEPH DUFFEY

Introduction

A s we approach the 1990s, the U.S. economy is at a cross-roads. On the one hand, our nation remains among the world's most important political and economic actors. The

JOSEPH DUFFEY is chancellor of the University of Massachusetts at Amherst and a professor in the Department of Sociology there. He previously served as assistant secretary of state for educational and cultural affairs during the Carter administration and as chairman of the National Endowment for the Humanities. In June of 1983, Chancellor Duffey was named executive chairman of the Governor's Commission on Mature Industries by Massachusetts Governor Michael Dukakis. He is a member of the National Business–Higher Education Forum and of the Executive Committee of the National Council on Competitiveness. Dr. Duffey has held academic appointments at several universities and colleges, including Yale. He has been a fellow at the Harvard University School of Government. He has lectured at Northwestern, the University of Southern California, the University of Alabama, and has published widely in journals and reviews.

The author wishes to acknowledge the contributions of his colleagues Tim Koechlin, Joan Stoia, and Jim Leheny. Their research and discussions helped shape the perspectives of this chapter.

market for U.S. goods and services is the world's largest, and the standard of living of our citizens is among the highest in the world. On the other hand, our prominence in general and the health of our economy in particular have deteriorated over the past two decades. U.S. policy makers have faced long bouts of inflation and unemployment, and now face unprecedented trade and federal budget deficits. The growth of productivity has been sluggish, and real wages in 1987 were no higher than in 1969. As we move toward the twenty-first century, the prospects for our economy, and the firms and workers that comprise it, are mixed. Policy makers and citizens are thus faced with some difficult decisons in the years immediately ahead.

This chapter attempts to shed some light on the nature and possible consequences of these decisions. By laying out some of the specific problems confronting policy makers, and tracing their historical roots, I hope to provide insight. By looking back, we may better understand where we are headed.

I agree fundamentally with those who argue that the U.S. economy is plagued by basic problems: the federal deficit, the trade deficit, and slow productivity growth are all signs of an economy that is less vigorous than it should be.

Yet I am cautiously optimistic about the future. The twenty-first century could very well be characterized by rising living standards, rewarding work, and a strong and positive U.S. world presence. But such a future must be created, it will not simply unfold. A prosperous twenty-first century will require fundamental changes in our attitudes about work, government, and the relationship between business and labor.

There are two areas that are particularly important. First, we must recognize that human capital is our greatest competitive potential. The talents of inventors, engineers, managers, and skilled workers will remain our best hope for economic achievement. Our ability to compete hinges on the ability to take advantage of a creative, well-trained labor force. Business and government should see workers as an asset, and not simply as a cost of production. Part of the secret of enhanced productivity lies in making people feel as though they are valued members of the economic community.

In 1952, writing in the magazine *Nation's Business,* Peter
Drucker wrote: "Productivity is an attitude." Drucker was describing the reactions of "businessmen, technicians, educators, workers and union officials" who had come to the United
States from every country of Western Europe to find out for
themselves what causes American productivity. These visiting
"productivity teams," organized under the Marshall Plan,
were seeking to find the causes of America's remarkable progress in techniques and processes. Drucker wrote: "I know of
no team that did not speedily discover for itself that techniques
are not the really important thing and certainly not the real
cause of productivity." Drucker quoted a team of British businessmen, primarily in the printing industries, who wrote, "In
America, productivity is an attitude of mind." Drucker observed that a number of the teams reported the same thing.
"Attitudes, social organization and moral value: these underlie
and explain America's industrial achievement." "Even in such
a seemingly 'technical' area as the use of machinery, the visitors see the main cause for America's lead in attitudes rather
than in capital," Drucker observed. "What it adds up to in the
minds of . . . foreign visitors is that this country avails itself of
a much larger percentage of its human resources than their
own," Drucker concluded.

The "social dimension" of productivity is of central importance. This fact has, however, been lost on many of today's
managers and policy makers. Increasing conflict between
labor and capital in the name of "cost cutting" will inevitably
diminish the prospects for a vital American economy in the
future.

Second, rebuilding the U.S. economy will require a new
sense of collaboration and trust among business, labor, and
government. The unrivaled dominance in world affairs enjoyed by the United States in the 1950s and 1960s was rooted
in a very specific set of historical circumstances. The world has
changed, and the United States is now one of many important
industrial countries. Too much rhetoric and exhortation about
competitiveness today relies on sports metaphors. The talk is
about winning a race, beating our adversaries. The challenge,

rather, is first to understand a new situation, both in terms of domestic reality and international economic order. The key to revitalizing the American economy is to recognize that we must adjust to these new circumstances, rather than struggle over who is responsible for the difficult situation in which we find ourselves. Rebuilding America requires that we move beyond scapegoating.

It also will require that we create a coherent network of programs and attitudes that promote long-term competitiveness. In an environment of distrust, business, labor, and government all have tended to be shortsighted: businesses seek short-term profits, workers want wage increases now, and government spends now and pays later. We need to learn a lesson from the Japanese and the Germans, who have made national commitments to long-term competitiveness. We must begin to create a genuinely American collaboration which is consistent with our culture, politics, and institutions.

Part II of this chapter discusses the current state of the U.S. economy in some detail, and attempts to trace the roots of the economic problems now facing U.S. policy makers. Part III discusses the ways in which economic and demographic changes have affected the prospects for American workers and concludes with some proposals about how changes in economic policy and labor relations might enhance both the competitiveness of the U.S. economy and the quality of life of its workers. Part IV includes a brief conclusion.

The Changing Role of the United States in the World Economy

The health of the U.S. economy has been a source of major concern for nearly two decades. The years since 1972 have been characterized by three recessions (including the two worst since the 1930s), some unprecedented price inflation, high unemployment rates, dramatic interest rate and exchange rate fluctuations, declining real wages, and, most recently, enormous budget and trade deficits. These developments are particularly notable when contrasted with the relatively

smooth and consistent economic growth that characterized
the two decades following World War II.

During the 1980s the United States experienced modest
expansion following a decade of stops and starts. The unemployment rate fell from a high of 10.7 percent in December
1982 to 6.3 percent in June of 1987. In 1980 the annual rate
of inflation was 13 percent. Between 1983 and 1987 it averaged between 3 and 4 percent. Former presidential economic
adviser Martin Feldstein wrote in the *Economic Report of the
President* in 1984 that these developments demonstrate "the
inherent vitality of the U.S. economy." Others are not as sure
as Feldstein. In 1983 Robert Reich of Harvard wrote in *The
Next American Frontier,* "Since the late 1960's America's economy has been slowly unraveling." Four years later, in the *New
York Review of Books,* Felix Rohatyn, investment banker and
economic commentator, offered this sober assessment of the
state of U.S. economic affairs: "The United States today is
headed for a financial and economic crisis. What appeared to
be a possibility five or six years ago . . . has now become a
virtual certainty." While Rohatyn's view is more pessimistic
than many economists', there is widespread agreement that
the U.S. economy is plagued by a number of fundamental
problems. The relatively good news of recent years is welcome. But many economists remain concerned about large
trade and federal budget deficits, fluctuations in the value of
the dollar, slow productivity growth, low rates of investment,
and accelerating rates of private borrowing.

The Reagan Recovery: Why Are
Economists Skeptical?

There has been much good economic news in recent years.
Economic growth and declining unemployment rates are always welcome, particularly given their elusiveness over the
past two decades. The inflationary spiral of the 1970s appears
to be broken. This is an important and impressive accomplishment. Why, then, are many economists unpersuaded that the
"Reagan recovery" signals the end of economic hard times?

There are several reasons. First, by the standards of past recoveries, this has been a weak one. Growth has been moderate, and it is difficult to feel satisfied with an unemployment rate of 6.3 percent. Second, it appears that recent economic growth has been fueled, to a disturbing extent, by public and private debt. The *Wall Street Journal* reports that the ratio of debt to gross national product (GNP) increased by 30 percent in the five years following 1982. This occurred after fifteen years of very contained fluctuations. Rohatyn sees "a worldwide pyramid of debt that cannot withstand the next major recession." Third, the apparent decline in the competitiveness of U.S. firms relative to those of Japan, Europe, Korea, Brazil, and elsewhere continues. The trade deficit remains enormous, U.S. productivity growth remains sluggish, and U.S firms in many industries are losing market share to foreign firms both at home and abroad.

How can this situation be explained? Many culprits have been named in the literature: uninspired managers, greedy workers, excessive government involvement in the economy, unfair trade practices by our competitors, differences between U.S. and Japanese cultures, and bad policy making have all been proposed. Theories focusing on some, and perhaps each, of these issues can provide insight into the U.S. economy. Much of the problem, however, can be explained by structural changes in American and international economic relationships. Changes there have tended to narrow the gap between the United States and other economies. The problems facing economic policy makers in the late 1980s, in short, have many roots in the history of these relationships since World War II.

The Historical Roots of the Current Economic Crisis

In the twenty-five years following World War II, the U.S. economy boomed. Real GNP grew at an annual rate of 4 percent. The rate of unemployment was, on average, under 5 percent. The average annual rate of inflation was under 3 percent. Productivity and living standards grew rapidly. The recessions over this period were, by historical standards, brief and shallow. This persistent prosperity led some economists to conclude that major bouts of instability and stagnation were things of the past. The United States was by far the world's most important economic actor. Japan and Europe had been devastated by World War II, leaving the United States with more than half of the world's usable productive capacity. In 1960 one-fourth of world exports originated in the United States. U.S. multinational corporations, exploiting their advantages in production technology, marketing, and access to capital, established and expanded subsidiaries around the globe.

The dominance of the United States in world affairs extended to the realms of politics and military affairs as well. The United States was the world's "hegemonic power." It had the world's most imposing military presence. Its firms were leaders in trade and technology, and its banks were leaders in finance. Its agricultural sector was the world's most productive, and its government the most influential. The dollar was the free world's principal currency. *Business Week* described the United States during this period as the world's "banker and cop."

This state of affairs had two important consequences. First, U.S. firms were effective and profitable competitors, both because of their inherent efficiency and market power, and because of the effectiveness of the U.S. government in securing favorable conditions for their growth. Second, U.S. statesmen, bankers, and businessmen were able to use their power—and the dependence of foreigners on U.S. firms and government— to maintain international economic stability. Under U.S. leadership, world markets were open to trade and investment, and exchange rates were predictable and stable. In short, the rules of international economics—among them the central role of the dollar—tended to favor U.S. firms. Yet the existence of a dependable set of rules facilitated the growth of the world economy as a whole. The result was more than two decades of international economic growth. Ironically, this growth played a role in undermining the vitality of the U.S. economy.

What Happened?

Unfortunately for U.S. firms, the world situation changed in a number of ways that tended to undermine their ability to compete internationally and produce profitably at home. Among the most important developments were the following.

1. The growth of the U.S. economy stimulated growth in Japan and Western Europe. Restrictions against German and Japanese remilitarization also played a role by effectively forcing these countries to allocate their savings toward research and development, and toward new plant and equipment. The revitalization of these economies was, in fact, an explicit objective of U.S. policy, for both economic and political reasons. The growth of these economies meant the growth of demand for U.S. products. Further, it was believed that economic growth would increase the likelihood that communism would not flourish in these countries.

2. European and Japanese firms enjoyed a long-term competitive advantage of sorts because of their status as "followers." (This concept is discussed by Robert Reich and Ira Magaziner in *Minding America's Business*.) As these firms grew, they were able to employ the best and most recent technologies and marketing strategies with little opportunity cost. U.S. firms, having made expensive investments in once current technologies, had to consider the high cost of writing off these investments when considering the employment of newer technologies. U.S. firms, as a rule, were enjoying high rates of return based on their superior size, experience, and market power. They had little economic incentive, in the short and medium run, to invest heavily in upgrading their production technologies. The steel industry provides a classic example. In *The Next American Frontier*, Robert Reich describes the undoing of the U.S. steel industry thus:

By the mid-1960s America's basic industries had lost the habit of competing. . . . Since profitability was more or less guaranteed, there was no reason to innovate in new products or processes. . . . Steel technology had progressed since most plants were built—a fact not lost on foreign competitors. But it would have been difficult and costly to fit the new technology into their old plants. . . . They saw no reason to go to this trouble and expense since industry profits could be maintained through careful coordination among producers.

3. Japanese and German firms were encouraged by competitive conditions to focus on long-term viability, often at the expense of short-term profits. James Abegglen and George Stalk (and many other commentators on the Japanese corporation) highlight "bias toward growth" as a distinctive feature of successful Japanese firms. This may be rooted, in part, in cultural differences, as Ezra Vogel and Michio Morishima each argue, but it is also the result of the different conditions under which Japanese firms have developed. Japanese firms have been forced, largely by the initial superiority of U.S. firms, either to innovate, invest, and grow, or to fail. U.S. managers, on the other hand, have been hard pressed to persuade their stockholders of the need to retool for the future at the expense of current profits. Between 1966 and 1972 Japanese steel firms increased their assets by an average of 23 percent, as compared to 4 percent among U.S. firms.

4. The economies of the free world have become increasingly interconnected. In 1970, 9 percent of goods produced in the United States were exported. In 1980, this ratio increased to 19 percent. Imports have increased similarly. The U.S. Department of Commerce estimates that by 1980, 70 percent of U.S. goods were actively competing with foreign goods. This change has two broad sources. First, productivity and demand growth in Western Europe and Japan rendered these nations more viable exporters and importers. Second, rapid developments in the technologies of transportation and communication have led to both the more general availability of mass production technologies and the greater technical viability of foreign trade and investment. This partly explains the rapid development of industry in Brazil, Korea, Mexico, Singapore, and other newly industrializing countries.

The post–World War II boom in the United States was built on a "mass production model," where low cost and high quality were achieved by way of large, standardized production runs. The United States and Europe no longer monopolize the techniques and managerial expertise necessary to employ this model successfully. It has thus become increasingly difficult for U.S. firms to compete with the relatively low wage rates of Korea and Mexico without the technological advantages they enjoyed two decades ago. In contrast to the early postwar years, the United States is now only one of several formidable industrialized countries.

5. The United States suffered a number of defeats in the international arena which, along with, and in part because of, its declining economic dominance, have undermined its effectiveness as the leader of the free world. The defeat in Vietnam, the nationalization of many U.S. subsidiaries abroad, the success of OPEC, and the Iran hostage crisis are outstanding examples. The declining economic, military, and political dominance of the United States made the maintenance of international economic stability—stable exchange rates, reliable trade agreements, coordinated macroeconomic policies—a much more difficult task. A pivotal concession to the waning of the "U.S. hegemony" was President Richard Nixon's 1973 announcement that the U.S. dollar would no longer be regulated on the basis of the 1944 Bretton Woods agreement. Thus, just as the world economy was becoming more open and competitive, it was also becoming less stable and less predictable. The economies of Japan and several other countries were surely gaining ground on the United States, but the world economy as a whole was more volatile.

6. The current crisis also has domestic causes. Through the 1950s and 1960s, real incomes rose as the economy expanded. In the late 1960s, rates of productivity growth—the foundation upon which economic growth and rising living standards are built—began to decline. Wage rates continued to rise, the high cost of the Vietnam War led to increasing federal deficits, and the demand for improved social services persisted.

Declining productivity growth has perplexed many economists. William Brainard and George Perry, coeditors of the *Brookings Papers on Economic Activity,* write: "In the most comprehensive study to date, Edward Denison examined seventeen alternative hypotheses and concluded that alone or in combination they could explain only a fraction of the slow-down." One of the more controversial attempts to account for the decline in productivity has been offered by Samuel Bowles, David M. Gordon, and Thomas E. Weisskopf in their 1983 book *Beyond the Wasteland.* They acknowledge that many "technical" determinants of productivity—the capital/labor ratio, raw material prices, and technical change—played a role in the productivity slowdown. But they argue that "social factors" also played a central role. The authors attempt to show that the decline in productivity growth is largely explained by declining worker satisfaction, and by an increase of 50 percent in the ratio of supervisory workers to production workers between 1948 and 1979. They contend that slow productivity growth in the United States has its roots in deteriorating capital labor relations. And Robert Reich, in a 1987 *Wall Street Journal* article, describes the situation similarly: "People who feel themselves to be respected members of the economic and social system are more apt to work productively within it than are those who feel the dice are loaded against them."

Bowles and his coauthors have not, in my judgment, made a fully convincing case for this assertion. But it is clear that a decline in social cohesion and social morals is a factor too often left out of analyses of declining American productivity.

In the late 1960s inflation rates began to accelerate largely as a result of declining productivity and unchecked demands on resources. In an attempt to curb inflation, the Federal Reserve Board of Governors, in 1974, pursued so-called tight money policies. At about the same time, OPEC oil prices tripled. The United States, and most of the world, entered a recession. The era of "stagflation"—the coincidence of inflation and slow growth—was well under way by the middle of the 1970s.

Reaganomics

When Ronald Reagan was inaugurated in 1981, his administration was faced with fundamental economic problems. Real

GNP had been lower in 1980 than in 1979. In 1980 the unemployment rate averaged 7.1 percent, inflation was at 13.5 percent, and the rate of interest charged by banks to their prime customers was over 15 percent. The basic thrust of President Reagan's approach to economic affairs was simple: the government should have a minimal role in economic affairs. Wherever possible, resources should be allocated on the basis of "market forces."

The Reagan administration and the Federal Reserve Bank pursued four broad policies of significant economic consequence: (1) in 1981 the largest tax cut in U.S. history was enacted; (2) the Reagan administration shifted government spending away from social spending and toward defense spending (all told, government spending increased); (3) the Reagan administration sought to "deregulate" the economy wherever possible; and (4) in the late 1970s and early 1980s Paul Volcker's Federal Reserve pursued restrictive monetary policy in an effort to "wring inflation out of the economy."

The results have been mixed. The Federal Reserve policy significantly reduced inflation rates, but at some cost. The economy entered a severe recession, and unemployment rates reached 10.7 percent—a post–World War II high.

The policies of the Reagan administration have created at least one major economic problem, and have done little to alleviate a second. The fiscal policies of the early 1980s led to an explosion of the federal deficit. Between 1981 and 1986 the federal debt—the sum of all previous deficits—doubled. The deficit has had dramatic effects on capital markets, the value of the dollar, the trade deficit, and government spending in the future. Further, many economists believe that the Reagan administration has done little to improve the competitiveness of the U.S. economy.

Mounting Debt and Declining Competitiveness

The huge increase in government borrowing, coupled with slow growth in the money supply in the early 1980s, led to higher real interest rates. Profit rates on financial investment

increased relative to profit rates on investment in plant and
equipment. This had two notable consequences. First, many
U.S. manufacturing firms, looking to invest their share of the
tax cut, opted for high-return, low-risk government bonds and
other financial investments, rather than increasing investments in plant and equipment as predicted and hoped. Second, foreign investors began buying U.S. financial assets in
large volume. This dramatically increased the demand for dollars, and thus the value of the dollar. The "strong dollar"
raised the price of U.S. goods abroad and lowered the price
of imports for U.S. consumers, thereby providing foreign
goods with an unearned subsidy. The trade deficit was thus
made worse by large federal government deficits.

The importance of stable and equitable exchange rates is
highlighted by Pat Choate in *The High Flex Society*. Between
1980 and 1985, Choate points out, the dollar appreciated 40
percent, then depreciated 20 percent in the following eighteen
months. The Department of Commerce estimates that an
overvalued dollar was responsible for about 50 percent of U.S.
trade losses between 1981 and 1986.

The volume of private debt has also boomed. Corporate
debt as a percentage of net worth has increased by over 20
percent since 1980, and household debt as a percentage of
disposable income has increased by nearly 25 percent. Bankruptcies among individuals jumped nearly 35 percent in fiscal
1986. In 1980 fewer than twenty banks failed. In early 1987 the
Federal Deposit Insurance Commission chairman, William
Seidman, predicted more than 150 failures. The debts of Brazil, Mexico, Argentina, and other Third World countries to
U.S. banks remain enormous.

The potential effects of a recession are serious. Lower incomes for households, firms, and Third World debtors will
leave them increasingly unable to pay their debts, and will
leave the world financial system vulnerable to a major crisis.
A recession, further, would only serve to exacerbate the federal deficit problem by lowering tax revenues and increasing
welfare and unemployment payments.

The strong dollar has certainly hindered the competitiveness of U.S. firms in the short run. It may have had significant long-term effects as well. The loss of foreign and domestic sales has brought some firms to bankruptcy. Declining profitability has denied trade-dependent firms the funds they need to retool for the long term. Many firms are carrying a heavy debt burden. Others have been forced to close down facilities and move operations abroad.

Little has been done to enhance the competitiveness of U.S. firms. The pressure to show profits in the short term is stronger than ever, and there is no significant indication that productivity in U.S. firms is improving.

What Can Be Done?

The future success of the U.S. economy lies in enhancing the productivity, flexibility, and specialized advantages of its firms and work force. The United States cannot match the wage rates of Taiwan and Mexico. It *can* potentially match anyone in its ability to provide an educated, creative work force, a set of institutions that facilitate rapid and sophisticated research and development, a stable business environment, and the largest national market in the world.

A program that includes improved educational opportunities, increased cooperation between management and labor, and the growth of demand has two advantages over a program of wage cutting. First, it more directly addresses the problems underlying the decline of U.S. competitiveness. That is, it is a plan that plays to the strengths of the U.S. economy, rather than encouraging U.S. firms to fight a losing battle against low-wage competitors. Second, it is a program built on cooperation and an improving quality of life, rather than conflict and austerity.

Further, firms must be given the incentive, in the short run, to invest in projects that enhance their long-term viability. Corporate tax cuts might be tied to incentives for increased reinvestment in training and equipment. The recent increase in hostile takeovers has, more than ever, focused the attention of managers and directors on short-term profits.

Prospects for the American Work Force

The U.S. economy has undergone dramatic changes over
the last two decades. These changes have had, and will continue to have, consequences for the quality and substance of
work life in America. At stake is the content and location of
new jobs, the organization of work, and the standard of living
of American workers. In the year 2000, a great many jobs,
production techniques, and enterprises will bear little resem-
blance to those in existence today.

The Shift from Manufacturing
to Services

Among the most significant trends affecting the future of
work in the United States is the steady growth in the ratio of
service to manufacturing jobs. Services now account for 90
percent of all new jobs in the United States. This shift has been
a point of contention among economists and policy makers.
Some argue that this trend demonstrates that the United
States is "deindustrializing." Others argue that the shift to
services is a "natural" next step for a mature industrial country, and that this structural change merely reflects changes in
our comparative advantage.

Indeed, our comparative advantage in many manufacturing
industries has declined. The key organizational and technical
aspects of the "mass production model" are increasingly available to firms in other countries. Further, advances in the technologies of communication and transportation have made
once remote low-wage sites accessible to firms from the United
States and other countries. This "transfer of technology"
surely has been facilitated by U.S. multinational corporations,
the U.S. government, and American universities. But to blame
our economic decline on this process misses the point. It is
nearly impossible, in the long run, to maintain technological
monopolies. Attempts to do so contradict efforts to promote
the development of Third World countries and our allies.

The significance of the shift from a manufacturing- to service-based economy cannot be overstated. It has implications for every important aspect of American work life. Some of the most notable areas are discussed below.

Income. Many economists and workers are concerned that the shift to services will mean a lower standard of living for American workers. Indeed, average wages in service industries are lower than those in manufacturing. The industries in which employment is declining most rapidly—auto and steel, for instance—tend to be those that pay best. The net effect of this shift has been a stagnation—a slight decline, in fact—of the average real wage paid to American workers. This is a particularly striking statistic when compared to the 50 percent increase in real wages enjoyed by American workers between 1950 and 1970.

While many workers have felt the income squeeze, the burden has been distributed unevenly. Displaced workers have been the hardest hit. In a 1978 study, Louis Jacobson found that permanently displaced prime-age male auto workers experienced, on average, a 43 percent drop in annual income over the first two years following displacement, and an average of 16 percent over the next four years.

The shift away from traditional manufacturing jobs has had a disproportionately harsh effect on minority workers, particularly black males and workers with low levels of education. Between 1973 and 1984, average real annual earnings of black males between the ages of twenty and twenty-four declined by nearly 50 percent. Unemployment rates among nonwhite workers remain more than twice that of white workers. In 1983 the ratio of average annual income of black men to that of white men was 52 percent, down from a post–World War II high of 58 percent in 1969.

There is reason to suspect that this trend will continue. The Department of Labor predicts that increasing mechanization will tend to slow the growth of low-skill service jobs. At the same time, relatively unskilled workers—a disproportionate number of whom are nonwhite—will be the fastest growing segment of the work force. Unless there are increased efforts to incorporate nonwhite workers into the economic mainstream, they will be increasingly frequent victims of unemployment and poverty.

Still, there is some reason to be optimistic about the net effect that the shift to services will have on the earning potential of American workers. While many new service jobs are part-time and relatively low paying, much of the growth in services will be in professional, technical, and managerial categories. Analysts predict that 40 percent of future job growth will occur in occupations at the high end of the education and skill range, occupations that generally will require either a college education or other post-secondary training.

The Location of Work. Changes in the composition of American output have had, and will continue to have, a significant effect on the geographical distribution of jobs. There has been a significant relocation of manufacturing jobs from the states of the Midwest and Northeast to the states of the Southeast and Southwest. Many of the highest paying and most challenging jobs in banking, financial services, corporate management, and government will continue to be concentrated in major urban centers. The low cost of data transmission has made increasingly viable the shift of lower tier jobs in finance and banking to offshore locations. Retail growth has been concentrated in the suburbs.

The complicated consequences of a firm's decision to relocate provide an example of what economists call "market failure." The firm makes its decision, for the most part, on the basis of the costs it will incur. But a plant closing entails significant social costs as well. Laid-off workers lose income and can relocate only at significant expense. Major changes in the geography of production affect the performance of the macroeconomy as well, by increasing the incidence of "structural unemployment"—a situation where able workers are idle in one location while labor shortages occur elsewhere.

Changes in competitive conditions require that some industries decline while others grow. The nature and location of work are thus bound to change periodically. To the maximum extent possible, federal and state policies should provide incentives for firms to consider social costs and benefits as well as profit in their location decisions.

Changes in Skill Requirements and the Organization of Work. Changes in technology, competitive conditions, and the growth of services have had, and will continue to have, an impact on both the skills required of workers and the organization of work. During the post–World War II period, U.S. firms were geared for routinized mass production. Successful firms in the twenty-first century will be characterized by flexibility, regular innovation, and the ability to satisfy the needs of specific customers. Workers will have more responsibility, and will be required to use higher order skills on the job. Increasingly, workers will be organized into teams, and there will be a greater emphasis on worker self-management. Skills in writing and problem solving will be important prerequisites to a greater and greater percentage of jobs.

Small businesses have generated the greatest share of new service jobs, in areas from consulting, personnel recruitment, and data processing to security and maintenance. Large firms are contracting out more and more services to such businesses. This is part of the broader trend toward smaller, more flexible workplaces.

Other Trends Affecting American Workers

A few other trends are worth noting: self-employment has become increasingly popular. Part-time, temporary, and at-home work are becoming increasingly common as well. The growth of these alternative arrangements is a positive development, on the one hand, as it offers businesses and workers increasing flexibility. On the other hand, part-time jobs generally offer lower pay, less stability, and fewer benefits than do full-time jobs. The growth of part-time work reflects, in large part, the relative hardship faced by American labor in the last decade or so. Lower wage rates have compelled families to

send second wage earners to work, and slack labor markets
have forced a larger percentage of workers to accept part-time
and temporary work.

Fewer than 20 percent of nonagricultural workers in the
United States belong to labor unions, down from a high of 36
percent in 1954. The growth of service industries and the
decline of highly unionized basic industries provide a partial
explanation. Further, high unemployment over the last fifteen
years has undermined the bargaining power of workers. The
decline of unions has accelerated during the Reagan administration. Firms have more aggressively opposed organizing
drives, pushed for decertification votes, and pursued union
"give backs."

Women's participation in the labor force has also grown
significantly in the postwar period. In 1960, 33.3 percent of
the labor force was female, and by 1983 the ratio was 45
percent. The percentage of mothers who work increased from
17 percent in 1955 to 50 percent in 1983.

Finally, income earned by nonwhites and women continues
to lag behind that of white men. We have noted that black men
actually earn less relative to white men than they did twenty
years ago. Women, on average, earn 65 percent of what men
earn for a week of full-time work. Discrimination on the basis
of gender or race is not only harmful to its victim, it wastes
important resources. When talented people are denied access
to jobs commensurate with their potential, productivity and
economic competitiveness suffer.

Policy for the Year 2000:
Some Recommendations

The prospects for American workers in the twenty-first century are mixed. American workers have experienced fifteen
years of slack labor markets, stagnating income, intensifying
import competition, and dislocation. A vital American economy that offers workers creative, rewarding work is absolutely
attainable, but the conditions for such a scenario will require
serious planning, work, and a resurgence of trust and coopera-

tion among business, labor, and government. It will require a
shift to an economic program that promotes not only investment in plant and equipment, but also investment in human
capital. Such a policy shift would be marked by the following
characteristics.

First, America needs to sustain a public commitment to a
strong national education system. The economic tasks before
us require an educational system that produces creative think-
ers, people who know how to learn. We are currently in danger
of losing our best competitive advantage, our highly educated
and skilled work force.

Second, we need better funded and more coherent networks
of job training programs. These programs would, for example,
provide retraining to displaced workers, facilitate the school-
to-work transition, and improve skills of older workers. We
should devote resources to the promotion of lifelong training
opportunities.

Third, we need to address the increasing tension between
work and family life by providing affordable child care.
Households headed by women are the most likely to suffer
from poverty, and more and more "traditional" households
are characterized by two wage earners. Citizens of a major
industrialized country ought not have to choose between parenthood and prosperity.

Fourth, the pressures of international competition require
that firms and industries be able to shift resources quickly. A
flexible work force is critical to a vital economy. Workers and
communities, however, should not be left to shoulder the social cost of plant relocation alone. Firms should be required to
demonstrate that benefits of their relocation outweigh the
costs. Dislocated workers ought to have a right to severance
pay and retraining or, if they choose to relocate, their costs
should be shared by the departing firm and the government.
We need to develop more "safety nets," like portable pension
plans, training and educational allowances, product development grants, and business start-up funds to minimize worker
dislocation.

Finally, we must stop wasting talent. "Acceptable" unemployment levels are too high. Unemployment not only denies a decent living for an individual, it drains government resources and lowers our national output by leaving able hands idle. Further, discrimination suffered by women, blacks, and other groups, beyond being morally wrong, is wasteful. By denying people equal access to education and employment, we are throwing away the chance for enhanced productivity and innovation.

One premise of this chapter is that the productivity and creative contribution of a worker to the production process depend on the extent to which workers feel they have a stake in their work, and that they are valued members of the economic community. Blaming workers for our declining competitiveness, union busting, and irresponsible capital flight is thus at odds with the end of promoting the long-term competitiveness of the U.S. economy. As Robert Reich wrote, "Social justice is not incompatible with economic growth, but essential to it."

Conclusion

The U.S. economy is at a crossroads. It is an economy saddled with public and private debt, and plagued by sluggish productivity growth and a massive trade deficit. At the same time, it enjoys the advantages of a highly skilled labor force, a well-developed research and development infrastructure, and the world's largest market.

A future characterized by declining living standards, widening disparities between rich and poor, and fewer opportunities for profitable investment is entirely possible. Yet, there is basis for cautious optimism. But a prosperous twenty-first century for America will require that we make a fairly major change of course over the next decade. Among the most important steps we need to take are the following.

1. Americans and U.S. policy makers must recognize that the world economy has changed dramatically over the last several decades, and that these changes have made it more difficult for U.S. firms to compete effectively. That is, it must be recog-

nized that there is a problem, and that its causes transcend bad policy, bad management, or excessive wage demands. The United States is now only one of many mature industrial powers, and this means more intense competition for firms and less margin of error for managers and government policy makers.

2. In order to compete effectively, the United States must play to its strengths. The future of the U.S. economy lies in enhancing the productivity, flexibility, and specialized advantages of its firms and work force. The United States cannot match the wage rates of Taiwan or Mexico. It can, potentially, match any country in its ability to provide an educated, creative work force, institutions that facilitate rapid and sophisticated research and development, a stable business environment, and the largest national market in the world.

An educated work force, whose members feel they have a stake in the economy, is a crucial precondition to increased productivity growth and innovation. Peter Drucker wrote in 1952 that despite the advantages enjoyed by the United States in technology, capital-labor ratios, and marketing techniques, European visitors were most impressed with the social dimension of productivity: the ways in which work was organized and the attitudes of people about their work. We need to make this social dimension of productivity a central policy focus.

3. More than ever, the fate of the U.S. economy depends on the ability of its firms to innovate in the realms of production technology and new product development. A large percentage of new innovations comes from smaller technical companies rather than large companies or government. An economic environment that promotes new ventures must be cultivated.

4. Firms must be given the incentive, in the short run, to invest in projects that enhance their long-term viability. High interest rates have induced more and more firms to engage in "paper entrepreneurialism," rather than upgrading their production facilities. Recent hostile takeovers have forced managers to show a profit now, and worry about tomorrow later.

5. The pursuit of these objectives will require a major shift in the relationship among educators, business, labor, and gov-

ernment. Increasingly hostile relations between labor and management serve only to inhibit productivity and innovation. The promotion of long-term competitiveness would be facilitated by establishing panels of business, labor, and government representatives who are charged with shaping detailed policy proposals which are in every American's interest.

6. Perhaps most crucial, the revitalization of the U.S. economy will require a change in many of our basic attitudes. It depends on changing attitudes of workers about their work. It will require that managers change their attitudes about the relative importance of short- and long-term profits. And it will require that business, labor, and government change their attitudes about each other.

4

Competitiveness: An Analysis of the Problem and a Perspective on Future Policy

LAURA D'ANDREA TYSON

The Meaning of Competitiveness

During the last several years, the dramatic and sustained deterioration in the U.S. trade deficit has created growing concern over American competitiveness. Indeed, competitiveness, a concept that did not even exist in national policy discussions until the last few years, has become a buzzword. Business, labor, education, and government leaders speak of the competitiveness challenge confronting the United States and offer a potpourri of sometimes conflicting policy solu-

LAURA D'ANDREA TYSON is associate professor in economics at the University of California, Berkeley, and a research associate of the Berkeley Roundtable on the International Economy. She has served as a consultant for several organizations, including the International Bank for Reconstruction and Development, the congressional Office of Technology Assessment, Wharton Economic Forecasting Associates, the Rand Corporation, the President's Commission on Industrial Competitiveness, and the Council on Competitiveness. She was assistant professor in economics at Princeton University from 1974 to 1977 and has published extensively on international economic issues.

tions. Initiatives in such diverse areas as trade legislation, educational reform, and taxes are defended or criticized on the basis of their likely effects on U.S. competitiveness. Like most buzzwords, competitiveness has symbolic significance. It draws national attention to the unassailable fact that the position of the United States in the world economy is weakening. America can no longer rest comfortably in the belief that it will continue to be the premiere economic power in the world. Although still the largest and one of the richest economies, the United States has lost position compared to many countries with which it competes in world trade. To some extent, of course, this was inevitable. At the end of World War II, as Paul Kennedy points out in the *Atlantic Monthly,* the U.S. share of world manufacturing output was close to one-half—a share never before attained by a single nation. As many developed countries rebuilt from war destruction and as many developing countries introduced ambitious development programs, some catching up was inevitable. But the pace and extent of the catch-up—or to put it differently, the pace and extent of the decline in the U.S. position—were not inevitable. They were influenced by actions at home and abroad. And, significantly for the future, there is no inevitability to a continued decline in the U.S. position, especially at the rate observed in recent years.

If competitiveness is to have more than symbolic significance, if it is to become a reliable guide for policy by public and private actors, it must be properly defined. The need for an appropriate definition is evident in current policy debates. Some people define competitiveness as a trade problem. The trade deficit is an indicator of competitive difficulties, and trade policy changes, even ones that threaten to reduce our access to foreign markets and our standard of living, are the solution. Others define competitiveness as a macroeconomic problem. Low U.S. saving rates and huge fiscal deficits have kept the U.S. cost of capital relatively high, and U.S. producers have not been able to finance competitive investment rates required for improvements in product and process technologies. The solution lies in a reformulation of our monetary and

fiscal policies to get interest rates down and national saving
and investment up. Still others define the competitiveness
problem as a labor cost problem. U.S. firms cannot compete
because U.S. wages are too high, and the solution is a decline
in U.S. wages and perhaps, incidentally, continued erosion in
union influence.

For the purpose of discussion here, competitiveness is defined, as it was in the report of the President's Commission on
Industrial Competitiveness and more recently by the Council
on Competitiveness, as "the degree to which a nation, under
free and fair market conditions, produces goods and services
that meet the test of international markets while simultaneously maintaining and expanding the real incomes of its citizens." There are two important points in this definition. First,
competitiveness implies an ability to compete in international
markets, with balanced trade over the long run, *without* an
associated decline in real wages, and *without* a continued de-
line in the value of the dollar that would cause falling real
wages over time. Second, competitiveness as broadly defined
implies an ability to compete in free and open markets. In this
sense, neither a worsening of U.S. trade performance occa-
sioned by trade measures abroad nor an improvement occa-
sioned by trade measures at home is a sign of change in U.S.
competitiveness.

Productivity, Technology, and Competitiveness

The critical determinants of competitiveness as defined here
are productivity improvements and technological innovation.
The key to the ability of U.S. producers to offer competitive
prices while increasing rather than cutting real wages for U.S.
workers is productivity growth. When inputs become more
productive, costs decline and producers can pay higher wages
and charge competitive prices without sacrificing profits. Behind productivity improvements, in turn, lie both human and
technological forces. Managerial and labor skills are the foundation for productivity performance—the better trained and
more flexible the work force, other things being equal, the

greater its productivity. And the more rapid the diffusion of technological improvements in production processes, the faster will productivity improve. Innovative new machinery and new materials are both driving forces behind productivity growth. Technological improvements also directly affect the competitiveness of U.S. producers in product markets. Improvements in product quality or serviceability and product innovations are often the source of competitive success in international markets. For products that compete on such features, including many of the high-technology products that account for about two-fifths of U.S. trade in manufactures, technological improvements in process or product design are significant influences on competitive outcomes.

In productivity performance and technological innovation, there are clear signs that the United States has been losing ground relative to its competitors. For the period from 1960 to 1985, U.S. productivity growth was the lowest among the advanced industrial countries by a substantial margin. In manufacturing, U.S. productivity growth picked up sharply in the economic recovery beginning in 1982–83 but still fell short of rates achieved by most of the other developed countries and many developing ones as well. As a result of more than twenty-five years of relatively poor productivity growth, the substantial advantage in productivity levels enjoyed by U.S. producers has narrowed dramatically and in some instances disappeared altogether. In several sectors, including steel, autos, machine tools, and semiconductors, productivity levels in several competitor countries now equal or exceed U.S. levels. The erosion in the relative U.S. position has been concentrated in manufacturing and has been particularly dramatic vis-à-vis Germany and Japan. When the United States had an apparently overwhelming advantage in productivity, the pace at which that advantage declined did not seem of concern. Now that the advantage has narrowed, the long-term differential in the pace of productivity growth is of paramount importance.

There are also several indicators of a relative decline in U.S. technological capabilities in recent years. Research and development (R&D) spending is the principal mechanism for generating commercial innovations. In the United States, according to Martin Baily's article in the October 1986 issue of *Science,* real industry-funded R&D spending rose by 6.2 percent per year from 1960 to 1969, but by only 2.4 percent per year between 1969 and 1977. Significantly, the slowdown in R&D spending was associated with a slowdown in industrial productivity, suggesting that a slower pace of innovation was behind weakening productivity performance. R&D spending as a percent of sales by U.S. firms has increased from the low level of the 1970s, and U.S. industrial productivity growth also has picked up, once again suggesting a link between innovation and productivity. But the growth in R&D spending by Japanese and German firms since the late 1970s has been even faster than that by American firms. At the national level, nondefense R&D spending as a percentage of gross national product (GNP) has grown more rapidly in Japan and Germany than in the United States during the same time period.

In the United States there has been a dramatic increase in real federal spending on defense related R&D while real federal spending on nondefense R&D has fallen as a percentage of GNP since 1979. Defense oriented research cannot replace civilian R&D. Past evidence suggests that America's reliance on defense as a technological engine can hurt rather than help competitive outcomes in commercial applications. In computerized machine tools, for example, U.S. suppliers concentrated on unusual aerospace and defense applications, thereby losing a dominant share in commercial markets in such critical areas as robotics. Many observers now argue that civilian and defense needs are becoming even more divergent and that the current boom in defense research is diverting resources away from industrial pursuits.

Lower rates of civilian R&D spending in the United States have been associated with continued erosion in the U.S. patent position. The number of patents granted to U.S. inventors is an indicator of the flow of new commercial technology. The number of patents granted to U.S. applicants peaked in 1972 and declined substantially thereafter. During the same period, the share of U.S. patents held by U.S. residents also declined, from over 80 percent in 1965 to 55 percent in 1986. At the same time, the share of U.S. patents held by foreigners increased, with two-thirds of the increase awarded to Japanese nationals.

At the industrial level, perhaps the most dramatic evidence of the erosion in U.S. technological leadership comes from the semiconductor industry. In 1977, the U.S. technological lead in semiconductors appeared unchallenged. But studies by the Defense Science Policy Board and the Berkeley Roundtable on the International Economy indicate that the Japanese have now achieved leadership in a range of critical areas, and in others they are fast gaining on their American competitors. There are warning signs of similar trends in the computer and telecommunications industries as well.

The apparent relative weakening in the U.S. technological position is particularly disturbing because it has come at a time of seemingly basic innovation in the machines and know-how that constitute manufacturing practice. In this period of technological transition, made possible by the application of microelectronics to production techniques through a range of industrial sectors, if U.S. firms fail to design, adapt, and diffuse new technologies of production as rapidly and effectively as their foreign competitors, they will face even more difficult struggles in international markets in the future.

Fragmentary but suggestive evidence indicates that even when U.S. firms introduce new, more flexible automation systems into their production processes, they encounter difficulties. For example, a study by Jay Jakimar in the *Harvard Business Review* (1986) compares the use of flexible manufacturing systems (FMS) in Japan and the United States for comparable products. The study reveals that the number of parts made by an FMS in Japan is almost ten times greater than in the United States, while the rate of new product introduction is twenty-two times greater in Japan than in the United States. Jakimar concludes that with few exceptions the FMSs installed in the United States show an astonishing lack of flexibility in use.

How Policy Has Weakened
U.S. Competitiveness in Recent Years

Despite supply-side rhetoric, U.S. policies during the last several years have failed to address the long-term competitiveness difficulties of the United States. Investment rates, while rising from cyclically depressed levels in 1981–82, have remained low compared to our major competitors, and the U.S. saving rate, already low by international standards in the 1970s, fell to record lows in the 1980s. Most economists agree that at least in the short run, the tax law introduced in 1987 will depress investment and saving rates still further. The quality of the U.S. labor force continues to suffer from long-term difficulties, resulting in higher illiteracy rates, poorer math and science training, and higher dropout rates than those reported in other advanced industrial economies. And despite the increase in civilian R&D spending noted above, the share of such spending in GNP remains lower in the United States than in Germany or Japan, as has been the case since the 1960s.

Indeed, our national macroeconomic policies, in the name of supply-side economics, have actually aggravated the competitive decline of the United States in recent years. The sharp appreciation of the dollar between 1980 and 1985, caused by the growing borrowing needs of the federal government and low U.S. saving rates, significantly weakened the already precarious competitive position of U.S. producers in world markets. In short, our macro policy choices superimposed a short-term erosion in U.S. competitiveness on a more fundamental long-term erosion. The existence of the long-term erosion is one reason why, even though the dollar has fallen sharply since late 1985, wiping out most of the appreciation against several major currencies, the U.S. trade imbalance has not improved.

A particularly disturbing aspect of the erosion in U.S. competitiveness, especially in recent years, has been its effects on the composition of jobs and wages in the U.S. economy. High-wage jobs in the United States are still disproportionately in the manufacturing sectors where the U.S. competitive decline has been the most severe. Many studies, including a recent one by Tyson and Zysman, show that surging imports and faltering exports played an important role in the rapid destruction of manufacturing jobs after 1979. Since manufacturing jobs on average pay much higher wages than jobs in the rest of the economy, the loss of manufacturing jobs meant a loss in high-wage job opportunities for U.S. citizens. Thus, it is not surprising to find that between 1979 and 1985, the average weekly wage of jobs lost—mainly in manufacturing—was $444, while the average weekly wage of jobs gained—mainly in services— was $272. This pattern of job destruction and job creation is one of several factors contributing to the surge in income inequality in the United States since the late 1970s.

At the national level, we have consoled ourselves about the decline in manufacturing jobs by talking about a "market-driven" transition to an information-based service economy. The problem with this line of reasoning is twofold: the pace of the transition has been accelerated by our eroding competitiveness in manufacturing; and many service activities, especially the high-wage, high-skill services in finance, software, business consulting, engineering, and the like, are what Stephen S. Cohen and John Zysman call "tightly linked" to manufacturing activities.

Where linkages between services and products are tight, services are often specialized for particular products or even for particular suppliers, and these services, together with the products they support or use, are best thought of as an inter-related system rather than as separate commodities. This is especially true for many high-technology products and their specialized support services. Under these circumstances, close frequent communication between producers of output and specialized services is common, and such communication in-volves more than just the exchange of price information and often involves a substantial element of risk on both sides that results in long-term contractual relationships. For tightly linked services, it is hard to imagine how a competitive erosion in product lines in world markets would not spill over into an erosion in related services. In other words, the health of the most valuable services the United States has to offer depends on the health of the manufacturing base that provides the major market for such services.

During the last couple of years, mainly as a result of the intransigence of the trade imbalance in the face of the dramatic fall in the dollar's value, concern over U.S. competitiveness has intensified. Supply-side economics has been largely discredited, leaving a legacy of huge fiscal deficits without the anticipated boost in U.S. growth and productivity performance. Confidence that market forces are pushing us to a brighter information-based service economy has weakened, replaced by growing anxiety that U.S. manufacturing producers can no longer compete effectively "on the shop floor." There is growing understanding that our huge foreign debt, reflecting several years of living beyond our means as a nation, represents an inescapable foreign claim on our future goods and assets. And, as the technologies of production and communication change rapidly, there is recognition that the competitive dynamics of the world economy are in a period of transition where the positions of individual producers and nations in the world's hierarchy of economic power and wealth are subject to rapid change.

In these new circumstances, the United States must fashion a new set of economic policies if it is to retain its position as a major economic power, perhaps no longer ahead of the pack as it was earlier, but as first among equals. We need a strong national commitment to bolster our national competitiveness and policies, institutions, and values that reflect this commitment. In short, we are after a true "supply-side" economics that strengthens our national productive potential over the long run.

Luckily, as we seek to design a competitiveness agenda for the nation, there are lessons to be learned from other nations that have started out earlier than we on paths to build national competitiveness. Perhaps the most basic lesson from foreign experience is that the old distinction between free trade and protection, which still holds sway in many U.S. policy debates, is outmoded. Protection is not the only or even the most important way governments affect the national competitiveness of producers over time. The experience of many nations, including the United States, shows that a whole array of government policies, none of them necessarily protectionist in the usual sense of the term, can "create" or shape the competitive advantage of national producers over time.

Creating Advantage by Macroeconomic Policy

State policies can create competitiveness at both the macroeconomic and the microeconomic levels. At the macroeconomic level, policies can affect competitiveness over time by influencing the quantity and quality of labor, capital, and technology. An advantage in capital-intensive or technology-intensive industries is not an immutable fact of nature, but the result of a host of interrelated economy-wide policies that affect the incentives to save, invest, acquire human capital, and innovate and diffuse technology. In each of these areas, U.S. policy can be shaped to strengthen U.S. competitiveness over the long run.

U.S. saving and investment rates are persistently lower than those of our most successful competitors in both the developed and the developing world. Despite widespread euphoria about the U.S. investment boom encouraged by tax cuts and economic recovery after 1982, the U.S. investment rate has remained below that of our major competitors throughout the 1980s, continuing a trend that characterizes the entire postwar period. As a result, the pace at which we supply our work force with modern equipment and technology has been slower, and this is reflected in our lower rate of growth of productivity. Nations with rapid productivity growth invest in plant and equipment at a much higher rate than nations with slow productivity growth. The United States has been a low-investment nation, and the effects on our productivity growth have accumulated over time.

Since there is a high correlation between national saving and national investment, despite the greater international mobility of capital, the low U.S. saving rate acts as a long-term barrier to a higher national investment effort. In this respect, U.S. saving behavior in the 1980s is disturbing. The gross private saving rate in the United States has remained well below the levels achieved by our major competitors, and the U.S. personal saving rate has fallen to new lows. On the government side, the growing federal deficit has induced very high rates of government dissaving, despite the fact that state and local governments have generated substantial saving. The financing requirements of the government deficit and private investment have exceeded the saving generated by the private sector. The excess has been covered by the inflow of funds from the rest of the world, an inflow that equalled about 15 percent of U.S. nondomestic investment between 1983 and 1985, and about 40 percent of the 1985 increase in GNP. Without the inflow of foreign funds, at unchanged rates of government dissaving, the result would have been much higher interest rates crowding out private investment to make room for government borrowing needs.

A sustained reduction in the federal deficit is a necessary condition for improving national competitiveness over the long run. Without a fundamental change in our macroeconomic situation, the United States will continue to run massive trade and current account imbalances. Under these circumstances, any possible salutary effects of competitiveness policies on U.S. trade performance will continue to be swamped by national borrowing needs. To the extent that policy initiatives, such as the proposed trade bill or a continued drop in the dollar's value, succeed in improving the trade imbalance and stemming the inflow of foreign capital without a decline in the borrowing needs of the federal government, further increases in the inflation rate and in interest rates can be expected.

Seen from this perspective, a necessary but by no means sufficient condition for an improvement in long-term competitiveness is a sustained, substantial reduction in the federal budget deficit. Without such a reduction, improvements in the trade balance are likely to occur at the expense of, rather than in support of, long-term competitiveness and are likely to be accompanied by worsening macro conditions at home and abroad. With competitiveness as the long-term policy objective, not just any mechanism to reduce the fiscal imbalance will do. Tax increases that further reduce business incentives to invest and innovate, that reduce private incentives to save, or that increase the cost of labor will hurt U.S. competitiveness, as will expenditure cuts concentrated on education, R&D support, worker dislocation assistance, and the like.

Given outstanding spending commitments on Social Security and defense and growing interest payments on the national debt, the only way to reduce the deficit significantly without eliminating not only spending programs that promote competitiveness but almost all other discretionary spending programs as well is some kind of revenue-raising measure. In 1986 only $282 billion was spent by the federal government for all items other than Social Security, defense, and interest payments on the national debt, while the total budget deficit was $220 billion. Thus to eliminate the deficit solely by cutting these other expenditure items would necessitate the virtual elimination of government.

Unfortunately the 1986 tax reform does not address our long-term competitiveness needs. Because of transitionally higher tax rates in 1987, the new tax law was projected to reduce the federal deficit in 1987, but this effect is not expected to persist in future years. The tax reform was avowedly revenue-neutral at a time when the country desperately needed a revenue-raising tax bill. It also eliminated important incentives to invest. According to Lawrence Summers in the *Harvard Business Review,* the tax bill raises the effective tax rate on most classes of investment by about 20 percentage points and increases the rate of return required on a typical investment project by 10 percent to 15 percent. In the long run, Summers estimates that this may well reduce the stock of plant and equipment by 10 percent to 15 percent and the economy's potential output by about 3 percent. And new evidence indicates that by curtailing individual retirement accounts (IRAs) and increasing the tax burden on capital income, the 1986 tax reform bill will probably discourage private saving as well.

If the debate about tax reform had focused on the need to restore U.S. competitiveness over the long run, a very different tax bill might have emerged. The investment tax credit, rather than being eliminated, might have been strengthened and targeted toward particular activities or industries. The same might have been true for the tax credit on R&D expenditures. Reductions in personal income tax rates might have been accompanied by the introduction of a value-added tax. The virtues of such a tax are that it falls on consumption, not saving, and that it can be rebated on sales to foreign markets under the General Agreement on Tariffs and Trade (GATT) rules.

Government policy can also affect competitiveness at the economy-wide or macroeconomic level over time by influencing the quality of labor resources. In a world where capital and technology are increasingly mobile, national competitiveness ultimately depends on the quality and productivity of national human resources. If the United States is to be able to compete in world markets with rising real incomes for its domestic work force, then this work force must have the quality, flexibility, and productivity required to make and sell products at prices competitive with those of similar products produced by lower paid workers elsewhere.

As a result of many well-known problems in our educational system, especially in grades K through 12, there has been a relative erosion in the quality of our labor resources. This shows up in a variety of indicators: compared to its major foreign competitors, the United States has more functional illiterates, graduates a smaller percentage of its population from high school, has a greater percentage of high school graduates uneducated in math, and produces a smaller percentage of engineers among its college graduates. Only 75 percent of high school students in the United States graduate on time. Estimates of the number of functionally illiterate adults in the United States run to the tens of millions. Forty percent of the thirteen-year-olds in the United States are reading below the skill levels for their age. A recent study of reading skills of seventeen-year-olds found that less than half of them performed at higher than basic or intermediate levels. A recent study of math students in several countries showed American twelfth graders well behind their Japanese counterparts and students from many other countries. Even the best U.S. students—those who learn calculus in the twelfth grade—performed poorly against Japanese students and were only on a par with other participating countries.

In the United States, much of the responsibility for developing a more skilled, motivated work force lies with the states and local communities that fund and oversee the nation's public schools and universities and with private employers that are responsible for forging better worker-management relations, more effective on-the-job training programs, and better employee incentives. That actions by both state and local communities on the one hand and private employers on the other can make a critical difference to worker quality and performance is suggested by a variety of evidence. New educational initiatives in Tennessee, New Jersey, and Massachusetts, for example, have had notable successes in raising indicators of educational excellence. And as a growing number of examples of Japanese takeover and management of U.S. firms and workers indicate, substantial productivity improvements in U.S. labor performance can be realized by changes in workplace organization and manager-employee relations.

Growing interest in proposals to strengthen the nation's schools has encouraged a needed infusion of new funds at the state level. From 1982 to 1987, support for education by state governments increased by 26 percent in real terms, although some of this increase went to make up for federal budget cuts. Adjusted for inflation, average teacher pay in 1987 was up 2 percent from its previous peak in 1972, while average wages in the rest of the economy remained lower than those realized in the early 1970s. At the federal level, the budget for the Department of Education has borne a disproportionate share of cuts in order to preserve defense and Social Security and to meet outstanding interest obligations without tax increases.

One promising development at the federal level is the proposed program of training and assistance for displaced workers, including but not limited to workers displaced by foreign competition. In new, more competitive international conditions, and in the presence of major technological changes in production processes, flexibility is the key to competitive success. And flexibility requires that workers be able to move quickly and easily from one task to another or one machine to another in the workplace, and from one workplace to another as market conditions change. As the Japanese and Swedish experience indicates, well-organized and well-financed programs to train and relocate workers support the kind of flexibility that is required, thereby enhancing the competitiveness of the overall economy.

Finally, government policy can affect competitiveness at the economy-wide level by its effects on the pace and direction of technological innovation and diffusion. In the United States, the federal government funds about 47 percent of all R&D spending. Federal funds for R&D are overwhelmingly defense oriented. During the Reagan years, real federal spending on nondefense R&D as a percentage of GNP fell, and the gap between federal spending on defense R&D and nondefense R&D hit a twenty-year high. R&D defense spending has focused mainly on "mega-projects" like the strategic defense initiative (SDI) that are likely to have limited spillover effects in commercial areas, at least in the short run, and that divert scientific and engineering talent from commercially oriented R&D programs. In contrast to the U.S. situation, in Japan, where government financing is a much smaller percentage of the total national R&D effort, it is expressly focused on commercial areas such as new materials, semiconductors, and biotechnology. The Japanese approach has been one of financing programs to promote cooperative research on so-called generic technologies that seem to have promising commercial applications. These programs have been financed to a significant extent by the companies participating in the cooperative programs, leading to a shared burden of the R&D effort between public and private actors. Joint financing and cooperation make economic sense, since the social returns to such R&D efforts are likely to exceed the private returns appropriable by any single firm.

Concern over competitiveness has led to a rash of new proposals for federal programs to support commercial R&D efforts in the United States. Examples of federal government programs to support generic research in commercial areas include National Science Foundation support for the express switching program and the national laboratory program in ceramics centered in the Oakville National Laboratory. Proposals to find a mechanism for the Department of Defense to help finance a major program of joint R&D in semiconductor manufacturing equipment and techniques are consistent with the need to find effective means for government to promote generic research, the benefits of which will be shared by a large number of commercial users. President Reagan called for the establishment of a number of new university-based science and technology centers for long-term research in critical generic technology areas, like new-materials processing and robotics for automated manufacturing.

In addition to devoting more of its research budget to commercial R&D activity, the U.S. government should consider policies to speed the diffusion of new technologies. President Reagan and Congress made several proposals to improve the diffusion of technological information from a variety of governmental agencies, including the federal laboratories and the Department of Defense. At the same time that better institutional mechanisms for the diffusion of technological information are designed, however, the incentive of those in the private sector to learn about and incorporate such information in their own production processes and products must be strengthened. R&D tax credit policy is an important determinant of this incentive as well as the incentive of the private sector to engage in its own R&D efforts. In addition to strengthening tax incentives for R&D investment by industry, the government should evaluate the efficacy and cost of promotional tax or credit schemes targeted at the more rapid diffusion of critical technologies, such as robotics. Japanese experience indicates that promotional schemes of this type can speed the introduction of critical technologies with beneficial effects for the competitiveness of both the using industries and the supplier industries.

Creating Advantage at the
Microeconomic Level

In addition to using policy to create competitive advantage at the economy-wide level, government can use policy to create competitive advantage in individual industries or activities. Although this is a widely accepted idea and practice in many countries around the world, in the United States it is fraught with theoretical and political difficulties.

A large and growing part of world trade consists of exchanges that do not reflect national differences in resource endowments, even those resources whose quantity and quality are influenced by government policy. Instead, such trade reflects apparently arbitrary or temporary advantage resulting from economies of scale, shifting positions in technological leadership, or from product differentiation and other forms of nonprice competition. For trade in these products, it seems obvious that national policies can have an enduring effect on trade flows and national welfare. This proposition has spawned a whole new area of trade theory among economists. The so-called new trade theory has concentrated on demonstrating that under certain conditions, national policies to promote or protect domestic producers in international competition can improve national welfare. There are essentially two different types of conditions that give rise to results of this kind. First, industries that are "imperfectly" competitive, most often as a result of economies of scale, earn higher returns than those available in the rest of the economy. Under these conditions, national welfare may be improved by government policy to win larger market shares for domestic producers in world markets and hence a larger share of world profits for the domestic population. A second set of conditions that provide a justification for welfare-improving policies draws on standard notions of externality or spillover effects. In lay terms, certain industries may be more important than others because they generate benefits for the rest of the economy, and government policy to promote them can improve welfare by fostering these spillover effects. Under both sets of conditions, the industries involved are defined to be "strategic" either in the sense that resources employed by them earn higher returns than they would earn elsewhere or in the sense that they generate special benefits for the rest of the economy.

Much of the empirical research on how government policy creates advantage at the micro level has focused on high-technology sectors and on Japan for case study evidence (see, for example, the works of the scholars at the Berkeley Roundtable on the International Economy—BRIE). This research indicates that the Japanese government has used a host of interrelated policies, some aggregate, some industry specific, some formal, some informal, to target certain industries and that these policies have had an enduring effect on Japanese trade patterns in specific sectors. Case study work by BRIE scholars has demonstrated the role of policy in the evolution of Japanese production and trade in the consumer electronics industry, the semiconductor industry, and the telecommunications industry. This work suggests that an interrelated set of protectionist and promotional policies has given Japanese producers the advantages of large-scale production and cumulative production and research experience that have been critical to their export successes in related products.

The Japanese approach to these and other industries is motivated by the goal of guiding or influencing the structure or composition of the economy in specific directions. In pursuit of this goal, the Japanese have used trade policies, such as tariffs, tangible and intangible nontariff barriers, and related policies, such as controls over direct foreign investment. But these kinds of policies have been used in conjunction with a variety of other policies, including tax and subsidy policy, financial and interest rate policy, research and development policy, and antitrust policy. The actual mix of policies has changed significantly over time, and some observers argue that both the extent and the strength of policy intervention have declined since the early 1970s. Nonetheless, the long-term effects of earlier or continuing policy intervention on trade patterns in targeted sectors persist because of the long-term nature of the advantages created by such intervention.

A careful examination of Japanese policy indicates that it has been what might be called "market conforming" or "market promotional" in its objectives. It has been designed to promote or accelerate the development of sectors deemed to be both privately and socially profitable and to manage the decline of sectors deemed to be privately and socially unprofitable. In the United States there is some support of and experience with policies to aid national producers as they adjust to competitive decline. In industries as diverse as apparel, steel, and automobiles, the United States has responded to severe import competition by a variety of protectionist measures designed to give the domestic industry time to restructure. Trade adjustment assistance programs for workers who lose their jobs from import competition also have been part of the policy response at various times. In no case have protection and adjustment assistance been linked to conditions specifying the pace and direction of industry restructuring. This has been left to "market" forces, despite the fact that market conditions have been distorted by protectionist measures, and despite the fact that there is evidence in the business literature suggesting that the most productive, efficient firms in a weakened industry may be the first to leave, weakening it still further. The U.S. approach stands in sharp contrast to the Japanese approach, where decline is managed by legally mandated recession and rationalization cartels in which government assistance to affected firms, workers, and communities is linked to a detailed program for reducing capacity at the industry and often the firm level. The French, too, have introduced explicit restructuring programs for industries in decline, such as the steel industry in the 1970s.

Even those who might be willing to entertain the idea that industry-specific policies may be market conforming and beneficial when used to moderate the adjustment costs associated with industrial decline are often unwilling to acknowledge that such policies may have beneficial effects when applied in industries that are growing and profitable. If industries or activities are profitable by market criteria, why might government policy to promote them be welfare improving? The answer to this question lies in the notion of strategic industries or strategic activities introduced earlier. If an economic activity is strategic in the sense that it earns higher returns than those available elsewhere in the economy or in the sense that it generates significant positive spillover effects in other parts of the economy, then market promoting policies to support such an activity can improve national economic welfare.

Japanese industrial policy seems to be motivated by such a perspective. For example, in the 1950s and 1960s steel and shipbuilding were promoted because they were believed to provide substantial spillover benefits in the form of infrastructure. From a traditional economics perspective, the spillover effects provided by the steel and shipbuilding industries are "pecuniary" in the sense that they are reflected in lower input prices to their downstream users. Because pecuniary externalities are reflected in market prices, there is no need for government policy—markets left to themselves will provide the optimal amount of investment and production. This conclusion holds, however, only as long as there are no "imperfections" in product markets and no "distortions" in capital markets. And these conditions are often at odds with economic reality.

Take, for example, the case of the Japanese steel industry in the 1950s. Because steel was an important intermediate input produced with economies of scale, policies to promote rapid expansion of high-quality domestic steel resulted in lower prices and reduced costs for steel-using industries. This encouraged the expansion of these industries which in turn fed back into further expansion of the steel industry and still lower costs. This virtuous interdependence between the steel industry and downstream users gave rise to a true externality—increasing private returns in the steel industry, resulting in increasing social returns in the downstream user industries.

Paul Krugman coined the phrase "linkage externality" to apply to this type of spillover effect resulting from increasing returns in the production of inputs and their effects on the costs of downstream producers. Such a notion underlies arguments for policies to promote infrastructure in the usual sense of transportation and communication networks.

In recent years, Japanese market promoting policies have concentrated on high-technology sectors, such as semiconductors, computers, and telecommunications. The Japanese view these industries, like steel and shipbuilding in the past, as providing infrastructure on which the future competitive success of a variety of sectors depends. A policy of promoting R&D, investment, and growth in these new "infrastructural" activities is viewed as generating beneficial effects throughout the economy. As the arguments above make clear, these industries certainly satisfy some of the conditions required for a linkage-externality argument for market promoting policies. Seen from a narrow perspective, they provide inputs for production throughout a broad spectrum of the economy, and they enjoy both dynamic and static increasing returns. Indeed, increasing returns have been nothing short of spectacular in semiconductor production in the last decade, with spillover effects on increasing returns in related computer and telecommunications equipment. Private increasing returns in this complex of industries, in turn, are the basis for social increasing returns throughout the economy, as the standard linkage-externality argument suggests.

Seen from a broad perspective, this group of industries provides the foundation for a fundamental revolution in production and communications technologies that is transforming how work is done and how life is lived. The spillover effects of this revolution are likely to be so profound and so widespread that any attempt to define them precisely, much less to quantify them, at this point in time is an exercise in false formalism. What seems certain is that such industries are "strategic" in the sense of providing both linkage-externalities in the form of spillover effects from R&D and innovation throughout the economy.

Even if one discounts the linkage-externalities and transformative effects of these high-technology industries—a position that is misguided in its shortsightedness—standard externality arguments about the returns to R&D and innovation provide a traditional case for market promoting policies. Economists generally focus externality arguments of this variety on the issue of appropriability. As long as the returns to innovation and R&D are appropriable, there is no divergence between private returns and social returns and hence no rationale for policy intervention. Appropriability can be better understood by examining different kinds of knowledge generated by R&D and innovation. Three kinds of knowledge, all of which are present in the high-tech electronics industries, can be distinguished: production process knowledge reflected in firm-specific learning curves that can be internalized within a firm; product design knowledge that can be reverse engineered, which, once generated, is available internationally; and knowledge that spreads beyond the firm but not necessarily easily beyond national or sometimes even regional boundaries. This third kind of knowledge seems to be the reason behind the development of geographically concentrated "high-technology" centers, with information embodied in people and spread through social and academic networks.

The economic literature on innovation and diffusion has focused on the second kind of knowledge—knowledge that is only partly appropriable by the innovating firm. For such knowledge, the evidence suggests overwhelmingly that the social returns to R&D and innovation are significantly greater than the private returns, and this is the most widely accepted rationale among economists for government support for R&D. The argument is particularly powerful for basic and generic R&D, which, by its nature, is likely to generate knowledge with benefits that extend beyond the innovating firm.

Until recently discussions of the spillover effects of R&D did not address the issue of the geographical concentration or dispersion of knowledge. Recently, however, both because of the apparent tendency of high-technology firms to cluster together in distinct communities and because of concern about the extent and pace at which technological knowledge diffuses across national boundaries, the issue has received considerable attention. Of particular interest to the question of how policy creates competitive advantage in trade is the idea that government support for R&D and innovation helps to create a national pool of innovative talent. The history of technological change in a variety of industries and nations indicates that technological change both supports and is supported by the creation of an ability to innovate embodied in a pool of specialized knowledge and in a specialized labor force. By its nature, this ability is not easily contained within firms or sectors but is much more easily contained within national boundaries. A nation that promotes R&D and investment in its high-tech industries is encouraging the development of a highly skilled pool of innovative talent, which, in the long run, given the mobility of goods, technology, and capital across national borders, may be the single most important factor on which national competitive advantage rests.

Finally, if high-technology industries are strategic because of their linkage and knowledge externalities, they are also strategic in the sense that they are characterized by imperfect competition. A variety of characteristics cause these industries to diverge sharply from the competitive model: significant learning curve economies and the advantages they yield to early entrants; product heterogeneity based on changing technological positions and changing product standards; the importance of marketing-distribution channels to market penetration; and implicit or explicit preferential or protectionist treatment for domestic producers in many national environments, most notably the Japanese.

From the point of view of U.S. firms and U.S. policy makers, the concentrated nature of these industries, the vertical linkages among them, and the government's role in coordinating joint activities among them in Japan are cause for particular concern. The Japanese computer industry consists of three large firms (Fujitsu, NEC, and Hitachi) that are also three of Japan's four largest semiconductor producers. These same firms control more than two-thirds of all telecommunications equipment production in Japan and dominate domestic and global markets in many consumer electronics items. They are also tightly linked to the largest Japanese producers of semi-conductor capital equipment. Given this market structure, it is reasonable to conclude that even in the absence of promotional policy measures, U.S. firms as sellers would face significant barriers to market entry in Japan, and U.S. firms as buyers would be unable to purchase frontier technology inputs from Japanese producers to compete with the same producers in downstream, higher value-added product markets.

The constellation of arguments indicating the "strategic-transformative" nature of high-technology industries provides a powerful prima facie case in support of market promoting policies in the United States. The evidence suggesting that the competitive strength of Japanese producers in these industries has been bolstered by such policies to the disadvantage of U.S. producers indicates that this case should be treated seriously in U.S. policy discussions of whether and how the United States should respond. It is not enough to argue glibly that closure of the Japanese market to U.S. firms simply worsens consumer welfare in Japan or that Japanese promotional policies simply lower prices to U.S. consumers, with a net welfare gain for the United States. These policy prescriptions apply only in a static, perfectly competitive world without adjustment cost and without externalities, a world that does not fit the high-technology industries.

We need policy prescriptions that reflect the strategic significance of high-technology industries and activities, such as semiconductors, computers, new materials, superconductivity, and biotechnology, to our future economic well-being. An obvious starting point is the introduction of cooperative R&D programs, financed in part by the federal government, and in part by firms in a few critical areas. The United States must redirect a significant fraction of its federal R&D dollars to nondefense, commercial programs if our technology lead is to be sustained. Instead of a strategic defense initiative that funds research in a weapon system that will never be used, we need a strategic commercial initiative that funds research in the most promising commercial directions.

Conclusion

The U.S. economy confronts a crisis in its international competitive position. The staggering trade deficits of the last several years and the foreign borrowing that has financed them cannot be sustained over the long run. At some point during the next few years, the U.S. trade position will have to adjust dramatically, with profound consequences for the level and composition of production and employment at home and abroad. Both domestic and foreign policy makers will have to grapple with ways to improve U.S. export performance and to reduce U.S. import dependence. Macroeconomic policy choices will play a critical role in these adjustments, as they did in the spectacular erosion in the U.S. trade deficit after 1982. Given the magnitude of the adjustment required and the underlying longer-term weaknesses in U.S. productivity performance, however, reliance on macroeconomic policy alone will prove risky. Reliance on exchange rate corrections, with or without a deceleration in U.S. growth rates compared to growth rates abroad, runs the risk of higher inflation rates, recessionary conditions, or more likely a combination of both, in the United States and in the rest of the world.

The adjustment process can be made easier by policies to improve the underlying competitiveness of U.S. producers. Higher productivity growth, better quality products, and innovations in product and process technology, like exchange rate adjustments and a recession in domestic demand, can improve the U.S. trade imbalance but with a far lower cost in relative living standards and in forgone output and consumption in the United States. What is needed to make the required adjustment of the U.S. trade position less costly is the development of a national competitiveness policy. Such a policy would represent the true realization of the supply-side objectives of the late 1970s rather than the distortion of such objectives as a result of the "supply-side" fiscal policies of the last six years. The process of strengthening the competitiveness of the U.S. economy is a long-term one. There are no quick fixes. Just as erosion in the U.S. competitive position was a long-term phenomenon reflecting years of policy inattention and failure, any improvement from changes in policy will be realized only gradually. The danger is that policy makers, frustrated by the apparent lack of success of prudent policy measures in the short run, may adopt misguided policies of protection that promise to improve the trade balance quickly but are destructive of real competitiveness in the long run.

Finally, in designing a national competitiveness policy, we face three principal constraints. First, as a nation, we cannot compete in world markets by cutting real wages: this approach will not work because there are millions of foreign workers who are willing to work at wages lower than those we can pay. It also will not work because it will threaten the foundations of our economic and political system. Second, a retreat to defensive protection will not serve as a long-term policy to support high wages and sustained productivity. Third, policies that are radically inequitable are unlikely to generate the broad political support required for a national commitment to long-term growth and innovation.

The opportunities we face are equally constrained. Ours is a world in which science and technology, capital, and management know-how are widely available. Consequently, we can only compete internationally in how effectively we develop, diffuse, and use technology and product and production know-how in our firms. Effectively using technical possibilities depends on management vision and worker skills. Simply put, in the long term, investment in science, education, technological innovation, and technological diffusion is all that will sustain us.

5

Integrated Process Management: A Management Technology for the New Competitive Era

MAREK P. HESSEL
MARTA MOONEY
MILAN ZELENY

> He that will not apply new remedies must expect new
> evils, for time is the greatest innovator.
> —Francis Bacon

Introduction

We view the erosion of U.S. competitiveness to be above all a problem of management. Problems of management require managerial solutions. Traditional reme-

MAREK P. HESSEL is associate professor at Fordham University in the Graduate School of Business Administration. Prior to joining the faculty at Fordham, Dr. Hessel served as assistant professor at Montclair State College in New Jersey, and taught at New York University. Dr. Hessel earned the M.S. degree in economics at Warsaw University in Poland and completed his Ph.D in operations research at New York University. He is the author or coauthor of several articles in scholarly journals and has given presentations internationally on topics concerning managerial technologies, game theory, and conflict resolution.

MARTA MOONEY is associate professor at Fordham University's Graduate and Undergraduate Schools of Business, where she has

dies, such as trade protectionism, tax incentives, and governmental regulation, are inadequate and misplaced tools; they simply will not do.

We submit that the problem stems from the inability of the traditional management system (or prevailing "management technology") to keep pace and fit with the new competitive environment it helped to create. The system has lost proper coupling with its own niche; it has become obsolete.

Fundamental principles of the traditional system remain deeply embedded in the way we think, even about its own transformation or improvement. The structure of this book best illustrates the point.

This book is organized into three principal topics that coincide with the three key factors of the traditional "linear" models of organizational change: (1) dissatisfaction with the status quo, (2) vision of the future, and (3) action steps for implementing the change. Each topic has been further fragmented into subtopics, and each subtopic has been assigned to specialists who prepared chapters (such as ours) for subsequent, hopefully integrative, discussion. An ancient, systems-defying principle of division of labor (and knowledge) has become almost intuitive in American management culture.

---

taught since 1976. With academic degrees in engineering, economics, and industrial relations, Dr. Mooney has held positions with Lockheed Aircraft Corporation, Systems Development Corporation, and Boise Cascade Corporation. She has published several articles on management and productivity, and her research activities currently focus on management technology and transfers of managerial technologies.

MILAN ZELENY teaches at Fordham University, as a professor of management systems. Dr. Zeleny has taught at several other academic institutions, including the European Institute for Advanced Studies in Management, Columbia University, the University of South Carolina, and the Prague School of Economics. He has lectured and published extensively in areas ranging from mathematical programing, systems analysis, and game theory to management systems, artificial intelligence, and knowledge engineering.

We assume that the benefits of simplifying individual tasks and parceling them out exceed the cost of weaving the separate pieces back together to form a whole cloth. (We often fail to see the paradox in simultaneously accepting that the whole exceeds the sum of its parts and that the whole can be reconstructed from its parts.) This implicit assumption is rarely questioned and almost never subject to scrutiny: experienced executives (of NASA for example) confronting a task too large to handle on their own move instinctively to break it down into smaller pieces and assign them to specialized individuals whose performance is then monitored and coordinated by other specialists.

The business success of today is starting to march to a different drummer: multipurpose machinery, multifunctional workers, flexible organization, multifunctional parts, knowledge orientation, and systems approach. In short: integration. In order to discuss even potentially lasting improvement in U.S. competitive performance, we have to seriously reevaluate this intuitive faith in task specialization, functional separation of workers and managers, and various managements "by results" or "by objectives." Radical rethinking of the currently reigning management theory and practice is required. We choose to view management as *technology,* a useful and necessary step in gaining insight into this process.

Management Technology

The word "technology" comes from Greek *technologia* (systematic treatment of an art). It is now widely understood as the totality of means employed to achieve practical purpose(s).

Following Zeleny's conceptualization, we propose to view technology as a triune of hardware, software, and brainware, embedded in a "support net." Hardware consists of the various physical/logical means for carrying out the tasks selected to achieve objectives and goals. Software is the set of rules and procedures guiding the use of hardware: the know-how, the knowledge of how to carry out the tasks. Brainware is the justification for the deployment of hardware and software: the "know-what" and the "know-why" of the technology in use. These three components form the *technology core.*

This core is embedded in a complex network of physical, informational, and socioeconomic relationships which support its proper deployment toward the stated goals and objectives. Figure 1 illustrates a scheme of the core and its support net.

For example, automobile hardware consists of the physical/logical organization of components that distinguish an automobile from, say, a motorcycle. Software consists of rules for maintaining and operating the automobile in different modes and under different conditions. Brainware consists of decisions about where, when, and why to drive, which route to take, etc. The support net consists of infrastructure of roads and facilities, rules of conduct and institutions for their enforcement, driving culture, style, and behavior.

To the extent to which any core requires and is in turn determined by the appropriate embedding, technology is neither a thing nor a tool, neither a method nor a logical design: technology, especially for managers and economists, is (should be) a form of *social relationship.*

Management as Technology

Management "hardware" consists of specific tools and methods applied to achieve organizational objectives and goals. Management "software" includes organizational procedures and guidelines for using various hardware components. The knowledge of which components to use, when, and why represents the (managerial) "brainware."

This core is again embedded in its support net: the requisite organizational and cultural structure that facilitates its proper deployment and use. The support net includes organizational patterns, task roles, formal and informal covenants, management styles and culture, and behavioral norms and habits.

The term "management technology" thus imparts the much needed rigor and seriousness to a much maligned discipline that bears primary responsibility for a nation's economic wel-

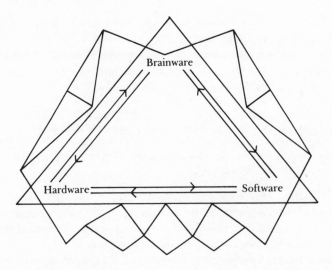

FIGURE 1. Technology Core and Its Support Net Embedding

fare. Trivialization of a vital discipline, via terms like "management methods," "management practices," or "managerial culture," makes it inherently difficult to maintain high professional standards for research, education, and practice.

Management technology framework encourages and allows scholars and practitioners to approach this vital field as a unified interactive system, not as a collection of disjointed elements. The studies of management technologies naturally connect with the studies of engineering technologies in order to enhance our understanding of management systems.

Limits to Technological Performance

Every technology is subject to physical, logical, and environmental limits to its performance. Benefits of incremental investments in technology diminish as these limits are approached, and even disappear once they are reached. A breakthrough toward a new technology—a shift to a different technology "regime"—becomes the only way to preserve or renew competitive advantage.

In *Innovation: The Competitor's Advantage,* Richard Foster introduces characteristic S-curves of technology performance (see Figure 2a). He insists:

What is important to remember is that, no matter how vigorously a competitor backs his own technology, it cannot escape the realities of technical limits and the implications of the S-curve. If a competing technology is present, the technology with the greatest potential will seize control of the market.

It is the same with any management technology. Being a form of social relationship, it emerges, develops, persists, stagnates, and declines. Its life span is finite, its usefulness determined by its own limits of performance.

Ideally, the core and support net of management technology evolve simultaneously, in a mutual codetermination. However, to the extent that core embedding in the net involves social and cultural persistencies, the development of the support net may (and often does) lag behind the development of the core. This lag explains the bottom part of the S-shaped pattern. Once the requisite support net begins to take shape, subsequent investments in the core start to produce higher yields. When the technology-spawned external socioeconomic opportunities have been exploited, additional performance gains tend to depend solely on the investment in the core. These gains diminish as the maturing technology approaches its performance limits, and ultimately they vanish altogether.

Discontinuity of Technological Change

The fundamental discontinuity and nonlinearity of technology transition are schematically illustrated in Figure 2b. In the context of management technologies, the discontinuous character of technological change is even more apparent. The support net itself changes: the very structure of the organization, the nature of individual tasks and their definition, connections of physical and informational flows, the nature of

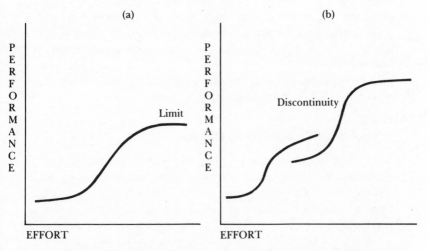

FIGURE 2. (a) The S-curve of Technology Life Cycle (b) The Displacement of a Mature Technology

coordination and control, the organizational culture, and so on. Newly emerging management systems are, therefore, in Zeleny's terminology, "high" technologies of management.

Some U.S. firms have attempted to acquire Japanese management technology. Their failure stems from the fundamental mismatch between the imported core and the existing support net. Although industrial robots are virtually the same in Japan and the United States, their respective performances are worlds apart. Product design, assembly line organization, employees' education and motivation, and management integration are understandably much more important than the hardware.

Typically, deployment of managerial hardware is a technical matter requiring only minimal investment in training. A much larger challenge rests with embedding the core in an appropriate support net. The net itself cannot be imported; it must evolve in a form compatible with the prevailing sociocultural patterns.

The "quick-fix" transfer of Japanese management practices into the U.S. environment, properly fueled by self-appointed vendors and merchants of "Japanese management," simply aggravates the difficulties. The new core is embedded in the wrong (existing) net; the net gets entangled with the core, sometimes reversing the direction of support; and the patience and determination to create the appropriate support net are missing (GM's Saturn project).

Timing of Technological Change

The timing of technological transitions—knowing *when* to shift resources to a competing (management) technology—is clearly the central problem of competitive management. Successful transitions are rare, leadership changes even rarer; inertia and clinging too long to existing technology prevail. Technologically threatened companies—and most U.S. companies are threatened in terms of their management technology—tend not to appreciate, or even recognize, the threat until too late in the game. Furthermore, even if they detect the threat, few firms react by embracing the new technology; they increase their efforts to "improve" the old one instead.

The art of technology management in general, and of management-technology management in particular, i.e., the art of negotiating the discontinuities of change, is not yet widely practiced.

The Managerial Challenge

Foster's notion of "managing across discontinuity" is the art surely mastered in Japan, Taiwan, Singapore, Hong Kong, and South Korea, and understood even by the "sleeping giant" of China itself. It is the formidable challenge of this management art that U.S. management must accept before the 1980s are over.

There is considerable evidence that major U.S. companies are operating at or near the performance limits of traditional management technology. There is even more convincing evidence that more advanced management technology is being practiced in Japan and other "business ecologies." The evolution and application of appropriate management technologies in the United States is a matter of competitive survival. It will take radical institutional, personal, and cultural changes to bring this process about, and to bring it about in time. Waiting passively for its slow natural course to assert itself (as it ultimately will) could only help the "Asian century" to begin even before the year 2000.

In the 1980s American businesses spent billions of dollars on advancing existing and outdated management technology through grantsmanship, research, training, consulting, and, quite recently, through a strange sort of "guru" management seminars of enlightenment and consciousness raising. The results were devastating. Anticipating any positive results from such strategies is demonstrably unrealistic within the dominant frame of management technology, which remains organized around the principles introduced by Frederick Taylor.

How can we continue to use a labor-oriented management technology in a mostly knowledge oriented business environment? We are not losing to cheaper labor out there, but to better brains. The well of the Tayloristic division of labor has dried up.

A nation's future competitive performance depends on investing in the new managerial technology, developing its appropriate support net, and successfully navigating the tricky waters between the old and the new—*managing across discontinuity*. From Zeleny's 1986 article "High Technology Management" in *Human Systems Management,* we excerpt the following cautionary words:

bureaucracy and management (support net) might resent introduction of technology which would restructure *it,* even though the task (production of a product, performance of a scientific project) would be enhanced on all performance criteria. This process often ends in *pathological states* of workers supporting managers and professors supporting assorted deans in (much too common) "reversed" institutions.

Success depends not on our admiration of past achievements, but on our understanding of current failures.

Evolution of Management Technologies

The primary objective of any management technology is to support continued competitive survival of the enterprise. That can only take place through explicitly catering to its internal and external customers. Effective performance of management technology depends on (1) its ability to meet the expectations of "customers" given, (2) the available technological means, and (3) the requirements of the competitive marketplace.

In Figure 3 we sketch the circular and codeterminant nature of interactions among these three factors. Competitively effective management technology allows full utilization of economic benefits offered by a particular competitive environment (or "business ecology"). (The term "ecology" reflects our understanding that global competitiveness is not a zero-sum game. As Starr and Ullmann point out in chapter 2, "In global relations, countries, industries, and companies must be mutually prosperous." The zero-sum fallacy is part of traditional economic lore, which has retarded the rates of change considerably.)

A business environment is in (dis)continuous flux: the competitors, consumer expectations, and production technologies all change with time. The ability of a particular management technology to accommodate such changes determines its life span.

Traditional Management

The function of traditional management emerged at the end of the nineteenth century. The rapid transition from economies of scope of a craft shop to economies of scale of a huge factory has been completed. Mass production, fed by emerging mass markets and fueled by fairly localized competition, has relied on extensive division of labor and knowledge. Management technology was the only missing ingredient, and the crisis of 1895–1900 might well have been rooted in its absence.

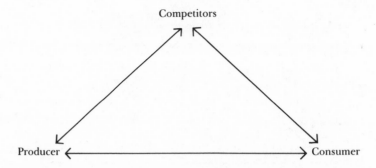

FIGURE 3. Competitive Environment of Management Technologies

Mass production required planning, organizing, coordination, and control efforts reaching well beyond anything imaginable in the craft shop. New management technology was needed to solve the enormous coordination problem brought about by the implied atomization and simplification of tasks of the emerging business enterprise. This environment of producer-consumer-competitor interactions, together with the demands it placed on the emerging management technology, is illustrated in Figure 4.

The founders of scientific management, mostly engineers by training, provided an elegant, consistent, and appropriately mechanistic solution: specialization through (1) simplification of individual tasks, (2) predetermined rules of task coordination, and (3) detailed monitoring of individual performance. The solution was general; its particular application was put in the hands of a new specialist: the professional manager.

Implicit in the task of simplification was the division of knowledge which, in the opinion of founders of traditional management, required corresponding functional specialization. The necessary coordinative function became the exclusive domain of specialized managers (who became totally, and in those days ideally, separated from workers).

The role of this functional specialization within the coordinative mechanism of traditional management cannot be over-

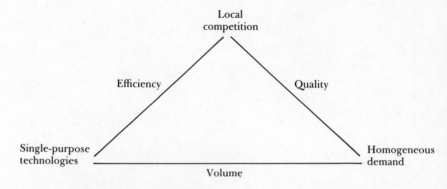

FIGURE 4. The Requirements for Management Technology in the Competitive Environment of the 1900s

emphasized. In fact, it has now achieved an untested (although testable) status of an organizing principle for all systems. (As somebody put it: "Creation of a specialty is a generalized solution to all organizational problems.")

Neither overspecialized workers nor even more overspecialized managers function in a vacuum: they perform their functions within an organization. This organization, the very heart of traditional management, in order to achieve its horizontal coordination, relies on a very specific pattern: total separation of operating and coordinative functions, combined with vertical communication channels of a command hierarchy.

In order to support one of the most rigid manufacturing schemes ever conceived (the dedicated assembly line), traditional management delivered a requisite organizational scheme of matching rigidity: the hierarchical command structure. (The very success of this intracompany command hierarchy even led the Soviet Union to extend the same principle to intercompany command: to the economy as a whole. Modern socialism was born, with its persisting, inevitable, and legendary inefficiencies.)

Undoubtedly, the success of this intracompany command hierarchy contributed to the tremendous economic development of the West, probably because the temptation to extend its influence to the economy as a whole was (and to some extent still is) so successfully resisted in the West. The opposite, and more natural, inclination—to extend the competitive efficiency of free markets down to the company operations level—unfortunately has been resisted with equal success.

Regardless of the missed opportunities, the traditional management technology has to be reevaluated today: the realities of the S-shaped curve are already setting in.

Performance of Traditional Management

The performance of traditional management technology must be measured against the very goals it sets for itself: cost-efficient production of high-quality standardized goods.

Efficiency Performance. The means of achieving efficiency have been a progressive simplification of workers' tasks and a progressive specialization of managerial functions. The efficiency performance of the traditional system thus necessarily rests on the balance between benefits of task atomization and the costs of task coordination. As the workers' tasks become more atomized, their coordination becomes more extensive, more complex, and more difficult. To the extent that the system relies on specialized coordinators, cost savings brought about by increasing the number of task-specialized workers are offset by cost increases brought about by increasing the number of function-specialized managers, as illustrated in Figure 5.

At some point the cost of task coordination must catch up with the benefits of task atomization. After reaching this point, further efficiency gains are precluded by the cost of mushrooming coordination structure: the technology reaches its limit; the management system runs out of fuel.

The evidence is overwhelming that American management has already reached this limit. It is important to realize that this limit, symbolized by stifling and ossified "corpocracy," is a technological normality and not an organizational degeneracy. It is a result of misplaced and hopeless effort to match the

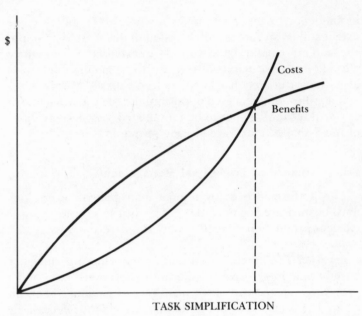

FIGURE 5. **Performance Limit to Traditional Management Technology**

complexity of the regulated system with the complexity of the regulating one (the widely misused and misinterpreted "law" of requisite variety).

The claims that "middle management halves the information and doubles the noise" are obviously correct, and the demands for "trimming the managerial structure," "getting rid of managerial fat," and "improving the company's strength-to-weight ratio" are entirely consistent with the phenomenon. But trying to meet these otherwise legitimate demands within the framework of traditional management technology, which itself brought them forth, is a rather meaningless and self-defeating exercise. The continued usage of traditional management technology can no longer be justified on efficiency grounds.

The recent emphasis on developing management information systems, decision support systems, communication support systems, and other such "supports" (or "crutches"), far from being a solution, is in fact the most telling indicator of the magnitude of the problem of coordination. Yet these new technologies continue to be developed within the old context of the technology of traditional management. Their effectiveness is therefore limited by the very technology they intend to support.

Instead we must look for a management technology that can break through the coordination limits of traditional management. Whatever specifics characterize such technology, it must reduce (if not cleanly sever) its reliance on the external (symbolic) coordination of the productive operations: it must be self-coordinative to a significant degree. Its coordinative mechanism must be integrated within the operating process itself; most of its managerial functions must be shifted to workers and machines. Such replacement of functional specialization with functional integration effectively flattens the coordinating structure of traditional management, without the "trimming the fat" sloganeering. The new management technology must be embedded in horizontal (process oriented) rather than vertical (position oriented) organizational structure.

Under these conditions, management is challenged with a new, more demanding, and more professional role: how to create, maintain, and enhance the conditions under which the operating system can coordinate itself. Can there be a simpler definition of management for the twenty-first century? Management ceases to function as a position and integrates itself as one of the crucial functions of the process itself.

Quality Performance. Product quality has been a proclaimed concern of traditional management from its very inception: witness the variety of quality standards, sampling techniques, statistical quality controls, and market research it spawned. But the continuing need to convince customers of the fulfillment of this promise (or contract)—exemplified by the increasing abundance, aggressiveness, expensiveness, and misinformativeness of advertising slogans—provides the most powerful evidence of the quality performance failure.

Traditional management technology is obviously and fundamentally unable to deliver the requisite quality to the customer, even if its symbolic commitment to quality persists and does not have to be challenged. Commitment and ability to deliver are two completely different things.

The reasons for the quality failure are equally self-evident. First, functional specialization separates the various dimensions of quality, and a customer's unified perception of it is either broken down or ignored altogether. Design quality is in the hands of design engineers, production quality rests with production engineers, and quality control is carried out by quality inspectors. The only real quality assurance—the quality design of the entire production process (which must start and end with the customer)—is out of reach for this management technology. Second, task simplification (and specialization) separates the worker from the product and from other tasks (and therefore from other workers). A one-task worker can hardly relate to the complex final product, to the process that delivers it, or to the other one-task workers on the line. It is unfair to expect that he or she would even care, and it is vulgar to tell that worker, "Let's work together." The system gives the worker neither responsibility nor opportunity for improving the quality of the process. Third, the complexity of the coordinative structure (management) hides the real impact of poor quality. The systemic separation of decision makers from doers dictates the need for buffering the production process against internal fluctuations and external perturbations (errors, slippages, miscalculations, and shocks) via increasingly massive in-process inventories. These "just-in-case" buffers further amplify the separation and independence of the individual steps (and workers) in the operating process sequence. The connections between individuals and process performance are cut, process deficiencies are covered up, and workers adopt the responsibility-free attitude ("It is not my job") that is so typical of socialistic command economies.

It is becoming clear that the more developed the traditional management system becomes, the worse its quality performance must be. The unprecedented avalanche of quality props and crutches (product recalls, cash rebates, long-term installments, "incredible" warranties and guaranties, and zero percent financing) is recent proof of the apparently unstoppable quality decline of U.S. products.

New management technology must assure full and meaningful worker and customer participation in the production process. Ultimate *knowledge of the process rests with the worker* who performs it; but knowledge without responsibility is either irrelevant or irresponsible. As Peter Drucker insists in his *Management in Turbulent Times*, "The . . . fundamental challenge is to convert the employee's knowledge into responsibility within the enterprise and on the job."

Ultimate *knowledge of the product rests with the customer*. New technology must be not only knowledge- and responsibility-integrating, but also customer- rather than product-driven.

Mass Production. The third goal of the traditional management technology was the mass delivery of highly standardized products. It certainly succeeded in doing just that, and admirably so. The only condition was the existence of relatively homogeneous markets and customers. The competitive environments of the 1920s and 1950s were famous for their homogeneity, localization, and undemanding mediocrity; they do not exist anymore.

The Competitive Environment of the 1980s

The competitive environment is never stable, always evolving, and ever changing. Population structure and dynamics, wealth accumulation and distribution, economic and social policies, development and decline of developing countries, new technologies, and similar factors all keep changing in a more or less continuous fashion.

In the 1980s the cumulative effect of small, continuous changes suddenly created a qualitatively new competitive environment. The movement progressed from the economies of scale of the assembly line to the economies of scope (or variety) of the flexible production or service delivery system, toward (as *The Economist*'s Nicholas Valery puts it) "a magic kingdom where elements of the mass production of Henry Ford and the craftsmanship of Peter Fabergé co-exist." In other words, the set-up costs have been successfully driven down to essential zero.

In Figure 6 we present the relationship between the new competitive environment and its appropriate management technology.

Because competition is global, demand by definition cannot be homogeneous. In fact, homogeneous markets do not exist—there is a heterogeneous market which is continually segmented and resegmented by population dynamics. "Markets" do not buy anything; *individuals do.* This fact in itself rings the death knell to mass production.

Single-purpose, dedicated technologies still persist (mostly thanks to the use of trivial financial ratios in U.S. decision making), but reprogrammable, multipurpose flexible technologies are rapidly emerging to match the turbulent, rapidly evolving environments.

Individual customers naturally demand high-quality customized designs of products and services (indeed, they demand the very right to design and thus become *prosumers,* integrated in the process itself). Flexible, one-digit set-up technologies make these new demands realistic, and global competition forces instantaneous response. The name of the game is flexibility and adaptability, effectiveness rather than efficiency, and responsiveness rather than costs. As turbulence, unpredictability, and change become the only constants of the new business environment, an institution's capacity for survival depends on its capacity to change, to adapt, and to avail itself of new opportunities.

Integrated process management (IPM) appears to be the management technology that fits the new environment's demands. Its historical embedding is outlined in Figure 7, where

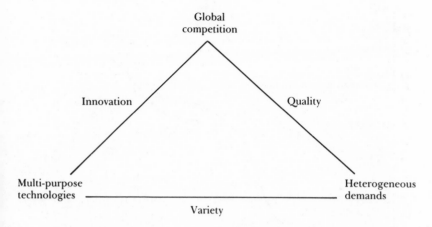

FIGURE 6. The Requirements for Management Technology in the Competitive Environment of the 1980s

we compare the S-shaped technology performance curves of major management technologies of the modern era.

The left-most curve covers the early period of the essentially "managementless" production system. Its life span ended around 1900, when the absence of appropriate management technology drastically slowed down the flow of benefits from otherwise powerful manufacturing technologies already in use. This end of the century crisis brought forth the first management technology: scientific management. This product oriented, specialist coordinated system then reigned supreme until the 1960s. During the following decade, its performance deteriorated at an alarming rate: the 1970s brought about zero or negative productivity growth in U.S. industry. The challenger, the new management technology of IPM, was already partially blueprinted by the likes of W. Edwards Deming and Joseph Juran in the early 1950s, and was adopted, improved, and further developed by Japanese managers in the next two decades.

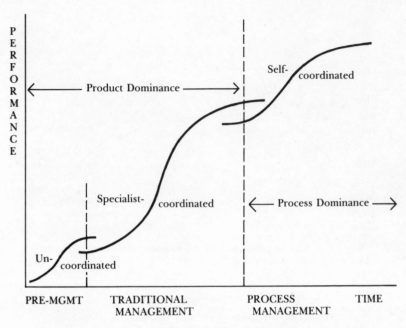

FIGURE 7. The Three Generations of Management Technology

Integrated Process Management

When knowledge becomes the major form of capital, as it did in the 1980s, management of the enterprise has to transform itself. Managing labor, land, money, or machines is fundamentally different from managing human knowledge. While the U.S. economy is structured, organized, and educated for the former (and has achieved some success there), world competitive enterprises now have rapidly shifted toward the latter. The management of human knowledge remains quite underdeveloped in the United States.

To put it more plainly, if it is the labor you are buying, you can afford to manage by traditional command, rigid hierarchy, and socialistic planning. You can simply say "do that!" and then reward the doer according to how your command was carried out.

If it is the knowledge you have to buy, forget the above paragraph. You cannot command "think that!" or "solve that problem!" or "be creative!" Everyone outside the centrally planned systems should know that. Getting knowledge from your employees requires fundamentally different skills and systems than getting merely their labor.

Who are the possessors of relevant knowledge in this new business environment? Clearly, customers and employees are. Customers know what they want, and employees know how to deliver it. Both customers and employees must be fully integrated into the enterprise. Because employees themselves can be viewed as customers, it is sufficient to speak of *customer integration* as being the single most important characteristic of IPM.

IPM consists of astonishingly simple solutions to extremely complex problems. As a whole it represents a total and uncompromising opposite to the traditional U.S. management system. For example:

- Because the customer is the ultimate determinant of business success, make the customer the driving force and dominant purpose of your business. In fact, make your customer a part of the business process.
- Because the most important determinant of job satisfaction is "work autonomy," organize your enterprise according to distributed autonomy principles, based on independent decision making and clearly assigned traceable responsibilities.
- Because the most powerful motivator is private ownership, turn your managers and workers into private owners, employees into "business associates," and workers into capitalists—all in *real* terms, not only as slogans.
- Because we now need knowledge more than labor, and because knowledge is an integral concept by its very nature, reintegrate the tasks and functions in order to reverse the

traditional process of specialization (division of labor and knowledge).

- Because "integrated customers" must get their products or services when and where they need them, and in the form and quality they prefer (in order to remain integrated), organize according to just-in-time (JIT) principles.
- Because the best way of dealing with future uncertainty is to acquire flexibility of means, expanding today's flexibility, rather than sharpening future forecasting, is the only proper and professional form of long-range planning.

Customer Integration

We are now ready to comprehend the true meaning of well-known statements that capture the spirit of IPM:

To increase productivity aim to increase quality of the process (Myron Tribus);
The product in the hands of the customer is still a part of the production cycle (Myron Tribus);
Our customer—our master (Tomáš Bat'a).

The emphasis is unmistakable and self-evident: the *customer* is the purpose and driving force of the enterprise and must be integrated into the process of production or service delivery. Improving the quality of such customer integrated process becomes the tool to assure customer satisfaction and to amplify the customer's role as a driving force of the enterprise.

Traditionally we have described the production process as a linear transformation of inputs into outputs (products or services). Such simplistic and one-directional schemes, characterized by a well-defined motive (plan), beginning (input), process (transformation), end (output), and object (customer)—all conveniently separate, separable, and autonomous entities—clutter most management textbooks even today.

This separation of components (nonsystems view) compels us to concentrate either on the management of input (human, financial, and material resources); on the management of output (product or service characteristics, advertisement, selling);

or even on the management of the production transformation itself (process). The inadequacy of such partial approaches is self-evident.

Serious practitioners and theorists of management are quite familiar with the original summary of the new approach by W. Edwards Deming; we reproduce its version in Figure 8.

The difficulty of the "old way" is not with any specific process component, but with the very system of their components' interconnections. The customer is allowed to remain an object, separated from the process, "out there" in the environment. The product is allowed to leave the production system and wither in the hands of the customer. No matter how loudly we proclaim our concerns for the customer or how elaborate are the institutions we establish to satisfy the customer (return policies, warranties, questionnaires, recalls), customer remains an external object separated in the environment.

This implies that a very important *real* linkage with the business environment has been lost. We have neglected to develop the capacity to learn about the business environment *directly* from customers' behavior. (Customers' complaints, a rich source of information and wisdom, become noise and nuisance in competitively declining cultures.)

Instead, we have chosen to establish an artificial and symbolic *information loop* of data gathering, market and consumer research, forecasting, and information processing. Instead of responding to customers' wishes directly and just-in-time, we have opted to *ask* them through a separate data-gathering loop: instead of measuring their behavior, we have measured their opinions.

True and real customer integration makes the function of traditional "cognitive" marketing at least redundant. There are two main reasons for the marketing bias: (1) the customer is viewed as the object and not the subject of production; and (2) traditional rigidity of means requires extensive planning and thus prevents just-in-time responsiveness of the enterprise. So, we are forced to plan by forecasting, and because customers cannot tell us, we have to ask them. Managers want to hear what's happening, not what consumers *say* is happening.

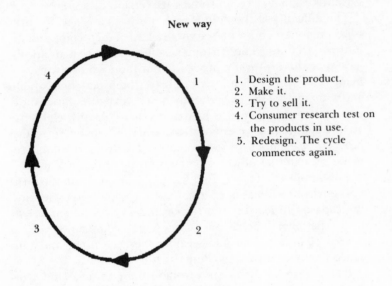

Old way

1. Design the product.   2. Make it.   3. Try to sell it.

New way

1. Design the product.
2. Make it.
3. Try to sell it.
4. Consumer research test on the products in use.
5. Redesign. The cycle commences again.

FIGURE 8. The Original Deming Cycle of Management Process

IPM by-passes the marketing bias by establishing the mechanism by which the customers "tell" directly about their wishes. Through appropriate just-in-time flexibility, IPM reduces increasingly wasteful reliance on forecasting, planning, marketing, and consumer "research."

Americans have mastered the decadent art of "selling the sizzle, not the steak" to such an extent that there is no "steak" any more. In fact, the prerecorded digital sound of the "sizzle" has become in itself the product aggressively hawked on the vulgar streets of business surrealism.

Traditional management philosophy is contrasted with IPM

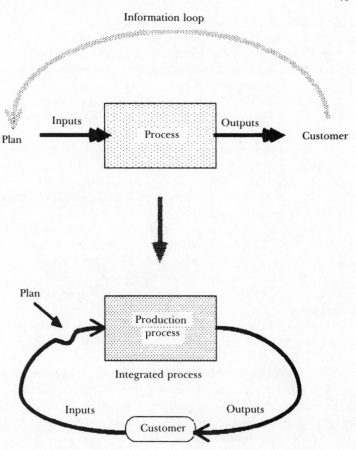

FIGURE 9. The IPM-cycle with Explicit Customer Integration

perspective in Figure 9. Note the *information feedback loop* of the traditional approach: this artificial contrivance further separates the real from the symbolic; it does not involve customers in the real process, but attaches them through the symbolic loop only.

Similar decoupling exists on the input side of the system: the separation of the enterprise from its suppliers, subcontractors, and prospective employees becomes absolute and is further amplified or aggravated by simplistic institutions of competitive price bidding, multisourcing, and outsourcing. Integrating our customers on the input side is thus equally desirable: suppliers should become an integrated part of the enterprise.

Because of the described separations of enterprise customers (including employees), some sort of planning is necessary. Because U.S. companies are organized according to the principles of command economy—forecasting, planning, maintaining a hierarchy of command, carrying out orders, and so on—this planning takes the form of computing (estimating, predicting, or forecasting) customers' and suppliers' respective environments "out there."

Such *planning as forecasting* of future states already has led to the downfall of socialist economies. Yet it is being increasingly practiced in "capitalistic" enterprises. The right form of planning for the new environment is *planning as expansion of requisite flexibility* (i.e., ability to cope with an ever larger variety of future states). This, strangely, is practiced in neither socialist nor traditional capitalist enterprises. Yet it has become the most powerful strategic tool of the most successful world competitive companies in *any* system.

IPM goes far beyond simply connecting the customer with the plan through an information loop. It actually integrates the customer into the system in real terms: it makes him or her an integral part of the process. The product (any output) in a customer's hands remains part of the production cycle. In this sense, the product is never finished; it is continually being worked upon and relentlessly improved.

Our scheme must therefore be transformed into a circular loop, connecting outputs with inputs via customer, with no beginning and no end. The entire loop becomes the process of our concern. We refer to this extended concept as the *integrated process.* Traditional process (in the narrow sense of production transformation) is only one of its identifiable components. The purpose is not to manage input, output, or process, nor any of these components in combination; the purpose is to manage the entire loop of the integrated process as a whole system. Hence, integrated process management. The *IPM loop,* the other loop in Figure 9, *is real:* it integrates all the material, human capital, and knowledge into circular *interflow* of information throughout the enterprise. The concept of customer has been expanded to include all categories of enterprise customers: consumers, suppliers, and employees. In the services, customer integration takes the form of self-service: direct contact between the producer of a customer-friendly product and its designated end-user. The traditional service provider, i.e., an overspecialized manipulator of the customer-unfriendly product, is thus effectively bypassed and eliminated from the process. Many unsuspecting service firms already have started on their inevitable journeys out. Japanese industrial giants have entered the do-it-yourself business in the meantime.

Newly conceived functions of planning and management can now be viewed as purposeful perturbations to the self-feeding and self-propagating interflow of the enterprise. Such perturbations create loop "indentations" (*in-formations*) to be propagated throughout the organization. The concept of information acquires its true and original meaning as "in-formation": a real effect rather than a symbolic coding of a real effect.

For example, a customer's actual buying and repeatedly using a brand of toothpaste is *in-formation;* a customer's *saying* (perhaps in response to a questionnaire) which toothpaste he or she might prefer to buy is *information.* It goes without saying that a world competitive enterprise can only be built on in-formation, not on information.

The integrated process itself becomes self-managing and self-maintaining, subject to described managerial and environmental perturbations. There are no separate "inputs" or "outputs": any *locus* along the interflow loop can be perturbed by external or internal in-formation. The question is not how to gather information about local conditions and communicate it up to the center for "synthesis" and decision making. The real question is how to provide the decentralized and autonomous *loci* of the interflow (employees on the line) with the strategic in-formation they need.

The IPM scheme of Figure 9 implies, among other things, that : (1) the quality of the integrated process must be continually maintained and improved; (2) responses along the interflow loop must be localized and just-in-time; both input (suppliers) and output (customers) sides of the enterprise must be integrated into a system; (3) vertical integration of operations must be increased along with the integration of labor and knowledge in order to reduce the damaging separation due to excessive specialization and division of labor; (4) the organization of the integrated process must be as flexible as possible so that important "in-formations" can be propagated rapidly and reliably; and (5) employees must directly share in the ownership, management, and decision making so that the necessary acquisition of knowledge and inflow of innovation can be assured.

In Figure 10 we outline the crucial difference between the two fundamental approaches toward handling environmental uncertainty and ambiguity: *forecasting* versus *flexibility*.

Instead of computing the environment "out there" (like long-range or strategic planning of socialist centralized hierarchies), IPM emphasizes the continuous build-up of the internal and increasingly autonomous *response flexibility*. In the new environment of turbulence, unpredictability, and discontinuous change, there is only one true long-term strategy to follow: to become sufficiently flexible in technology, labor, and knowledge to respond just-in-time to the ever widening variety of environmental perturbations (in-formations).

Conclusion

We have argued that the cause of the "malaise Américain" is its management. The government did not cause the rise of U.S. industrial competitiveness in the past, and it has not been responsible for its subsequent decline; least of all can it be relied upon to bring about its renaissance in the future.

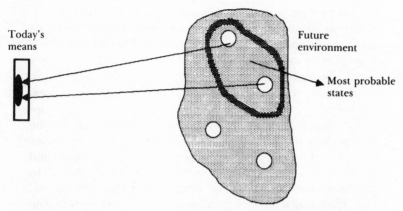

Classical long-range planning (strategic planning, strategic management) computes the turbulent and ever-changing future environment as precisely as possible (by identifying most probable states) with respect to fixed goals and attempts to match current means via requisite adjustments.

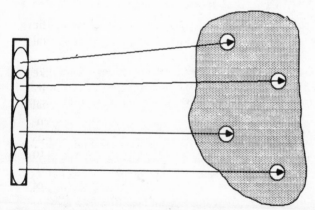

IPM-strategy builds requisite flexibility into today's means (technology, job skills, knowledge, organization) in order to respond to ever wider range of states of the future. The ultimate long-term strategy for dealing with change is to be continually and just-in-time changeable: flexibility has become a strategic tool par excellence.

FIGURE 10. Flexibility as a Strategic Planning Tool

The only useful policy that government *can* pursue is to create the conditions and disseminate the information necessary for widespread national adoption of IPM and its variants. Government can encourage the use of IPM by private enterprises, demand its adoption by governmental institutions (to facilitate rapid privatization), and force its usage throughout the military sector.

We are convinced that American business and management schools now stand ready to take an active and fully cooperative part in the long process of restoring American management to the very top of world competitive systems. It will achieve this not through catching up, not through imitating, but through new leadership, propelling itself into the twenty-first century—now.

Appendix
Practical Roots of IPM

As any useful and successful management system, IPM too has arisen directly from practice and experience of business and not from artificial theory or research. The theory of IPM is only now, after the fact of its emergence, being developed for the purposes of knowledge building, transfer, sharing, and enhancement. Its practice (although admittedly ignored by the media and academia) has always been vigorous and very impressive.

Zeleny has carefully selected a few cases from significantly different times and environments. One of the typical practical embodiments of IPM was the so-called Bat'a system in Czechoslovakia in the 1920s and 1930s. The most successful current "prototype" is Lincoln Electric Company in Cleveland. The Fletcher Jones stores in Australia, JZD Agrokombinát Slušovice in Moravia, and Au Bon Pain fast-food chain in Boston demonstrate the eminent applicability of IPM across time, geography, political systems, and type of business. Further, even the truly successful and winning companies in America (i.e., *not* those traditional and failing ones described in *Search for Excellence*) can attribute their winning performance to employing significant subsets of the IPM management technology.

Bat'a System

The Bat'a system integrated the following components into a single functional whole:

1. decentralized organization (distributed autonomy), rooted in departmental autonomy, self-management, direct and immediate profit sharing, and full individual responsibility for quality;
2. automation and "robotics" support for fully flexible production layouts, combined with semiautomated statistical self-monitoring of performance;
3. employees' full coownership of the enterprises based on long-term employment contracts and earnings reinvestment programs;
4. customer satisfaction (via product quality and its continuous improvement) as the dominant strategic principle of the enterprise;
5. maximum possible vertical integration: only a few suppliers, no middlemen, and direct contact with the customer;
6. total quality of employee life (not just of "working life"): from the workplace, through personal health care, to employee housing and social services—all self-imposed as primary company responsibility;
7. extensive "in-house" management and business education and training through Bat'a School of Work and Management;
8. no subsidies, no debt, no public stocks, no preferential customs or quotas, and no unions (all employees were coworkers or "associates").

Tomáš Bat'a was an extraordinary entrepreneur—perhaps the greatest business and management genius ever. He:

- fell in love with the machines ("thinking to the people, labor to the machines!" proclaimed the factory sign);
- eliminated all "middlemen" and ran his own network of retail and repair stores and outlets all over the world;
- made the customer and the public not only the purpose but the very foundation of his enterprise ("our customer—our master" and "service to the public" were not slogans, but explicit and serious principles of business);
- made employment stable and long term: part of each employee's earnings was reinvested in the company, each worker becoming a capitalist and company coowner in the process;

- claimed that the quality of employee life was the primary concern of the employer and *not* of the state; his company provided family housing (with gardens) and built a social infrastructure of hospitals, museums, churches, swimming pools, leisure facilities, sport stadiums, roads, and so on;
- sought total self-reliance, independence, and vertical integration: railroads, waterways, airports, land, forests, and even local government all became part of the enterprise concerns;
- strived to operate with no debt and with no credit; established his own company savings and investments bank, never went public: all stocks were held by the employees; yet, all state taxes were paid according to the highest principles of integrity.

Each machine (referred to as "electrical robots" since 1926) was jointly owned and under full responsibility of a designated group of workers. The process of continuous innovation and improvement was installed, and a total system of rotational preventive maintenance mastered.

Assurance of continually high-quality output was based on rewards to individuals for quality improvements and penalties to teams for quality failures; because of flexible layout and individual worker responsibility, all line breakdowns and stoppages were ultimately eliminated.

Total strategic flexibility was achieved by breaking the "classical" large factory plant down into smaller, semiautonomous, and independently competing workshops, and by making *all* machines self-contained, independently powered, and motorized, while educating multifunctional workers, fully rotational within their technological groups. This allowed all changes in product styles and types to be achieved quickly by pulling out or inserting machines temporarily ("decoupling the line") to rearrange machine sequences and layouts.

Lincoln Electric Company

Lincoln Electric Company, the world's largest manufacturer of welding machines and electrodes, is also one of the highest-paying factories in the world, characterized by the highest quality and the lowest prices at the same time. It appears to be fully resistant to Japanese competition.

James F. Lincoln began a stock purchase plan for all employees in 1925, a suggestion system in 1929, the bonus plan in 1934, and a pension plan, promotion from within, and continuous employment by 1944. (It is interesting to note that Bat'a visited Cleveland in the early 1920s.)

James F. Lincoln, in his remarkable book, *A New Approach to Industrial Economics,* describes a number of leading principles that are virtually identical with the Bat'a system and IPM:

- money needed for expansion is supplied by the customer in retained earnings. It is obvious that the customer's interests, not the stockholder's, should come first. The customer is Lincoln's most important constituency;
- "The last group to be considered is the stockholders who own stock because they think it will be more profitable than investing money in any other way," writes Lincoln. Financing for company growth should come from within the company—through initial cash investment by the founders, retention of earnings, and stock purchases by those who work in the business. Lincoln does not rely at all on borrowing, and debt is limited to current payables;
- product quality is the highest and assured, as reflected by the very short or nonexistent warranties: the AC-225 welding machine is only warranted for one year. Lincoln has never handled a warranty claim; yet Lincoln is the undisputed price leader in its field;
- Lincoln also never has had a formal organization chart; routine supervision is nonexistent. Functional integration is awesome: a typical production foreman coordinates as many as 100 workers. Under such implied structure, production workers (about 3,000 employees) have two or three levels of supervision between themselves and the president; workers operate several machines, while supervisors are busy with planning, record keeping, and improvements;
- there have been no layoffs at Lincoln since 1949. A typical Lincoln employee earns about twice as much as other factory workers in the Cleveland area; the labor cost per sales is well below industry averages;
- management is the coach who must be obeyed. Employees are the players who must be respected and given full execution responsibility: they alone can win the games.

Au Bon Pain Company

In the early 1980s Ron Shaich (Harvard M.B.A.) and Len Schlesinger (Harvard professor) wanted to create a company where they would want to work. Shaich remembered his business school case study of Lincoln Electric. They also learned from Golden Corral Corp., another food service operation: give unit managers a piece of the action, turn them into owners.

At Au Bon Pain, they learned that it is a waste of time to try to tinker with the system: "We had to turn assembly-line foremen into shop-keepers; we had to bust the system wide open."

In early 1986 they heard the crucial piece of practical wisdom from Pete Harman of Kentucky Fried Chicken: "You know, at a private company, you don't have to be greedy. You can share it with your good people, and it all comes back to you."

Why not tie store managers' incentives to "controllable" profits (profit less rent and depreciation)? They could then adjust their use of labor, shrinkage, and controllable expenses depending on the level of business they did. Overnight, managers began solving the problems they used to dump on the company. The system does not accept excuses.

Because of the profit sharing and because half of the bonus is retained in a reserve fund, most successful managers are increasingly "locked in." They are in the same position as company owners: they have to solve their own problems, hire and fire their own people, set their own wage scales, and cut their own deals. What they cannot do is to compromise on food quality and customer service.

The company's top management officials comment proudly on the system they created: "We're out of the picture, it's a closed loop." It's a closed loop: the circular integration (study Figure 9 again) has been achieved. "*This,* is the kind of company I'd like to work for," says Shaich.

It is a pity that Shaich and Schlesinger had to reinvent the wheel themselves because their own business education was tragically deficient in providing the principles of distributed autonomy, self-management, and self-coordination, the Bat'a system, or IPM.

Fletcher Jones Company

The Fletcher Jones Company started in 1924 with men's clothing in Warrnambool, and was established in Melbourne, Australia after 1928. In 1974 Fletcher Jones (FJ) had thirty-one stores and 3,000 employees.

The phenomenal success of this company is described by Fletcher

Jones himself in his book *Not by Myself*. Truly, he, like Bat'a and Lincoln, did not do it alone.

This company is fully rooted in real, not symbolic, employees' ownership: all employee shares bring the same dividends and the same rights as any public stocks and are given to *all* employees. In the 1970s the Jones family owned 30 percent and employees 70 percent of the company. FJ stocks are limited to FJ family and employees only: there are no absentee stockholders, stocks are not for sale on the stock exchange, and no outsider can buy them. If a shareholder takes a leave of absence, the shares must be sold back to the firm. If an employee retires, the shares retain their original vesting until the employee's death, at which point they can be inherited by his or her survivors, but *then* must be sold back to the firm.

JZD Agrokombinát Slušovice

This is a remarkable story of a collective farm deeply embedded within the most rigid and most centrally controlled socialistic system on earth. The only comparative advantage the farm had was its proximity to Zlín, which was until 1948 the site of Bat'a Enterprises, the *genius loci* of the modern management paradigm.

Since 1969 the collective farm director Ing. F. Čuba, CSc. started to expand traditional agricultural production through vertical integration, horizontal expansion, and innovation.

Today they have 3,000 employees who produce food, electronic computers, agricultural machinery, fertilizers, and top race horses. There are weekly "technical councils" which propel the best technical and organizational innovations immediately into practice; employees enter contracts that give them full responsibility and also full benefits for their tasks (e.g., drivers lease their automobiles into their own full care and maintenance); 100 computers comprise a fully decentralized information system.

Their microcomputers, TNS, originally produced for their own use, are now produced at the rate of 2,000 pieces a year, the largest computer production in Czechoslovakia. Guaranteed delivery time is three months, and a computer leasing service is also available. At least 100 software programs, ranging from optimization of feeding schedules to management of warehouses, are available.

The enterprise is totally dedicated to social services for its employees. This so-called *agroservis* provides home delivery of groceries, buying of larger consumer appliances, apartment painting and repairs, car rental, and so on. All the rooms in the Hotel Slušovice are equipped with color television. Their construction department built a department store in Zlín in nine months, even though materials like window glass had to be brought from West Germany. There are at least twelve separate types of production, ranging from computers, horse saddles, and cigarettes to cognac, milk products, and racing cars.

The example of Slušovice provides crucial evidence of the applicability of the Bat'a system across time, across cultures, and even across political systems: managing across discontinuity.

IPM–run Companies in the United States

In 1981 Richard E. Cavanagh and Donald K. Clifford of the McKinsey Institute started research into 100 very high-performing, high-growth, midsized businesses in the United States (*The Winning Performance,* Bantam Books, 1985).

The 100 businesses selected are not comparable to so-called excellent companies (*Search for Excellence*) or to the Fortune 500, as is also observed by Stoner, Taylor, and Wankel in this volume. For example, their average sales growth per annum is 18 percent (while the Fortune 500 is 7.8 percent, and the "excellent companies" about 12 percent), and earnings for the period 1978–83 were 20 percent (the Fortune 500 were 6 percent, and the "excellent" group was 10 percent).

Typical examples of the "Winning 100" companies include Automated Data Processing, Inc. (thirty-seven years of consecutive increases in quarterly earnings, all over 15 percent), Cray Research, A.T. Cross, Cullinet Software, Harvey Hubbell (twenty-one years of uninterrupted increases in quarterly earnings), Loctite, Pall Corporation (the Fortune 1,000 highest return to shareholders over the last twenty years), Safety-Kleen (the U.S. highest return to shareholders over the last ten years), and so on.

It is natural to ask what these companies have in common and what are the major characteristics of their management *systems.* Cavanagh and Clifford went even further and asked management experts worldwide (both academics and practitioners) about the "success criteria" *they* would expect to see at such extremely successful midsized high-growth companies.

The results illuminate the gap between the "conventional wisdom" of seasoned management experts and the reality of winning (as op-

Conventional Wisdom of Expert Consensus of Opinion	Reality Found in the Winning 100 Companies
1. Success found in rapidly growing industries of the "rising sun" type.	1. Industry does not matter: industries do not win, companies do.
2. Relatively small, able to penetrate even the biggest markets.	2. 98 percent were niche players: the smaller the market, the larger the profit.
3. Low-cost producers, achieving economies of scale, running down "experience" and cost curves.	3. No low-cost producers but high quality, innovation, new markets, new products, new ways.
4. Low-price providers.	4. Customer is willing to pay for what he or she wants.
5. Either minding their own business, knowing what to do and getting on with it, *or* miniconglomerates, but both related to the first four points.	5. Neither: new product with existing skill, or new market with existing product.
6. No-nonsense management: employees need to be told what to do, and managers would tell them.	6. Employees=shareholders: 30 percent of the stock owned by people who worked there. Label "employees" not used.
7. Their mission: create wealth.	7. Mission: customer service, innovation, motivation.
8. Management by exception: if it ain't broke, don't fix it.	8. Do it better, always, *especially* when things go right.
9. Leadership: cool, rational, professional.	9. Intuitive and creative, yet good with facts and figures.
10. Entrepreneurs: somewhat disorganized, undisciplined, and materially motivated.	10. Values, priorities, and strong culture!

posed to "making it") in the world of practice. There is a difference between being good or "excellent" (in the U.S. sense) and being a long-term winner on the domestic and international scenes (26 percent of the "Winning 100" earnings comes from overseas).

It is safe to conclude that the "Winning 100" companies are being run according to principles and practices that are almost the exact opposite of experts' conventional wisdom. The implications for business and education are staggering and humbling at the same time: there are few business schools in the United States today that would teach the "winning system" rather than conventional wisdom.

The table on the preceding page lists major characteristics of the "Winning 100" companies as predicted by experts and as actually identified in practice.

The left side of the table is remarkably consistent with the interrelated statement of conventional wisdom of the traditional management model. The right side summarizes the exceptionally high-performance practice of people for whom business is an embodiment of their values, vision, and enthusiasm about the business. The "Winning 100" study shows clearly that IPM, in all of its extensions and versions, is (and was) being practiced widely, although, as always, by true "winners" only.

6

The Challenges of
Competitiveness: A Labor View

DOUGLAS A. FRASER
B. J. WIDICK

Introduction

In a persuasive study aptly entitled *Manufacturing Matters: The Myth of the Post Industrial Economy,* Stephen S. Cohen and John Zysman define competitiveness as "the degree to which

DOUGLAS A. FRASER was the sixth international president of the United Auto Workers union from 1977 to 1983. He is currently a professor of labor studies at Wayne State University and the Jerry Wurf fellow and lecturer at the John F. Kennedy School of Government at Harvard University. Mr. Fraser began working for Chrysler Corporation at the age of eighteen and rose through the ranks of UAW, serving in various local capacities before joining the UAW staff in 1947. Mr. Fraser played a key role in several important Chrysler/ UAW negotiations, including those that resulted in union representation on the Chrysler board of directors. Mr. Fraser is an officer of many labor, civic, and governmental bodies.

B. J. WIDICK is a former professor of industrial relations at the Graduate School of Business, Columbia University, where he taught for twenty-two years. He served as a visiting professor at Michigan State University in 1976 and as associate professor of economics at Wayne State University, where he did his graduate work. Prior to his academic career, Professor Widick was involved in several unions, as a nation can, under free and fair market conditions, produce goods and services that meet the test of international markets while expanding the real income of its citizens."

Labor has long held a similar view. It understood the need to be competitive, without doing so at the expense of a lower standard of living. Labor has long recognized the potential for international trade to improve the living standards of America, and to promote economic growth and development in all countries.

The difficulty has been that competition in the markets has been neither free nor fair. A case in point is trade relations with Japan, which exercises a policy of protectionism at home while arguing for free trade elsewhere. This has been a contributing factor to the accumulation of the huge U.S. trade deficit. The standard American piecemeal responses to unfair competition in the form of antidumping and countervailing duty laws have not been able to redress the imbalances, nor are they likely to do so. Another factor that has shrunk the markets for our exports has been the massive debt accumulations and interest payments of many Third World countries. The strength of the dollar compared to weak currencies like the yen in the past has had negative effects on exports, and has accelerated imports.

At long last, the high cost of uncompetitive U.S. business practices has come into question. Among those practices are excessive management compensation, the negative impact of authoritarian managements hostile to labor, short-term time horizons that exclude long-range strategies, and many cases of excessive preoccupation with mergers and acquisitions. Taking those practices into account, along with negative government and trade policies, we can see why the authors of *Manufacturing Matters* would argue that the competitiveness of the American economy was eroding.

However, countervailing forces have emerged that suggest

---

research director of the United Rubberworkers Union, vice president of the Akron Newspaper Guild, and UAW staff member.

that final judgments may be premature. These forces include favorable indications of new flexibility in crucial labor-management relations, the completion of modernization of many manufacturing facilities, and an alert recognition by key industrial leaders of the challenges ahead. Early results have been substantial gains in productivity, better product lines, and an awareness of the importance of quality to make America competitive. It should be noted that none of these developments or changes came easily.

While labor has resisted bearing the full brunt of change in terms of job losses, dislocations due to plant closings, and the ensuing devastation to the communities involved, it also has tried to meet the challenge by demands for equity, and by preparing the work forces for different days. But labor's flexibility and its sense of social responsibility must be shared by business and government to prevent the quest for "competitiveness" from being unacceptable to the affected sectors of the population and important political constituencies.

We suggest that an examination of issues in trade, competitiveness, and the auto industry will bear out our contentions.

Response of the U.S. Industry to Japan's Challenge in Autos

In contrast to the normal bargaining and friction that occur in trade relations between the United States and other nations, the relationship between the United States and Japan reached a stage of high tension in 1987 because it had become increasingly clear that, while Japan professed free trade, it practiced neomercantilism, an integral part of which is protectionism. The consequences are described by Stephen Cohen in his 1985 study, *Uneasy Partnership.* Japan did not have a trade problem with the United States; it had a trade problem with the world. The complaints voiced by the European Community countries and the developing countries in Asia were remarkably similar to those in the United States. The disdainful Japanese responses to complaints of other countries are also remarkably consistent: "try harder to export to our market and accept the fact that our outpouring of manufactured goods exports reflects our harder work and our lack of raw materials." Cohen wryly observes that it was difficult to believe that the rest of the world was wrong and the Japanese were right.

To begin with, in comparing the American and Japanese auto industries, some basic factors affecting them have frequently been underestimated, if not overlooked. Japan's industrial resurgence was facilitated by General Douglas MacArthur's dictums, including a loosening up of the semifeudal social relations of that nation. The auto industry was made a strategic target for growth by the Ministry of International Trade and Industry. The government role included protectionism, tax breaks, low-cost financing, and the molding of a docile work force. The economic open door policy of the United States, which welcomed imports, plus the effects of a strong dollar relative to a weak yen were stimulants for entry into the rich American market, especially since Europe denied Japanese penetration. Furthermore, the Japanese home market was limited. Aided by an American statistician, W. Edwards Deming—a man whose views were ignored in the United States—the Japanese pushed quality. This, combined with price advantages, enabled the Japanese to blitzkrieg the American market, which was filled with discontented consumers listening to auto critics like Ralph Nader. The result was the equivalent of shock therapy for the American Big Three.

For the past two decades, the Big Three suffered frequent and damaging blows to their reputations. The public perception was brutal: Chrysler became viewed as a basket case, Ford was drowning in red ink, and General Motors was the next *Titanic,* sinking without an orchestra playing. A rash of books, articles, studies, and media coverage pinpointed every fault, real or imagined, of the Big Three. Much of this is recorded in two major studies done at the Massachusetts Institute of Technology (*The Future of the Automobile,* 1984) and at the Harvard Business School (*Changing Alliances,* 1986). They include invaluable historical analysis. Certainly, there is much merit in their harsh critique of management policies. The authors are rather dubious about the industry's future, unless major changes take place, or have occurred. Our chapter examines that question.

Undeniably, the American auto industry has experienced much trouble in recent decades. Foreign competition, especially from Japan, has been a major cause of that trouble. Imports took a quarter of the market to the cheers for Japanese quality and price. Only when the national consequences of the potential collapse of the American car industry were visible did the nation take a second look. Working with alarmed auto and other business interests, the United Auto Workers union aroused public pressure, which forced a "voluntary restraining" program for Japanese imports and provided the Big Three with a "breathing spell" for recovery. The crisis character of the situation alerted political interests. Before a 1983 congressional committee, Maryann Keller, a nationally recognized auto expert long known for her free trade views, urged national legislation involving a restraining policy on imports.

Meanwhile, profound changes were taking place within the Big Three. In their seminal work, *New Deals: The Chrysler Revival and the American System,* Robert Reich and John D. Donahue give a microscopic analysis of the agonizing process by which the Chrysler turnaround came and succeeded. As the authors note, Chrysler, the fourteenth biggest industrial firm in the United States, was facing bankruptcy. Under the dynamic leadership of Lee A. Iacocca, and with the vital cooperation of the United Auto Workers union and its congressional allies, the Carter administration was persuaded to guarantee Chrysler loans—a decision the Reagan administration found unwise to change. Chrysler did bleed for cash all through 1980 and 1981, but fresh money let it continue a retooling campaign. The payoff came in 1983, when Chrysler was able to produce 2 million vehicles, earning a stunning $2.4 billion net profit.

Under the distinctly Iacocca-style management, and working within the framework of American-style union-management relations, the Chrysler success continued in 1985 and 1986. The company restored thousands of workers to the payroll, after its drastic earlier cuts among blue and white collar employees. It made its stockholders (who ignored their brokers) very healthy. The federal government made $311 million on its loan guarantees. The bankers and other creditors hit a bonanza when they rolled over Chrysler debt in the form of preferred stocks, and warrants rose from $3.50 to $18 in one year. Iacocca made millions in salary, bonuses, and stock option rewards. Nevertheless, a study, *The Chrysler Bailout Bust,* by James K. Hickel for the conservative Heritage Foundation, criticizes this performance as a bust. It even projected that Chrysler would be less competitive in the future.

After all, a "sin" had been committed against the theory that the "marketplace" was where the problem should have been solved, no matter what the social costs. Neither Chrysler management, nor the union, nor the city of Detroit was upset by the criticism. A major company had been revitalized, thousands of jobs had been saved, and the city retained its biggest taxpayer as a consequence of the Chrysler bailout.

Besides, in June 1987 Chrysler received an accolade in a *Fortune* magazine article praising its "production whiz" Dick Dauch, who turned the company's manufacturing around in a manner envied by the Japanese. The article also noted that Chrysler had an $816 cost advantage on compacts and a $3,310 advantage on sports cars compared to the Japanese.

Chrysler's acquisition of American Motors in 1986, a brilliant move on all accounts from all quarters, has also strengthened the corporation in every respect. Obviously, writing off Chrysler did not appear to be a sound judgment.

The gloomy forecasts for the American auto industry received another jolt in the mid-1980s with the dazzling performance of the Ford Motor Company. How ironic that a best-selling anecdotal book, *The Reckoning,* by David Halberstam, should compare Ford unfavorably with a Japanese success story: Nissan. However, the myths about the number two Japanese auto maker were exploded in a *Wall Street Journal* story late in 1986, which pointed out that Nissan was falling victim to the kinds of problems that had beset Detroit. Nissan was troubled by labor problems and misdirected short-term decisions, and was losing millions of dollars overseas and at home. In sharp contrast, Ford sold about 5.9 million motor vehicles in the world in 1986, posted a $3.3 billion net profit, and had a hefty $8 billion cash reserve. Obviously, there was something to be said for Ford-style management.

To many critics, the largest of the Big Three, General Motors, had a "bad" year in 1986, after recording fabulous profits earlier—a fact that astonished the critics who wrote GM off in the late 1970s. General Motors "only" sold 8.5 million motor vehicles in the world in 1986, as many as Toyota, Nissan, and Mazda combined. After an unusual but deliberate one-time billion dollar write-off mainly for plant obsolescence, General Motors' net profit in 1986 was $2.9 billion. Meanwhile, as it was finishing its streamlining in 1987, with remarkable changes in production and products and with innovative labor relations, General Motors was in a position to join Ford and Chrysler as top seeded competitors at home and abroad.

General Motors' innovations included a joint venture in 1985 with Toyota at the new United Motors Manufacturing Inc. in Fremont, California—Ford had worked out one with Mazda in a new plant in Flat Rock, Michigan, Chrysler with Mitsubishi in Indiana. The imaginative "Saturn" project, involving a $5 billion investment, was scarcely a sign of stodgy management. GM gobbled up H. Ross Perot and his sophisticated data systems company, as well as his caustic comments. The purchase of Hughes Aircraft was not only a lucrative gem, but gave General Motors a fresh laboratory for research and technological development.

"Changing Alliances," a four-year Harvard Business School study by Davis Dyer, Malcolm S. Salter, and Alan M. Webber, charges that "the failure of the U.S. auto industry to change has caused deep and irreparable damage." In view of the visible evidence of the drastic changes within the Big Three, that categoric judgment is open to serious challenge. Even their own study states elsewhere that

the American automobile industry of the late 1980's scarcely resembles that of only a decade ago. For example the Big Three produces in coalition with Japanese partners. The Japanese call the shots in design and supply of the most important parts and components of shared vehicles. GM was endeavoring to strengthen its ties to Toyota, Isuzu and Suzuki; Ford with Mazda, and Chrysler with Mitsubishi; and all three have found partners in other Asian countries as well.

Actually, the relationship between the American and Japanese companies is more complicated. Chrysler owns at least 15 to 20 percent of Mitsubishi stock, GM has large holdings in Japanese companies, and Ford's arrangement with Mazda in the Flat Rock plant suggests a new and unexplored relationship whose consequences remain unknown.

While the Harvard study's flat judgment that "the outcome is evident; and the Big Three is losing to the Japanese" could apply to the past, it is premature for forecasting the future, as the Ford and Chrysler successes remind us. The study underestimated the remarkable productivity gains of the American auto industry arising from the modernization of its facilities, as well as other factors.

The productivity rate of the American auto industry climbed from 1980 through 1985 at an average 6.7 percent annually. During the same period, unit labor costs declined almost 8 percent. It may be stated without equivocation that by 1987 unit labor costs in the American auto industry were competitive with producers anywhere, according to our private sources.

The impressive auto industry productivity records may help explain further a favorable report on June 16, 1987, by the Bureau of Labor Statistics, which declares:

The United States led the industrialized world in improving its manufacturing efficiency last year and was the only major country to reduce effective labor costs. The 3.5 percent increase in U.S. labor productivity in terms of output per hour was more than double the average improvement of nine major competitors, outpacing gains of 2.9 percent in Great Britain, 2.8 percent in Japan and 1.9 percent in West Germany and France, the Labor Department said. It was the first year since 1950 . . . that the U.S. outpaced its major competitors. Measured in dollars, U.S. labor costs per unit of output fell by nearly 22 percent when compared with its major competitors, with Japanese costs up 42.6 percent over 1985 and labor costs in West Germany up 39.8 percent.

Earlier, the Council of Economic Advisers in its March 1987 report had made a very pertinent comment on the issue of cost competitiveness. It stated:

In sum, the deterioration of international cost competitiveness in U.S. manufacturing during the first half of this decade was the result of the real appreciation of the dollar, not sagging productivity growth or excessive wage increases.

Perhaps these figures may help explain to skeptics why the labor movement rejects the contention that "high wages" are the cause of our competitive troubles.

Coincidental to the gains in productivity, another favorable development has given promise of making an important contribution to the competitiveness of the industry. It is the belated recognition by much of management of the value and need for blue collar worker input into all phases of the production process, and the invaluable role of the union in representing the constituency. This new attitude has been a radical departure from the traditional view that "management knows best." Gone are the days when any suggestion by a labor leader would be dismissed with the comment, "If you want to talk about cars, join our side of the table," as a General Motors executive told Walter Reuther when he proposed the building of small cars.

The blue collar worker, much maligned as either an Archie Bunker or a mere robot, has at long last been recognized for his or her invaluable work: the worker is now seen as a human being with much to contribute besides physical labor. This was the significance in the new concepts of union participation on all levels of the Saturn project, the Quality of Work programs at GM, the employee involvement policies at Ford, and the teamwork projects at all the companies.

There needs to be a reminder of another innovation within the auto industry, which was criticized by most of the business press and all management. It was the daring proposal in 1979 by Lee A. Iacocca to place the president of the United Auto Workers union on the Chrysler board of directors. Cries of "socialism," among other negative responses, could be heard.

While skeptical union leaders—and there were many—adjusted to the idea when they saw the value of labor input on the highest levels of corporate decision making, most management still shuddered at the idea. Since 1980 the United Auto Workers union has been represented on the board. The idea proved fruitful for both management and union, and so far there is no evidence that it has compromised the union, or caused the downfall of capitalism.

Obviously, our analysis of the auto industry, in terms of the competitive issue, differs from the pessimistic outlook explicit in the major studies reviewed. Ford and Chrysler have made a turnaround, and belatedly, General Motors is joining them. However, we must point out again that there were huge social costs involved in this transformation. Drastic job cuts and plant closings reduced direct auto employment from 776,299 in 1978 to 563,313 in 1986.

Fortunately, the collective bargaining system in the auto industry functioned to provide by negotiations important cushions to ease the economic shock—a system that most American employees do not have. The United Auto Workers union has negotiated, among other programs, supplemental unemployment insurance, job banks, and joint retraining programs designed to soften the brunt of permanent job loss.

In the summer of 1987, negotiations between the United Auto Workers union with Ford and General Motors again tested the viability of this uniquely American system of free collective bargaining. The persistent turbulent character of the industry—its ups and downs—fueled the desire for job security, which was the top union demand.

Issues like "outsourcing," the impact of joint ventures, plant closings, and the continuous upheavals in the parts industry all contributed to the intensity of feelings and negotiations at the bargaining tables. This was evident in the preliminary discussion of the 1987 negotiations between the union and Ford and General Motors. It made for a tough bargaining climate, in which the stakes were recognized by the negotiators.

Traditional adversarial relations were unlikely to be fruitful in the face of new competitive challenges in the marketplace.

The costs of overt conflict appeared too great for either side to accept as a modus operandi. A protracted strike struggle could signify a permanent loss of markets and jobs. Hence, a new climate was evolving in the bargaining process. Survival was necessary for both sides, and the parties involved knew this. In these circumstances, bargaining had become a tougher challenge, and the outcome a clear harbinger of the future.

However, there is a much broader dimension to labor's concern about competitiveness than the status of the auto industry, important as it may be to the American economy. Labor is also concerned about the impact of current trade policies, the consequences of the Third World debt of our export markets, and the whole question of tariffs; these factors affect not only the auto industry but our entire economy and its competitiveness. Labor has strong views on these subjects, which we present next.

Needed: a Managed Trade Policy

Much of this section is drawn directly and verbatim from UAW testimony and publications, reflecting official positions with which we concur.

Labor believes that drastic changes in trade policy are needed if we are to reduce the U.S. trade deficit and assure that international trade contributes to our objective of a diversified, full employment economy that produces an equitable distribution of income and expanding opportunities for workers.

The desperate need for a new trade policy is captured in a single indicator—the massive U.S. trade deficit. From $36 billion in 1980, the deficit has grown each year, until it reached *$170 billion* for 1986. This ballooning figure is responsible for the loss of millions of jobs, especially in manufacturing industries where a 1980 trade surplus has fallen to a deficit of more than $150 billion. In automotive products, the 1986 deficit exceeded $50 billion, compared with an $11 billion deficit in 1980. The deterioration in the trade balance characterized nearly all sectors of the U.S. economy, including agriculture and high-technology industries. Millions of unemployed and underemployed Americans and thousands of depressed communities can explain their plight by pointing to the employment cutbacks and plant closings resulting from trade problems.

In nearly every industry, U.S. exports have stagnated, while imports have skyrocketed. Once strong U.S. exporting industries have seen their share of world markets decline, just as domestic industries have lost market share to the growth of imports.

The fact that administration officials responsible for trade policy could allow this incredible trade deficit to accumulate is the most powerful argument favoring the need for a managed U.S. trade policy. The United Auto Workers union, along with other worker representatives and a variety of business interests, described the danger posed by our passive trade policy years ago, yet were ignored by administration officials.

There are those who attribute the deterioration in U.S. trade performance to macroeconomic policy, exchange rates, and the insufficient international orientation of U.S. businesses. These and others point to the trade deficit as a sign of lack of "competitiveness" in the world market. These explanations all have one thing in common—they minimize the role of the U.S. trade policy in creating the severe problems of the economy.

All these explanations of the nation's international trade problem ignore the basic responsibility of those in the administration in charge of trade policy—to assure that international trade helps achieve our national objectives for full employment and income growth. If macroeconomic policy is inconsistent with this objective, there should be a voice in the administration making this case; if exchange rates are causing distress for U.S. producers, the cries of those adversely affected should be heard by the administration; if opportunities for exports are visible, the government should facilitate taking advantage of them. Yet, even in those areas where the trade policy apparatus of the administration could have acted, it failed to do so. Where action has been taken, as with exchange rates, it has come only reluctantly because of intense public pressure and congressional initiative.

The claim that U.S. businesses are not interested in foreign markets is especially irritating to those who have watched in anguish as American companies close domestic operations and move abroad. While many companies have joined this parade overseas only in the last few years of intensified international competition, the internationalization of production by U.S. firms has been going on for decades. These overseas operations have not only replaced U.S. exports, but they have in many cases replaced production for the domestic market with imports. Commerce Department data for 1982 show that U.S. multinational corporations accounted for 46 percent of all U.S. imports and that, of that portion, one-third was shipped from their own foreign affiliates. The foreign involvement of American firms is extensive. It has been used to build the profitability of individual firms, regardless of the consequences for American workers and communities.

In the auto industry, imports of assembled vehicles and parts by the domestic producers have grown dramatically in recent years, and current plans call for continued increases. Cars imported by U.S.–based auto producers for sale under their own nameplates were only 6 percent of total car imports in 1984, but were expected to reach 20 percent in 1988. They will be entering the United States from Mexico, South Korea, Taiwan, West Germany, Japan, and Australia. The impact on American employment and production will be severe, especially in the small car segment, where most of these imports are concentrated. A similar process has begun in midsized and heavy-duty trucks, as domestic producers bring in trucks from Brazil and Japan to sell as their own.

To discuss another current explanation of the serious trade problems of American industries—that they lack international "competitiveness," we note that, on the one hand, the large trade deficit has made it painfully obvious that U.S. producers are having difficulty competing with international trade. On the other hand, simply saying this does not shed any light on *why* these difficulties exist. The number of specific proposals of those addressing this issue is extremely high, ranging from increased funding for foreign language study to changes in U.S. antitrust and tax laws to changes in industrial relations and worker compensation. Many of these proposals have been poorly thought out, or are intended to achieve an objective that has nothing to do with "competitiveness." Many of the proposed changes in industrial relations fit into this category. Labor support for additional investment by U.S. industry in this country and for additional funds for education are long-standing and predate present initiatives. Labor continues to support public policies and industrial policies that help its members achieve their individual potential while strengthening our economy, but these policies alone would not eliminate our problems in international trade.

While economic policies certainly have an impact on trade flows, the trade policy carried out by the administration is the true indicator of how that administration sees the relationship of international trade to the rest of the economy and the role of the United States in the world economy. Historically, the open U.S. market has been used to encourage economic development in politically friendly countries and to assure American firms that moved overseas of a market for their products. When the United States was far and away the world's strongest economy, the impact of the open market on domestic employment and production was small, and demand for U.S. exports was strong. The Reagan administration ignored the changing worldwide situation and carried on as those before it—its trade policy was to keep the U.S. market as open as possible while seeking to open markets in other countries to a similar degree.

In today's world economy, however, the presumption that an open U.S. market has no important adverse impact on the domestic economy is both shortsighted and dangerous. The number of countries interested in, and capable of, exporting to the United States has increased dramatically, including developing as well as developed nations. Advanced technology and capital are exported daily around the globe to take advantage of low wage rates, tariff or nontariff trade barriers, tax abatements, investment incentives, and other government policies to attract foreign investment. In addition, industries abroad have been given government assistance in a wide variety of ways to stimulate growth in capacity much greater than domestic demand. The large and open U.S. market has been a consistent magnet for the production of these industries, including steel, autos, textiles and apparel, electronics, and, most recently, semiconductors, personal computers, telecommunications equipment, petrochemicals, and more.

These factors have contributed to the increase of U.S. imports from $253 billion in 1980 to $362 billion in 1985 and approximately $385 billion in 1986. Even with this incredible increase in imports, the Reagan administration insisted that there was no need to take action to defend the jobs of the millions of American workers displaced.

Because of its commitment to a wide open U.S. market, the Reagan administration responded to the political demands for action on the trade deficit by focusing on expanding U.S. exports. This took the form of negotiations over a limited number of narrowly defined unfair practices that restricted U.S. exports and initiation of a new round of multilateral trade talks aimed at reducing barriers to expanded trade. The reason so many domestic interests concerned about trade have focused on eliminating unfair trade practices abroad is because the administration has made it clear that it is one type of problem that may be pursued. Despite the attention given to export promotion by the administration, U.S. exports in 1986 would probably be *lower* than in 1980 in current dollars. Taking inflation into account, exports have declined substantially. In fact, government policies abroad limit markets for U.S. exports in many ways.

The Reagan administration placed most of its trade effort on getting a new round of multilateral trade negotiations (MTN) under way and making certain that trade in services and investment issues, now uncovered by international rules, were included. The reasoning is that the United States has an advantage in service industries and could greatly expand such exports if barriers abroad were eliminated. Looking at the trade statistics for services reveals several important points: (1) services trade consists of travel and transportation, proprietary rights (fees, royalties, profits on foreign operations), and business services—only this last item was the focus of administration interest; (2) the U.S. surplus in business services was $3.6 billion in 1985 with exports of $7.6 billion—this hardly made a dent in the $170 billion 1985 merchandise deficit; and (3) business service imports are growing nearly as rapidly as exports—there is no reason to believe the U.S. surplus will grow substantially, even with new trade rules. Unfortunately, the prospect for overall U.S. gains in the new MTN round are no better than in the services sector alone.

How, then, should we judge the trade policy of the Reagan administration? There are some basic criteria we propose using. Has the policy improved employment levels and living standards? Has it enhanced the prospects for equitable economic growth? We believe that the administration's commitment to concepts of the past, its laissez-faire response to the problems of U.S. industries, and its ineffective efforts to convince foreign governments to allow open access to their markets have contributed to a serious deterioration in U.S. economic capacity and potential, to an increase in poverty and a decline in family incomes, to higher unemployment than is warranted, and to increased income inequality.

This is a failed trade policy, and we need a new one if the future is to improve for workers, their families, and their communities. We can achieve this brighter future for Americans in a way that recognizes the legitimate aspirations of workers in poor and less developed nations: we can share growth, rather than pit one nation against another.

The first result of a realistic appraisal of American interests in the world economy would be a strong effort to reduce the worldwide U.S. trade deficit and the large worldwide surpluses of other nations. The current imbalance is widely acknowledged to be unsustainable and harmful to stable economic growth; yet the U.S. deficit continues to grow. Since the U.S. deficit is the only counterpart of the large worldwide surpluses run by Japan, West Germany, Taiwan, and other nations, the solution is to reduce the imbalances in tandem. The fact that nearly all other countries of the world keep a tight rein on their merchandise and current account trade balances means that the passive policy of the Reagan administration toward imports concentrated the worldwide deficit (and the economic dislocation resulting from it) in the United States, allowing movement toward greater international balance through U.S. action.

The rising indebtedness of the United States to foreigners adds further immediacy to the need for bringing the trade deficit down. The United States has surpassed Mexico and Brazil to become the world's largest debtor, creating obligations to make payments abroad for years to come. These payments are lost to the U.S. economy—they cannot be used to fund investment or consumption. The living standard of Americans is threatened as a result. Even when the annual trade deficit starts to decline, our foreign debt will continue to grow.

The longer the U.S. trade deficit remains at the unprecedented levels it has reached in recent years, the more wrenching will be the process of restoring balance. The ability of U.S. producers to respond to opportunities for growth becomes further compromised by the continuation of shrunken markets and financial constraints.

Dealing with the immediate problem of the trade imbalance is only the first step in developing a U.S. trade policy that defends the interests of American workers. We also need new policies to respond successfully to the problems facing individual industries hurt by imports and those suffering from lost export markets. U.S. trade policy must, in both cases, attempt to strengthen domestic production, stimulate necessary investment, and increase the stability of employment for workers in the industry.

The auto industry makes a good case study of how our trade policy toward industries injured by imports must be changed. In this case, as in most in which action is taken, the Reagan administration was concerned only with heading off congressional action to defend the industry from a sharp increase in

the share of the domestic market supplied by imports. The
Voluntary Restraint Agreement (VRA) negotiated with Japan
in 1981 was an insufficient policy response in several respects:
its initial three-year duration was too short to permit an adequate reaction by domestic manufacturers to the increase in
demand for small cars; the limit of a number of vehicles rather
than a share of the market allowed imports from Japan to take
a larger market share during the severe recession than was
anticipated; Japan's exports of auto parts and trucks were not
restrained, allowing the total automotive industry trade problem to grow; and no specific commitments to U.S. investment
and production were obtained from domestic producers in
return for the restraints.

When the three-year term of the VRA expired, the administration chose to negotiate only a one-year extension. Following this, the administration announced that the industry, as of
early 1985, was on its own. But by then there was a new factor
at work in the U.S. auto industry. One objective of the restraints, to convince a range of Japanese auto producers to
build cars in the United States, was at least partially achieved.
However, the domestic industry is now facing another import
crisis because of the failure of the administration's auto trade
policy to take into account the reality of the world auto market
and the difference between the interests of the domestic industry (workers, part producers, etc.) and the multinational U.S.-
based firms that are its most important producers.

The world auto market outside the United States is characterized by government-imposed domestic content requirements, local production requirements, and import restrictions
(high tariffs, informal restraint agreements with exporters,
strict import quotas, etc.). By setting a relatively short period
of restraint on imports into the United States, the administration was telling the U.S.-based companies that the United
States would once again be the only open auto market and that
it would be a target for the excess capacity of existing auto
producing nations and the new capacity of countries aspiring
to become auto exporters (South Korea, Taiwan, Mexico, Brazil, Yugoslavia, Malaysia, Australia). This signal was not lost

on the Big Three. They proceeded to use the absence of constraints on their actions, which they had insisted upon when the VRA was negotiated, to make arrangements to increase their own imports of parts, including engines and transmissions. The companies correctly anticipated an extremely competitive U.S. market in the postrestraint period, and they focused their domestic investment on their profitable vehicles, thus ceding the expanding market for small cars to importers (including themselves). Because the companies could raise their own profits by selling imported rather than domestically produced small cars and by cutting costs through the use of imported parts and components, the companies protected themselves from the inadequate trade policy of the administration.

While the Big Three have been protecting themselves by becoming importers, Japanese auto makers have built U.S. plants, or have plans to do so, for the same reason—to protect their U.S. sales and profits. The auto workers union welcomed these investments and the jobs for American workers they produced. But the union was disappointed at the low level of U.S. content in the vehicles assembled here.

The current trends in the auto industry produced an import share of 35 percent and an additional share of nearly 15 percent for low U.S. content transplants in 1988.

The effects of these developments will be a serious erosion of employment in the U.S. industry. There are about 500,000 jobs in this industry at stake, nearly one-third of current industry employment, as a result of the trade policy pursued by the Reagan administration. This would produce untold hardship for the workers and communities affected, and reduce the size of an important, high-technology domestic industry.

This type of analysis of world market conditions and of the interests of U.S. firms should be conducted for all domestic industries facing serious import competition. The interests of American workers and the domestic economy must be assessed *before* imports, U.S. company outsourcing, or foreign investment weaken domestic production beyond the point of recovery. Many essential U.S. industries (machine tools, semi-

conductors) are perilously close to that point, and a managed
trade policy is needed to preserve them.

U.S. export industries are in similar need of a trade policy
that defends U.S. production and employment. The Office of
the U.S. Trade Representative has catalogued the variety of
barriers imposed by foreign governments against our exports,
and the list is extremely long. The vast majority of these barriers have been in place for years; yet they were ignored by the
Reagan administration and previous administrations.

Instead of actively pursuing the removal of tariff and nontariff barriers to U.S. exports, U.S. trade policy has, among
other things, pursued investment treaties with our trading
partners to make it easier for U.S. companies to *invest* abroad
rather than to sell abroad. This approach may allow *companies*
to benefit from supplying foreign markets, but it hurts American workers and domestic production capabilities in two ways.
First, it replaces exports with foreign production, both in the
country where the investment is located and in other markets
formerly served by U.S. exports now supplied by the new
plants. Second, it creates for the company new capacity that is
often shipped back to this country, replacing the domestic
operation's sales to the domestic market. This is not a policy
that promotes U.S. exports.

The Reagan administration began to use the unfair trade
practice statute of U.S. trade law to let other countries know
what it considered unacceptable behavior in international
trade. Unfortunately, the first set of self-initiated cases covered
problems that are not likely to set precedents to open up large
numbers of U.S. job opportunities. Cases should be chosen for
their domestic impact, not their public relations value.

There is one area of unfair trade practices, in which the
Reagan administration opposed taking action, that should be
used to set a precedent in defining unacceptable trading practices—the denial of internationally recognized workers' rights.
The American sense of fair play is violated when products
made under repressive labor conditions are exported to this
country and displace our workers. There are many countries
around the world that have built an advantage in international

trade by preventing workers from exercising the right to organize and bargain with employers, by failing to adopt minimum
standards for conditions of work, or by allowing forced or
child labor. The United States should officially repudiate any
trading advantage obtained in this way and retaliate against
the exports of such countries. Without a change in the current
U.S. indifference toward the plight of workers abroad, trade
policy will continue to be viewed with distrust by union members and all American workers. A provision, sponsored by
Congressman Donald J. Pease of Ohio, to make denial of internationally recognized worker rights an unfair trade practice
was included in the trade bill approved by the House of Representatives in 1986.

The government's treatment of industries that file petitions
for relief from imports must also change. Under current law,
an unnecessarily tough standard of injury due to imports must
be met before an industry even receives consideration for
trade relief. If a petition passes that hurdle, the president may
refuse to impose quotas or higher tariffs to defend the U.S.
industry. In the recent past, findings of injury to the copper
and shoe industries were ignored by the president, and no
action was taken to defend their declining U.S. production.

Labor strongly believes that domestic industries deserve
support from the government when imports cause serious
damage. An industry that is found to be injured by imports
should be assured of some relief through government action.
The discretion allowed the president in current law has resulted in lost jobs and output by many industries, because
their imports received *no* assistance from the U.S. government.

The purpose of trade policy in the area of domestic industry
relief from imports should be to facilitate strengthening the
industry in the context of the U.S. economy and the world
marketplace. Present policy is to let struggling industries fend
for themselves and to assist only the small number that meet
the stringent conditions of U.S. law or are able to generate
enough political pressure to force the administration to act.
Companies left on their own have often made choices that

undermine the U.S. industry, by moving plants abroad, purchasing imports to meet domestic demand, or giving up and going out of business, leaving the market even more open to imports. The administration must take a more active role in shaping the economic future of America if we are to maintain our industrial strength.

Another government trade policy that has a double negative effect on U.S. production is the failure to take a firm position on the debt crisis facing a number of developing countries, especially in Latin America. This region has traditionally been a strong market for U.S. exports. The way the debt crisis in Latin American countries has been managed by the International Monetary Fund (IMF) and the World Bank in conjunction with international banks—with official U.S. government support—has forced the countries to run large trade surpluses to generate the money to pay back the banks. To accomplish this, Latin American debtors have slashed their imports and stimulated exports. The United States is the primary trading partner of these nations, and our exports have been hit hard by the cutback in Latin American imports; our industries have faced serious import competition because of the increase in their exports. American workers in agricultural and construction machinery, aerospace, and machine tools have lost export jobs, and auto parts workers have lost jobs due to the increase in U.S. imports.

There is *no* U.S. trade policy that addresses the problem of Latin American debt, despite the fact that the program the government is pursuing amounts to protectionism for the bankers, assuring that they are paid in full, while hundreds of thousands of American workers lose their jobs because of the trade impact. This is a serious failing in current trade policy. A new trade policy should demand a fair distribution of the impact of the debt crisis that requires the banks to share in the burden.

The austerity measures imposed on the domestic economies of countries facing debt problems and the need of these countries to generate funds to repay loans by running large trade surpluses have a direct effect on U.S. employment. Workers in aerospace, auto, agricultural machinery, and construction machinery have lost jobs because of the severe cutbacks in imports and the imperative to increase exports of Latin American debtor countries.

In 1981, prior to the first crisis of Latin American debtors, the UAW had 108,000 members making agricultural implements and construction machinery for companies like Caterpillar, Deere, and J. I. Case. By 1986 UAW membership in these industries had fallen to 53,000. This is a drop of 55,000 members, or 50 percent, in five years. While several factors contributed to this huge employment decline, the loss of export markets played an important role. From 1981 to 1986, U.S. exports of such equipment fell from $13.8 billion to $7.1 billion. Of this $6.7 billion decline, the shrinking of exports to Latin America accounted for $2 billion.

U.S. trade in civilian aircraft has also suffered during the years of austerity in Latin America. Exports fell by 40 percent from 1981 to 1986, and imports have begun to increase. The positive trade balance with Latin America in this important industry dropped by more than half between 1981 and 1986.

Finally, in the auto industry, we have seen U.S. exports to Latin America fall from $3.6 billion in 1981 to $1.5 billion in 1983 before turning up to $2.7 billion in 1986—a level that is still 25 percent lower than in 1981. In early 1987, one of our largest auto export markets in Latin America, Brazil, added automotive vehicles and components to its list of products either barred from import or facing new barriers. The reason for the new restrictions was Brazil's need to generate a larger trade surplus in 1987 than in 1986 in order to meet debt repayment obligations and reduce the need for additional loans. At the same time, exports of auto industry products from Latin America to the United States have grown by more than 400 percent, from $0.8 billion in 1981 to $4.2 billion in 1986. This important source of export earnings is certain to grow in the future, since both Mexico and Brazil have targeted this industry for further export development. The U.S. trade balance with Latin America in auto products has gone from a $2.8 billion *surplus* in 1981 to a $1.5 billion *deficit* in 1986.

In these four industries together, the U.S. trade surplus of
nearly $8 billion in 1981 has nearly vanished entirely. Exports
have declined by $3.7 billion, and imports are up $3.6 billion.
There can be no doubt that the debt crisis has been the major
determinant of this trade pattern with Latin America. The loss
of markets in Latin America due to austerity measures has
contributed to the many plant closings and layoffs we have
experienced since 1982, especially in auto parts and agricultural machinery.

Are there alternative U.S. policies that could halt the decline
in the U.S. industrial base and, at the same time, meet the
aspirations of Latin American workers for decent jobs and
improving living standards?

First, we must look at the present policies and their impact
on the economies of Latin American countries. With the support of the U.S. government, the debt crisis in Latin America
has been managed by the IMF and the World Bank in conjunction with international banks. Their traditional program of
debt management has been to force debtor nations to run
large trade surpluses to generate the money to pay interest to
U.S. and other banks. To accomplish this, imports have been
slashed and exports stimulated. The IMF also encourages
other changes in domestic policies such as eliminating government subsidies to industries and lifting price controls on consumer staple goods.

At first glance, these programs seem to have produced advantages for the developing countries at the expense of U.S.
employment and production. However, the conditions imposed by the IMF often distort economic development. An
emphasis on increasing a debtor nation's exports may come at
the expense of the production of basic goods required to meet
the needs of the people.

The international debt crisis is hurting workers in both the
Third World and the United States. Yet the government has
no trade policy that addresses the problem of Latin American
debt. It supports the repayment of interest and loans *in full*
and at current interest rates, while the living standard of workers declines in the Third World, and hundreds of thousands

of American workers lose their jobs because of the trade impact. An alternative policy would require the banks to share in the burden by writing off some debt and reducing interest payments.

Some Concluding Observations

Surely, our survey of recent innovations and other developments in the U.S. auto industry suggests that it has turned the corner. It gives many indications of being competitive in domestic and world markets, although at a painful price to many employees and communities. Perhaps this is a harbinger for other U.S. manufacturing sectors.

Of course, permanent competitiveness depends on favorable factors larger than the industry itself. These include fair trade practices, new and workable approaches to the impact of Third World debt, and carefully managed fiscal and monetary policies—all ingredients for a healthy economic climate in which fair competition prevails and the economy grows.

The current intense debate over this spectrum of issues is in itself a hopeful sign, reflecting widespread dissatisfaction with stand-pat policies and the status quo. Vigorous debate among many of the key players in management, labor, and the government over current economic issues is a vital component by which the nation sets and achieves its goals. Fortunately, this debate has begun.

In this context, it may be stated with assurance that labor expects to remain actively involved and play a responsible role in searching for more effective responses to the problems of mutual concern in our society.

The following policy statement of the United Auto Workers union is a sample of labor's agenda for the future.

Our Agenda for the Future

The first fifty years of the UAW were linked inextricably with the culmination of the industrial age. It is not necessary to subscribe to the more exaggerated visions of the robot revolution to agree that something new and different is occurring in plants and offices, that programmable automation is gradually but effectively altering production, distribution, and even the consumption of goods and services. In this new age, the UAW need not alter its basic dedication to fight for better working conditions and living standards for American workers. In the cybernetic age, as in the past, this goal will be sought in collective bargaining and in the political arena. The key elements on labor's agenda continue to be:

- Notification and consultation of workers when new technology is introduced—production processes that do not take into account the input of workers will not be effective.
- Reduction of working hours without reduction in income, and restrictions on overtime so that rising productivity does not erode jobs in plants and offices.
- More job and income security to make it possible for workers to welcome technology rather than fear it.
- Training in the new skills demanded in the "high-tech" workplace of the future.
- Protection against increases in stress levels, new health and safety hazards, and automated monitoring which could accompany new technologies into the workplace.
- Government policies that can provide a successful framework for the traumatic transition facing the U.S. economy, especially including:

    1. A trade policy that protects the jobs and living standards of American workers.
    2. Industrial and labor-market policies that will provide assistance to companies and workers as the U.S. economy restructures to meet the challenges of the new international economic order.

7

On Waiting for Neither Godot Nor the Apocalypse: Practical First Steps to Move U. S. Managers Toward World Class Managing

JAMES A. F. STONER
ARTHUR R. TAYLOR
CHARLES B. WANKEL

Introduction

The first two chapters in this book describe the unsatisfactory nature of the current U.S. competitive situation. The next sets of chapters offer a vision of what U.S. manage-

JAMES A. F. STONER is professor of management systems at Fordham University and previously served on the faculty of Columbia University's Graduate School of Business. He has taught in Europe, Asia, South America, Africa, and North America for a variety of organizations, including Arthur D. Little, Bell Telephone Laboratories, IBM, and the Royal Bank of Canada. Dr. Stoner has published several books and articles on management.

ARTHUR R. TAYLOR is dean of Fordham University's Graduate School of Business Administration and chairman of Arthur Taylor & Company, a private investment firm. He has served as vice president for the First Boston Corporation, executive vice president of the International Paper Company, and, from 1972 to 1976, as president of CBS. Dean Taylor is a director of several corporations and is affiliated with numerous cultural and educational associations.

ment practices and the society's supporting values, institutions, and policies might look like if the United States were to regain a leading role in domestic and international competitiveness. This chapter describes specific, concrete steps that the reader can take to assist U.S. managers in moving toward the vision of world class managing presented by Hessel, Mooney, and Zeleny in chapter 5 and Godfrey and Kolesar in chapter 8. The remaining chapters in this section suggest other things the reader can do to assist the remainder of the U.S. society to move toward actions and policies consistent with world class management in U.S. business, governmental, and not-for-profit organizations.

Crisis and Commitment

Many astute observers of American business have noted that two characteristics stand out about those American companies that have made the commitments and transformations associated with moving toward world class managing. First, for an organization to make the move, its top management must lead the way. Second, to make such a commitment the top management and the rest of the organization must be ener-

---

CHARLES B. WANKEL is assistant professor of management at the University of New Haven and has served as assistant dean and an instructor in management at Fordham University. Mr. Wankel has consulted for many businesses in a variety of industries, including IBM and McDonald's Corporation. He has given presentations in Malaysia, Singapore, and Poland, and has published widely on the impact and value of technology on international business and marketing.

A major portion of this chapter was written from interviews with a wide variety of academic and business leaders. Not all of them can be acknowledged, but the authors of this chapter can and do want to thank, in particular, Anthony G. Athos, Robert DeFillippi, Thomas P. Ference, David B. Gleicher, Donald Hambrick, Harold J. Leavitt, and William Newman. Naturally, they do not share any responsibility for the specific statements and recommendations included in this chapter.

gized by the recognition of a crisis situation. The Ford Motor Company, for example, experienced such a crisis with its 1980–82 loss of $3.26 billion.

This chapter does not challenge this understanding of the transformation process. It may or may not be an accurate description of the experience of American organizations over the last few years. Its logic would appear to be strong. Indeed, how could an organization successfully undertake the changes associated with the type of managing described by Hessel, Mooney, and Zeleny and by Godfrey and Kolesar without top management's full commitment, leadership, constant prodding, pushing, and support? And what can shake American managers out of their moment-by-moment, financial-markets-required-and-rewarded attention to maximizing quarterly profits except a clear and immediate threat to the very survival of their organization and, hence, a threat to those same quarterly profits in the very near term?

Although we accept the key role top management must play and the attention-getting value of a competitive crisis, we see severe limitations to these two factors as primary models of how U.S. organizations can move toward world class managing quickly and in large numbers.

First, if we emphasize too strongly the key role of the CEO, chairperson of the board, or other top managers, we risk inviting all other managers and individuals in the organization (and outside) to sit back and wait for top management to take the lead. Not only is such a perspective inherently disempowering—waiting patiently, or impatiently, for someone else to take action on something very important to us is almost always disempowering—but it also suggests no movement. No positive momentum can be started until the CEO yells "Charge!"— and even then, he or she must rouse the troops out of the passivity many will have sunk into during the long wait. Therefore, emphasis on the key role of top management runs the risk of inviting the organization's members to wait for a solution to arrive, speculating on its probable impact, and why it might be delayed. We see such a stance as not unlike those of Samuel Beckett's Estragon and Vladimir, who were consumed by speculation about the certainly impending, though never occurring, arrival of Godot who would rescue them from their situation. We use the word "apocalypse" in the title of this chapter to call attention to some disadvantages of "competitive crisis" as a motivator of change. There are at least three major problems with waiting for crisis as a spark to ignite the motivation for transformation. First, by the time an organization has reached and sensed the existence of the crisis, the crisis may be beyond remedy. In terms of organizational survival, "crisis" may—for some organizations—be apocalyptical.

In addition, as Marek Hessel has reminded the authors, there is considerable research to support the perspective that crisis as a motivator may be a fairly fine-tuned phenomenon. "Too little crisis" and we are not energized to act. "Too much," and we are in panic and are more likely to take the wrong actions in our frenzy, or to freeze in inaction rather than to adopt a constructive problem-solving orientation. Finding "just the right amount of crisis" may be a tricky task.

And finally, as a motivator of change, the crisis model puts organizational members in a particularly disempowered position—the classic "double bind": if they take constructive day-to-day actions ("Band-Aids") to move the organization forward, they may thus postpone the day of reckoning with the crisis, which in turn will delay the start of the necessary major corrective actions. The small improvements they make in the short-run may be of much less benefit to the organization than the costs of delaying the start of the necessary major corrective actions. On the other hand, if they do not continually attempt to move their organizations forward in every appropriate manner of which they are capable, they are clearly not doing their jobs. Those are certainly two quite unattractive alternatives from which to select.

The Approach of This Chapter

Now that we have introduced some of the issues regarding the top management leadership and competitive crisis models for transformation to world class managing, we shall attempt to build upon some of the *opportunities* we see in the models and to offer some additional perspectives which go beyond these two models. Then we shall identify specific steps the reader can take.

These models and suggested actions are offered, in a sense, as "first steps toward FIRST STEPS." Their full accomplishment would obviously create a major impact on the quality of U.S. management practice. However, we anticipate, and hope, that they will stimulate many readers to develop their own "models" for facilitating the sort of transformation we envision and to use those models to develop their own *action* steps. Therefore, we strongly exhort readers to implement appropriate ones of the specific steps we have suggested, and also to develop and implement their own first steps. We advocate this approach in the spirit of W. Edwards Deming's response to the question "what should we do to implement your fourteen points?" He often replies, "Just start!"

Additional Perspectives on Facilitating the Movement Toward World Class Managing

Introduction

We see it as ironic, and even paradoxical, that the top management leadership and competitive crisis models are potentially disempowering and at the same time are means for moving toward a way of managing that is striking in its ability to empower organizational members. If we want to assist managers to move toward world class managing, our models should contain perspectives which empower both ourselves and those target managers. To do that, we have chosen to emphasize the opportunities and possible solutions which lie in some models and to give short shrift to the problems and barriers to transformation that those same models can be used to call attention to.

This approach was not chosen in a cavalier manner, and it has its risks. For example, careful analysis of barriers that are initially seen as interfering with the desired change frequently leads to creative solutions, while quick actions that appear at first to seize fleeting opportunities frequently run afoul of unrecognized barriers. Although we recognize that the dangers of rash action are real, we are distressed that organizational and individual transformation models too frequently disempower their potential users by identifying so many potential barriers and so many steps that must be taken to get a result that many individuals become discouraged and give up before they even attempt to take the first step. We do not believe that Thomas Peters and Robert Waterman, Jr., have exaggerated the dangers of "analysis-paralysis." Therefore, we shall emphasize the "openings for action" that each model or perspective offers. And we shall leave for others the task of saying why nothing can be done.

Overview

We shall start with a short statement about the opportunities for action in the top management leadership model. We shall then propose that organizations far from crisis may, in fact, be even more open to movement toward world class managing than organizations in crisis. Next we shall suggest that systems' models of organizations suggest multiple opportunities to influence managers and their organizations. We shall present an optimistic hypothesis about how some influence attempts may be more likely to have desirable rather than undesirable consequences—and offer some guidelines for increasing the likelihood that the desirable consequences will dominate. Finally, we shall argue that movement toward world class managing may be achievable much more rapidly than is frequently assumed.

Empowering Perspectives on
Top Management Leadership

It has been suggested that individual contributors, first-line supervisors, and middle managers trained in the philosophy and techniques of world class managing, but working in organizations not yet following those management practices, are in potentially frustrating situations. In such circumstances, one important contribution they can make to their organizations would be to influence managers higher in the organization toward making a commitment to this way of managing. Reports of such actions are now beginning to emerge. At the GOAL (Growth Opportunity Alliance of Greater Lawrence) conference in Andover, Massachusetts, in October 1986, Earl Conway, manager of cost and productivity improvement in Procter and Gamble, described how an engineer trained in statistics captured his interest in the work of Deming and how Conway, in turn, worked with others to sell this approach to managing to higher-ups in P&G. He refers to this as "internal marketing." Through numerous dialogues and exchanges, dozens of top executives were sold on the Deming principles over what Conway views as a long period of time. A key step in this process was bringing in Deming for several days to lecture to about 500 P&G people.

In a similar manner, Donald Petersen, president of Ford, was influenced by James Bakken, who in turn had been influenced by William Scollard, who had taken home over the Christmas holidays in 1980 the videotape of the TV special "If Japan Can, Why Can't We?"

These chains of influence can probably be traced even further down these organizations. Conway's engineer and Scollard at Ford probably also were influenced by others. The point is that rather than waiting for top management to take leadership, individuals throughout the organization have the opportunity to "lead" the top management toward world class managing. To do that systematically, three steps have been suggested: (1) selecting the target person to influence; (2) taking actions that encourage a willingness in that person to be open to the speaker's ideas ("creating the listening"); and (3) speaking into that "listening" with suggested action steps.

In selecting the target person, such characteristics as power in the organization (the higher in the hierarchy, the better, presumably) and style would normally be important. Style dimensions such as skills in empowering and enrolling others, energy, enthusiasm, and the ability to formulate and articulate a vision would be important. Other important factors might include one's relationship with that person and perhaps that person's career stage and dominant career needs. In creating the listening (that is, getting the person ready to pay attention to what is said) at least two factors are important. First is determining what is important to the listener: quality, productivity, profits, the long term, his or her own current career needs, being able to empower others, being a leader, or whatever. Second is creating a platform for speaking to the listener, that is, establishing credibility through such behaviors as performing excellently, utilizing the techniques of world class managing, and so on.

And finally, in speaking into the listening, the task is to address the objectives the listener cares about, to show how the philosophy and techniques of world class managing can assist him or her to move toward those objectives, and to offer practical first steps to start that movement.

Movement Without Crisis

Some argue that implementing world class management practice in an organization is a major upheaval that will not be readily entered into by an organization unless it is under crisis conditions. Three major points are missed by those who emphasize managerial reluctance to try new approaches unless a crisis forces changes in priorities and activities. First, there are many well-managed organizations that continually "try on" promising new management approaches and discard old ones which are no longer effective. Second, in a well-managed organization, many of the pieces of world class managing may already be well in place, and the addition of the missing pieces may not be greatly disruptive. And third, there may be some types of organizations that are likely to be particularly attracted to world class managing approaches and outcomes.

Family-controlled or strongly influenced firms are one important example of such organizations. For such firms, the world class managing emphasis on quality, the long term, and commitment to employees and customers is likely to be particularly attractive. Many of those firms are protected to a considerable extent from the moment-by-moment obsession with share price and quarterly profits that inhibits the management of so many publicly held firms. Large family-controlled or strongly influenced organizations are more prevalent in the economy than most people realize. Indeed, Richard Beckhard has suggested that more than 95 percent of all U.S. firms are family-controlled, and these firms employ about 42 percent of the American work force. The larger and more effective of these organizations may become leaders in this type of management.

Now that a number of authors, managers, and consultants are beginning to reach a stage of understanding of world class management approaches which allows them to communicate the key elements of those approaches reasonably effectively, it is starting to become clear how consistent those approaches are with many of the practices of well-managed organizations in general. For example, the "commitment to the customer" that Peters and Waterman and Peters and Nancy A. Austin identify as a driving force in well-managed companies is quite consistent with the customer satisfaction commitment in world class management. Similarly, Peters and Waterman's "bias for action" looks a lot like the Deming (or perhaps Walter A. Shewhart) plan-do-check-act cycle. The companies Peters and Waterman, Peters and Austin, and Donald K. Clifford, Jr., and Richard E. Cavanagh discuss may be much more open to adding some additional effective approaches and tools to the ones they are already using than would a group of crisis plagued companies. So, in addition to efforts devoted to organizations peering over the edge of the abyss, and perhaps even in preference to such efforts, now may be the time to place much greater emphasis on building on the strengths of successful organizations.

Systems Models of Organizations

In the behavioral sciences, looking at organizations as systems of interconnected, interacting components (what has been called the biological analogy) has opened up powerful opportunities for understanding and working effectively in organizations. Unfortunately, this perspective—as a guide to change—has often been discouraging and disempowering to managers. With "everything connected to everything else," the task of predicting the final outcome of a change effort has often seemed quite complex and confusing. And the feeling that to "change one thing, you have to change everything" can make the change task seem overwhelmingly difficult. Without denying the complexity of organizations and the complexity of the transformation task, we believe four empowering perspectives on organizations-as-systems deserve greater emphasis.

First, the supplier(input)-organization(processes)-customer(output) loop emphasized in the Hessel, Mooney, and Zeleny chapter suggests that suppliers and customers are logical partners in the transformation process, and can be invited to participate actively in it. For example, Stephen F. Bruce, the manager of quality assurance for Ford Motor Company's North American Automotive Operations, has described how vendors who move toward self-certification of parts quality have allowed the company to use parts without further inspection. Ford's suppliers get additional business from it as they improve. The quality of Ford cars was a factor in the increase in its market share from 16 percent in the early 1980s to over 20 percent by mid-1987.

Second, the perspective that everything is connected to everything else suggests that there are many, many places a change effort can begin. Third, the law of persistence—if one part of a system persists in its behavior, and if it cannot be isolated or eliminated by the other parts of the system, those other parts will tend to align themselves with the behavior of that part—argues for making changes in the desired direction, protecting one's flanks, and "hanging in there" (persisting).

And fourth, the consistency hypothesis—in an organization (or society), behavioral changes which move the system toward more effective total performance will tend to reinforce and increase the effectiveness of existing behaviors contributing to effective total performance and will tend to facilitate the undertaking of new changes in behavior which will contribute to additional movement toward more effective total performance. In other words, things that work will tend to support other things that work and will tend to make it easier to introduce still other things that work—not always, but more frequently than otherwise.

Summary

Our suggestions for practical first steps to move American managers toward world class managing will be based largely on two perspectives consistent with the arguments above: (1) looking for any (and every) entry point in any (and every) organization with any (and every) manager—or non-manager—by any (and every) person who "buys into" the basic "vision" of world class managing described by Hessel, Mooney, and Zeleny and by Godfrey and Kolesar; and (2) accepting the perspective that, on balance, any movement toward the "vision" is more likely to be helpful than harmful.

These two points suggest that anyone who buys into the vision can do something to facilitate movement. In fact, if it is not already clear that everyone can do a great many things, it soon will be. So this perspective is inherently empowering, except for those of us who choose to disempower ourselves through being in a state of "overchoice," having too many attractive alternatives.

To sort the alternatives a bit we shall suggest some priorities for action: (1) obtaining the commitment of particularly influential individuals and organizations to this transformation in American management practice; (2) facilitating the adoption of the remaining pieces of world class management practice by already excellently managed organizations that have most, but not all, of the pieces in place; and (3) generating public support for this way of managing among organizations in the United States that currently practice it by sharing their experiences in moving toward and achieving world class management status.

Practical First Steps

How to Listen to the Suggested First Steps

These practical first steps were initially presented at The American Assembly program on global competitiveness. The purpose of that Assembly, like all Assemblies, was action. Therefore, we requested the participants to listen to our suggested first steps in three contexts: (1) actions they themselves could take—soon; (2) actions they could induce others to take—soon; and (3) most importantly—actions we failed to suggest. Now that The American Assembly conference is over, we make the same invitation to you, the reader. In particular, we invite you to listen for the suggestions that are *not* stated— the practical first steps that only you can see at this moment, that only you can achieve, and that have many more potential positive impacts than the ones listed below.

In reading these suggestions, please remember that for some of the steps you are uniquely well-suited to take action: the editor of *Business Week* was your college roommate—call him! You are a major recruiter for your company from an important business school—discuss with the dean the match (and mismatch) of what is currently taught with what is needed to improve U.S. competitiveness, and what your company can do to assist in improving the match. You once did a favor for H. Ross Perot before he was "the H. Ross Perot"—and he remembers it. Call him and describe the special role he can play; etc., etc.

And finally, as you read, please listen in the context that you are a busy person with many other commitments. So please listen for things you can do easily and efficiently now. Listen for things that you will enjoy doing, things that will reward you enough to energize you to do a few more. So look for things that will yield some "quick successes."

The Structure for the Recommendations

The recommendations for practical first steps suggested below focus primarily, but not exclusively, on encouraging individual managers and organizations to move toward world class managing by providing more information on this way of managing (sharing the "vision") and by attempting to remove some of the barriers to managing this way. They are divided into five categories, the first four of which tend to group similar sets of action takers together and the fifth, which contains a few ideas for increasing dissatisfaction with existing management practices.

The first four categories involve: encouraging individuals and institutions that are very influential with managers to take a leadership role in influencing this transformation; encouraging specific groups of organizations to take a leadership role by transforming themselves and sharing that transformation publicly as it evolves; encouraging key institutions to support the movement of individual managers and other organizations; and encouraging leadership from some less traditional sources than the ones listed above.

Although it is not difficult to develop ideas for increasing dissatisfaction with existing practices, we have decided not to include many items in the fifth (dissatisfaction) category. This decision is based largely on our belief that not very much more needs to be done to create dissatisfaction with current managerial and organizational performance.

Our experiences suggest that—with the possible exception of the presidents and board chairpersons—the managers, non-managers, customers, and suppliers of many American organizations are already dissatisfied with the level of performance of the management system of their organizations. And many of the steps in the first four categories oriented toward sharing information on this way of managing are likely to increase even further the existing level of dissatisfaction with old practices.

In addition, we are concerned that some of the logical steps to increase dissatisfaction further may simply increase fear and non-problem-solving behavior.

In making our suggestions for practical first steps, we have attempted to identify specific individuals who, if committed to this transformation, can make important contributions. Our intention in "naming names" is to encourage readers to contact these individuals directly or through mutual acquaintances. Enough such contacts should increase the likelihood that the desired commitment will emerge.

Encouraging Leadership from Highly Influential Sources

Business Media Leaders

Publicly avowed, consistent, and coherent editorial support of movement toward world class managing approaches by the editor-in-chief of *Business Week,* Stephen B. Shepard; *Forbes's* editor-in-chief, Malcolm S. Forbes; the managing editor of *Fortune,* Marshall Loeb; the *Wall Street Journal's* managing editor, Norman Pearlstine; and the *New York Times'* publisher, Arthur Ochs Sulzberger, and business editor, Frederick Andrews, would make a powerful start in communicating the potential for all U.S. managers to move in that direction. These five publications have repeatedly published stories on organizations that fit many or all of the characteristics discussed by Hessel, Mooney, and Zeleny and by Godfrey and Kolesar. It is a short step to shift a few more research and editorial hours to developing enough of a knowledge of this way of managing to justify a professionally competent and responsible "buy-in" to this approach to managing (or, of course, to reject it) and then continuing to use research and editorial resources to investigate, chronicle, monitor, and advocate this transformation.

Many other national and regional publications would also follow fairly quickly—and a few, of course, would make the shift before the "big five" listed above—or already have made that shift. Of course, if Andrews, Forbes, Loeb, Pearlstine, Shepard, and Sulzberger combined their public support with reports on the progress of their own organizations toward world class managing, the impact of their support would be greatly enhanced. (Perhaps they also would enjoy some enhancement of the performance of their already quite successful organizations.)

Business Heroes

Lee Iacocca and H. Ross Perot are superstars of the business scene of the eighties. If they were to write short books supporting this approach to managing and describing the consistencies between it and the ways their own organizations are (or were) managed, the books surely would be best sellers and could have a significant impact. Each author could have a particularly interesting story to tell. Iacocca's would be interesting because Chrysler is perceived not to have made as deep a commitment to world class management approaches as has rival Ford but maybe a bit more than GM, whose very public commitment seems to have weakened considerably in the last three years or so. For Iacocca to write such a book, he virtually would have to make a public commitment as deep and personal as Donald Petersen's at Ford. And Perot's book would be awaited particularly eagerly in this context because many observers believe the termination of his relationship with GM arose precisely from his dissatisfaction with GM's failure to make as deep a commitment to world class management approaches as Perot desired.

Many other business leaders also could make a significant contribution in this way, especially if they chronicled their organization's evolving transformation and their own personal odysseys. It is not clear that Citicorp has committed itself to all the tenets of world class managing, although it is generally recognized to be a very well-managed organization. John Reed at Citicorp would seem a natural chronicler of his organization's transformation, especially given the fiercely competitive internal management style at Citicorp (labeled by more than one wag as "a bunch of hungry sharks swimming in a very small tank"). What would, or perhaps does, world class management—with its high premium on collaboration and teamwork—look like at Citicorp? Or how about Armand Hammer, world class entrepreneur and deal maker? What kind of a story could he tell if he were to lead his enterprises in this transition as he enters his nineties? In the process, he would "sit at the feet" of the great gurus of almost the identical number of seasons—W. Edwards Deming and Joseph Juran.

The Transformational Leadership Role for Union Leaders

For more than a decade, some union leaders under the QWL (quality-of-work-life) or other banners have been shifting from a mostly adversarial role vis-à-vis management into a collaborative one in many key areas. Increasingly, these areas transcend concern for day-to-day working conditions to issues of organizational effectiveness, survival, and growth. Notable have been the United Auto Workers' Irving Bluestone in the seventies and Lloyd McBride of the United Steelworkers in the early eighties.

Throughout the leadership and rank and file of organized labor there are many individuals who have both the capabilities and the "organizational platform" to play a leadership role in transforming the relationship between their unions and the employing organizations. Among these leaders are Stanley Hill and Jack Schenkman of the Amalgamated Clothing and Textile Workers Union, Jan Pierce and Morton Bahr of the Communications Workers of America, Lynn Williams of the United Steelworkers of America, and Owen Bieber and Don Ephlin of the United Auto Workers Union.

Communicating to their membership a vision of the role unions can play in bringing organizations and people to world class performance levels would be a powerful contribution. Communicating the possibilities that lie in world class managing approaches to the management of the employing organizations with which they negotiate might be even more effective. And demonstrating the effectiveness of world class managing techniques by utilizing them in the day-to-day managing of the unions themselves might be the most effective step of all.

The Superstar Business Gurus

Peter Drucker is probably the most respected and widely known writer, philosopher, and lecturer on the business scene. His work is so consistent with and supportive of world class managing approaches that it would probably be possible to assemble from his existing writings a complete text on the subject. Were he to write still one more book on the topic, directly focused on how the transition should be managed, it would have a wide audience. Another best seller from Tom Peters also would find wide readership. He has two-thirds, or perhaps three-quarters, of the puzzle in place by recognizing the importance of devotion to customer satisfaction and product and service quality (which he tends to identify as "excellence") and to creating an environment that liberates the energies and commitments of employees. The main things he needs to complete the puzzle are the simple numerical tools and concepts which can make improvement of processes a continuous phenomenon.

One more candidate would be Ken Blanchard, who—like Tom Peters—has many of the pieces of the puzzle in place. Blanchard is particularly effective at communicating the role of managers in supporting their "subordinates" in achieving a strong customer focus and working toward excellence. He is also quite experienced in the process of working within organizations to bring about their transformation. And he certainly has learned, as has Peters, how to write wildly successful popular books on managing!

Presidential Candidates

Many observers have cited President Reagan's posture that "we're all right, Jack, and it is the rest of the world that is out of step with us and needs to adjust" as a significant barrier to acknowledging the need for transforming management practices. It would be both an attractive part of a political platform and a boost to U.S. management practices for a presidential candidate to make a public commitment to redressing management inadequacies. Such a posture would be particularly attractive for candidates if it is stated realistically and accurately: that many pieces of the world class managing puzzle are in place in a large number of companies, but the other pieces must be added to achieve the transformation necessary to maintain an economy strong enough to support a leading position in world affairs and to meet domestic needs. Actual or potential presidential candidates should be quick to grasp the validity of the argument and to see its potential power. As a few leading candidates start to speak effectively about this transformation, others may be influenced to align themselves with this perspective and members of Congress will begin to listen as well.

Encouraging Leadership from Specific Businesses and Organizations

The Young Presidents' Organization

One group of managers that could be particularly influential is the YPO (Young Presidents' Organization), a group of company presidents who became heads of their organizations before they reached forty years of age. This group might, for example, establish its own mini–Deming/Juran Prize for the member company (and its president) that made the most progress toward world class management in the previous two years. The members are obviously in the ideal position to transform their own organizations and are also well placed to influence other top managers of small and moderate sized and family oriented firms—the types of firms that most nearly reflect the YPO membership. They are also seen by some outsiders as quite competitive with each other, and thus might be attracted by a chance for something like their own Deming/Juran Prize. As a relatively small organization composed of individuals who see themselves, in many instances, as the epitome of the "can-do" spirit of leadership in management, they could also, very likely, move quickly on establishing such a prize.

Transforming Outstanding Organizations

The best managed companies in the United States are looked to as models of management by business publications, academics, and managers of other organizations. To the extent that they have achieved all of the elements of world class management practice, they represent support for other companies and their managers to move in this direction. To the extent that they have many of the pieces in place, they offer the opportunity both to show the value of putting the remaining pieces in place and to demonstrate the process of making that movement. Ford Motor Company's willingness to share reports on its progress in this direction has been a valuable resource for managers, students, and scholars. The leaders of other companies have the same opportunity available to them to improve their own companies and to make a difference in many other companies by sharing the results.

Various companies have been put forth as excellently managed companies, most notably by Peters and Waterman, Peters and Austin, and the "100 Outstanding Companies" in Clifford and Cavanagh's book *The Winning Performance*. Through these books and other articles, many of these companies have achieved considerable media prominence. Although some have failed to live up to the hype they received, especially some from the original Peters and Waterman sample, and the actual process of their selection in some cases has been questioned, many have continued to perform well, and those committed to world class managing approaches would make good copy. The leaders of those companies might be particularly open to adding the remaining pieces to their management tool kit for the types of reasons already advanced.

Encouraging Support and Leadership
from Key Institutions

Transforming the Business Schools

Universities are notoriously slow to change, and business schools are no exception. This slowness to change is a valuable quality in many respects and at many times. However, as competition for students and for a wide variety of resources has become more severe in recent years, the attractiveness of new approaches and new markets has increased quite dramatically. The Fordham Business Schools made a major commitment in revising their curricula to reflect their interpretation of world class managing, and the Brigham Young Graduate School of Business has been rumored to be moving in this direction. To the extent that the earlier chapters in this book are on target in their conclusions about the need for moving toward world class managing and about the advantages of doing so, business schools as a whole will be moving, at some pace or other, in this direction—and the ones that move the fastest will enjoy the greatest benefits in terms of image, improved market position, and improved access to resources.

One possible step in this direction would be a conference of business school deans addressed to a topic very similar to the one for this book. The conference could focus on what is and can be taught in business schools to improve U.S. competitiveness. It is sadly ironic to hear Deming report the responses he has received from a variety of students at a number of first-rate business schools when he has asked them "what have you learned in any of your courses that would help you to improve the U.S. balance of trade?"

Foundation Support for
Transforming U.S. Management

The Ford, Carnegie, and a variety of other foundations have a long and distinguished history of contributing to the progress of management and business education in this country and abroad. They are natural places to look for support as business schools begin to make the commitment to revise their curricula, and—we hope—their own internal management, to reflect our emerging awareness of the effectiveness of these management approaches. In addition to being supportive of schools that desire to move in this direction, the major foundations can also play a leadership role by providing the carrots that will move key schools along much faster than they would otherwise move.

An exciting possibility in the area of foundation leadership rests with the MacArthur Foundation, which has established an enviable reputation for innovation and willingness to break old rules in its development of new programs and new approaches. Thornton Bradshaw, a MacArthur Foundation director with a special interest in managerial transformation, could play a major role in carving out a special niche for the foundation in this area. Possible activities include supporting the development and dissemination of new curricula, creating a national level Deming/Juran Prize, creating a special group of MacArthur Fellows especially well-suited to play major roles in this transformation, etc., etc. Obviously, from the MacArthur Foundation and from Bradshaw we would expect some additional ideas which go beyond these in boldness and originality.

A Deming/Juran Prize

Proposals have existed for a number of years to establish in the United States a set of prizes similar to the Deming Prizes which have been awarded in Japan since 1951. Because of his major contributions to world class managing, it might also be appropriate to honor Deming's contemporary, Joseph Juran, who also has had a major impact on both Japanese and Western management practice.

A Deming/Juran prize is a natural step to take to call attention to the importance of world class management approaches and to provide clarity about what is involved in managing in that way. The development and communication of standards for such a set of prizes also will further both research and conceptualization in the field of management as a whole and this portion of the field in particular. One early and articulate proponent of U.S. Deming Prizes is Myron Tribus, who chaired the Task Force on U.S. Competitiveness and has remained active in this area after retiring from his position as director of the Center for Advanced Engineering Study at the Massachusetts Institute of Technology.

A Deming/Juran Prize could have a home in a great many possible institutions, including universities, professional societies, government agencies, foundations, a newly created institution set up specifically for that purpose, and so on. In Japan JUSE, the Japanese Union of Scientists and Engineers, provides a model that has worked well in that country. And certainly, Deming and Juran might have some preferences.

Encouraging Leadership from Nontraditional Sources

Starting to Work on the Quarterly Profit Barrier

Perhaps the single greatest barrier to achieving a commitment by top management officials to transform their organization's management practices is the pressure to protect and increase the company's quarterly profits. This pressure is exacerbated by the perception that movement to world class managing approaches will require investing in the future of the organization. Management officials are reluctant to invest funds that will appear as expenses this quarter but will not yield a return until some time in the future.

The recent activities of today's robber barons—the corporate raiders and "greenmail" experts like T. Boone Pickens, Carl Icahn, and others—make the quarter-by-quarter obsession of many top executives a not unrealistic posture if they desire to retain control of both their organizations and their own careers. Also, the moment-by-moment evaluation of those who manage pension funds and other large pools of institutional funds often encourages a churning of portfolios in response to actual or anticipated fluctuations in short-term corporate performance. (The churning can still occur even if, as some research has indicated, it is not effective in yielding high performance by the pension fund managers who engage in it.)

It will not be easy to reduce the tendency of top managers to focus on quarterly profits and increase their focus on longer-term factors. Closely held and family oriented firms are particularly attractive candidates for the adoption of world class management approaches, because they are less likely to be infected by the quarterly profit disease. To the extent that leveraged buy-outs yield similar closely held situations, they may offer promising opportunities as well.

Two separate approaches to this quarter-by-quarter issue may offer some first steps toward new possibilities. The first relates to new investing groups and criteria. The other relates to possible actions by institutional investors.

New Investing Groups and Criteria

Some investing groups and fund managers have become convinced that traditional management practices will yield sub-par corporate performance, not just in the long run, but also in the fairly immediate short run. They are also convinced that the companies most likely to survive and prosper, and hence to be good medium- or even short-term investments, are companies that are implementing the most effective management approaches available. These are not, of course, particularly profound observations; however, when they lead to favorable evaluations of companies moving toward world class management and to the ability of the funds' managers to look beyond quarterly profit fluctuations, they represent the beginning of a shift in stock market evaluation criteria. Some investing groups are looking specifically for traditionally managed companies to acquire and then to transform along the lines of world class managing approaches. To the extent that these groups are successful, they will tend to influence other investing groups.

In the course of our research for this chapter, we discussed one particularly intriguing possibility. Two companies—a multibillion dollar service organization and a new venture in its early planning stages—are each starting to investigate the possibility of issuing a new class of stock. The stock could be sold only every 100 years and—in the interim—could be willed only to members of the owners' immediate families. The main purposes of this class of stock would be to guarantee commitment to the long term by top management and to protect the companies from the current, moment-to-moment obsession with quarterly profits and from the depredations of corporate raiders.

One Group of Institutional Investors

In a cover story on the conflict between managers and shareholders over the control of corporations, *Business Week*'s writers noted that some institutional investors reported their investments are so large in some companies that they cannot readily adjust their positions if they lose confidence in a company's management. Rather than being guilty of churning their portfolios, they feel "locked in" to their investments. Therefore, they feel it imperative that they be able to influence the quality of management of the companies in which they have large positions.

One group discussed in the *Business Week* article is the Council of Institutional Investors (CII), a group of managers of large blocks of public institutional funds. This group is cited largely for its efforts to prevent entrenched management from protecting itself by paying greenmail or creating poison pills to deter corporate raiders. It also might take a leadership role in supporting the movement toward more effective management practices by the companies in which it has large positions. Harrison J. Goldin, comptroller of New York City and cochair of CII, could play a major role in encouraging this movement, as could John B. Neff of the Vanguard Group. He was mentioned in the article as one of the managers of large portfolios of private funds whose holdings are so large in some instances that they also cannot easily liquidate positions in companies with sub-par management.

Boards of Directors

A particularly promising vehicle for developing commitment to the transformation of management practices is a company's board of directors. Although the historical performance of boards has been less than impressive—achieving in some instances the status of exemplars of lethargic incompetence—both the legitimate tasks and the oversight capabilities of most existing boards are consistent with movement toward world class management.

Such problems as the reward systems and selection processes for board members and the filtering of information to the board through top management have been discussed extensively. These problems will not be overcome easily, but a major step in breaking out of this situation would be to provide a vision of what the board can do to improve the company's chances for survival in the medium and long run. Certainly, the vision of world class managing presented by Hessel, Mooney, and Zeleny and by Godfrey and Kolesar provides one attractive game plan available now for boards of directors. To support board members who wish to move in this direction, a series of case studies of boards and board members who have provided true leadership for their companies would be particularly valuable. Such publications as the periodicals *Corporate Board* and *Directors & Boards* are natural media for communicating the basic characteristics of world class managing, its importance for company survival, and ways and examples of moving toward this form of management. Case examples in which board members play leadership or strongly supportive roles in such transformations will be particularly valuable.

Novels, Movies, Television

Novels, movies, television shows, and documentaries are all tempting—and risky—opportunities to communicate the possibilities and some of the techniques of this way of managing. Examples of each are not hard to find. Eli Goldratt's foundation, the Goldratt Institute (in New Haven, Connecticut), reports that his novel on this transformation, *The Goal,* has sold more than 100,000 copies. *Gung Ho,* which captures some elements of this way of managing and misses some others, was successful enough as a movie to give rise to a short television series. And the number of television documentaries has grown rapidly since "If Japan Can, Why Can't We?" was first aired in 1980.

It is certainly likely that some novels, movies, and television shows will present perspectives on world class managing techniques and approaches that will be confusing, quite negative, or inaccurate. Accurate criticisms of actual implementation efforts also will arise in these media. This situation is inevitable. However, it does not argue against the encouragement of projects that deal with the positive possibilities of this approach to managing.

Professional Sports Teams

One particularly attractive—and high-risk—area for drawing attention to this way of managing and of providing highly visible models of it is the field of sports. In terms of attracting a great deal of attention, the public commitment of a team with an undistinguished record, like (until 1987) the Minnesota Twins, or one with an outstanding record, like the Boston Celtics, would be very successful. Much of the risk of athletic teams as exemplars of this way of managing would lie in the limited number of observations of success or failure imposed by the one-season one-observation interpretation which would tend to dominate. Perhaps a greater risk is that implementation would be poorly executed, and the wrong lessons would be drawn from the results.

In spite of these and other very serious reservations, the high visibility of athletic teams, the quick feedback of multiple games played each athletic season, and the large number of dollars involved for the owners and players—which is likely to cause the participants to take such a managerial "experiment" very seriously—do offer some significant attractions for encouraging "experiments" with sports teams.

Adding a Bit More Dissatisfaction

Wake Up, Cousins!

A June 1987 article by a Columbia University economist spoke of "diminished giants," comparing the halving of Britain's share of world industrial production from 1870 to 1913 (from 32 to 14 percent) with the reduction of America's share of the total world gross domestic product from 1950 to 1980 (from 40 to 22 percent). This comparison would make a good basis for a lecture series by a distinguished English citizen touring the United States under the battle cry: "Wake up, cousins!"

Business School Alumni Conferences

As the first step in reorienting their curricula toward increasing U.S. competitiveness, and as a means for calling attention to the need for such a reorientation, the deans of American business schools could convene alumni conferences under titles like "The Fall of the American Empire . . . and What We Can Do About It."

Summary

We have suggested a variety of actions that can be taken to speed up the process of moving toward world class managing by American managers. For many of these actions we have

212 STONER, TAYLOR & WANKEL

indicated key "players" who could provide particularly effective leadership in these activities. In other cases we have referred more broadly to specific institutions or tasks that can be undertaken. In all instances, readers have a variety of opportunities available to them.

First of all, they can take action to facilitate the occurrence of the actions, commitments, and events described. Second, they can modify and edit the suggested actions and target individuals to take advantage of their own unique information about the suggested actions or individuals, and then take action on the modified proposals. Third, they can accept the invitation extended earlier, and develop their own ideas for practical first steps to move U.S. managers toward world class managing practices. Then they can share those ideas, encourage others to take action on them, and take action themselves. We hope that a great many of us will do all three.

8

Role of Quality in Achieving World Class Competitiveness

A. BLANTON GODFREY
PETER J. KOLESAR

The Quality Crisis

The authors of this chapter speak frequently on quality management, and we often open these discussions or lectures by showing the list in Figure 1 and asking, "What do these industries have in common?" Most audiences are puz-

A. BLANTON GODFREY is chairman and chief executive officer of the Juran Institute in Wilton, Connecticut, and an adjunct associate professor in Columbia University's School of Engineering. Prior to joining the Juran Institute, Dr. Godfrey held several positions with AT&T Bell Laboratories. He has taught and conducted research at Florida State University, where he earned advanced degrees in statistics. Dr. Godfrey has published extensively in the area of quality control and quality assurance.

PETER J. KOLESAR is a professor in the Graduate School of Business at Columbia University and holds a joint professorial appointment in the School of Engineering and Applied Sciences. He began his career in 1959 as an industrial engineer with Proctor and Gamble, and has held numerous teaching, consulting, and engineering positions with a variety of corporations and institutions. Dr. Kolesar has published widely in scholarly journals.

WORLDWIDE COMPETITION — EVIDENCE OF THE CHALLENGE

AUTOMOBILES	FOOD PROCESSORS
CAMERAS	MICROWAVE OVENS
STEREO EQUIPMENT	ATHLETIC EQUIPMENT
MEDICAL EQUIPMENT	COMPUTER CHIPS
COLOR TELEVISION SETS	INDUSTRIAL ROBOTS
HAND TOOLS	ELECTRON MICROSCOPES
RADIAL TIRES	MACHINE TOOLS
ELECTRIC MOTORS	OPTICAL EQUIPMENT

FIGURE 1. What Do All These Products Have In Common? *Adapted from Stephen Wheelwright, March 20, 1984.*

zled because, as you can see, the list includes both high- and low-tech items, consumer and industrial products, and hard and soft goods. What is the common characteristic shared by athletic equipment and electron microscopes, by automobiles and hand tools, by apparel and earth moving equipment? This list, which, as best we can tell, originated with Professor Stephen Wheelwright of Stanford University, shows some American industries and products that lost 50 percent or more of their share of world markets since 1960.

Indeed, the 1980s have been very trying for American industry. We have seen markets we dominated erode or completely disappear, even in the high-tech, innovative markets that American industry created. No video cassette recorders are American designed and made, no compact disc recorders, no 35mm cameras. With the dreadful exit of General Electric from TV production in 1987, only Zenith remains in the business. The remaining television plants in this country bear the names of Sony, Sharp, Mitsubishi, and Matsushita. The fourth largest American automobile manufacturer, Honda of America, is gaining fast on number three, Chrysler.

The broad picture of the sudden decline in the international competitiveness of U.S. manufacturing is no less startling: a 1986 overall trade deficit of $170 billion, $59 billion of that with Japan alone, and of that about $30 billion in that most American of industries—automobiles. And that $30 billion is with "voluntary" export restrictions by the Japanese. In 1986 we even had a trade deficit of $2.6 billion in high-technology goods and, still worse, a trade deficit in agricultural products that is clearly understated by ignoring the importation of billions of dollars worth of illicit agricultural products. During 1986 and 1987, the U.S. dollar suffered (enjoyed?) a substantial de facto devaluation the purpose of which was to help alleviate the trade imbalance. Yet as a few of us predicted, the trade deficit continues apace. These facts are so shocking that we must remind ourselves that this is the country of Eli Whitney and Henry Ford, of George Westinghouse and Thomas Edison, of Alfred P. Sloan, John Rockefeller, and Henry Kaiser. We invented the telephone, the airplane, the computer, the transistor, and the laser. We invented and then perfected the production line. We are also the nation of Frederick Taylor and Elton Mayo, of Walter Shewhart, W. Edwards Deming, and Joseph Juran.

Of course, the next question is "how and why is all this happening?" Many explanations have been offered. There is no shortage of theories—indeed, we have gathered some twenty or so that purport to explain this downfall. Our list includes such well-known macroeconomic explanations as the dollar-yen exchange rates, the low U.S. propensities to save and to invest in capital, low investment rates in civilian research and development (R&D), and the high U.S. military spending in general and on military R&D in particular. Social and political characteristics of the United States, such as our high labor and management mobility and turnover, the power

of our industry-wide unions, the alleged sloppy and unproduc-
tive attitudes of American workers, and the unwillingness or
inability of our government to plan ahead and create an industrial policy, also make our list of explanations. Since much of
the problem seems to stem from our inability to compete with
Japan, the social and historical advantages of the Japanese
people, including their propensity for hard work; their cultural, linguistic, and racial homogeneity; and the rebuilding of
Japanese plants after the devastation of World War II, also
make our list. Some very specific comparisons are striking:
examine the differences in the pay and reward systems of
Japanese and American managers and workers, consider the
collaborative relations Japanese firms have with their suppliers, and study the differences in the capital structure of Japanese and American firms. Eventually such explanations get
down to the level of attributing Japanese industrial success to
their ability to copy—but not innovate; to their installation of
quality circles (there was something of a quality circle fad here
some years ago); to their proficiency with mathematics and
statistical quality control charts; or even to their incredibly
complex Kanji writing system, the mastery of which, it is said,
makes all other intellectual feats simple by comparison. And
so it goes, theory after theory, until we come to the alleged
pernicious impact of the short-term profitability goals of many
Wall Street investors, particularly the pension fund managers.

There is, we believe, a germ of truth in almost all these
explanations. Yet they do not directly address what we and
many other observers see as the root cause of the Japanese
success, which is that in industry after industry the Japanese
have consistently been able to produce higher quality and
lower cost goods. Thus the thesis of this chapter is that the
fundamental answer to both questions is the same: *quality*. The
failure of American competitiveness is largely a failure to manage for quality, while the key to the Japanese success is an
almost compulsive and fanatical attention to managing for
quality. The only long-and short-term remedy for the United
States is to recapture quality dominance or at least quality
parity in key industries. We believe this intensely. While we

probably cannot prove our thesis scientifically, we will later in the chapter offer convincing arguments by looking at some case histories.

How the Japanese have achieved mastery of quality is not a mystery or miracle. The "secret" is no secret at all, and its key is not high technology or robots, nor is it government assistance or macroeconomic forces. It is a *management system*. It is important for all Americans, and most importantly for Americans in influential and decision-making positions throughout industry, government, the communications media, Wall Street, and the universities to understand, appreciate, and learn the basics of this new management system. Why so? Because it is the most powerful system for the creation of goods and services that the world has seen—one that is rather universally applicable. There are cases to show that this system can be employed in both high- and low-technology industries, in mass and in one-of-kind production, for creating services as well as goods, in both the public and private arenas, for consumer end products as well as for industrial commodities, intermediate parts, or heavy capital equipment. Unless it is mastered, other efforts to improve competitiveness will avail us little. In the following sections of this chapter we shall lay out the essentials of modern quality management, then discuss the steps that the management of individual firms can take to get the system installed in their enterprises, and finally discuss steps that can be taken by other segments of U.S. society to enhance and support the success of this mission. There are important contributions to be made by all Americans in carrying out this agenda.

How Quality Matters

Let us start by taking a fresh look at why quality is so crucial. To be sure, "quality" is a necessity for customer acceptance, but even more than that we shall see by a series of cases that quality, productivity, and worker satisfaction are mutually supportive—and there is a lot of evidence that quality leads to the other two.

Joseph Juran is at least partially responsible for the very wide circulation in production circles of the Motorola–Matsushita/Quasar story. In the mid-1970s the Japanese electronics giant bought out a color TV plant that had formerly been run by Motorola. Prior to coming under Japanese management, the Motorola factory had been running at a rate of 150 to 180 defects per 100 sets. Three years later the defect rate had dropped to 3 or 4 per 100 sets! As a consequence, the cost of service calls dropped from $22 million to less than $4 million, the number of in-plant repair and service people was reduced from 120 to 15, and personnel turnover dropped from 30 percent to 1 percent per year. All this happened with effort and investment, including modified product designs that were less prone to field failure, changes in manufacturing processes to make them less prone to defect generation, and more reliable defect-free parts. In short, Matsushita utilized many of the basic quality management principles that leading American experts on quality had been preaching here for twenty years. They did not use a revolutionary new technology, nor a new work force. The key was intensive quality oriented management that brought with it the targeted increases in quality and *simultaneous* and concomitant decreases in cost. (Classical management and economic theory do not account for this possibility. We all have been led to believe that higher quality comes only with higher costs, haven't we?)

A second quality story that is vitally important to America is that of NUMMI (New United Motors Manufacturing Incorporated), the joint venture of GM and the Toyota Motor Company. In this venture Toyota is making the cars, a version of the Toyota Corolla, and GM is selling them under the Chevrolet "Nova" label. Toyota does the manufacturing in a GM plant at Fremont, California, which had been closed by GM due to low quality and low productivity. By all accounts, under GM management the Fremont plant was an industrial nightmare with poor quality performance, low productivity, wildcat strikes, and incredible absenteeism. Then Toyota took over the operations and now NUMMI has the highest quality and productivity of the entire GM system. How so? It was largely through implementing ideas similar to those used at the Quasar plant and also through a series of quality management techniques that rely heavily on innovative employee relations and workplace reorganization that make it possible for NUMMI to utilize the skills and talents of the workers in ways that simultaneously enhance quality, productivity, and worker satisfaction. Yet NUMMI is not a particularly high-tech operation; indeed, actual production technology used in the plant is not as advanced as that utilized currently at some other GM plants. Moreover, the workers are some 2,500 of the 6,000 UAW workers who were laid off when GM closed the plant. These successes of Matsushita at Quasar and Toyota at NUMMI show that quality and productivity go hand-in-hand and can be achieved in America by American workers—but using Japanese management techniques, if not Japanese managers themselves. There are similar stories of manufacturing success achieved here in the United States by other leading Japanese firms, including Sony, Honda, and Nissan.

Equally interesting and perhaps even more important to us are some "all-American" success stories. In their own ways, Hewlett-Packard, Xerox, Harley-Davidson, and Corning Glass Works have demonstrated the tremendous power of modern quality management. In each of these American firms, there have been instances of quality oriented product and process redesign, of the use of quantitative and statistical methods of quality improvement and process control, and very heavy participation in quality/productivity improvement by all levels and functions of management as well as by the hourly employees. For example, Harley-Davidson, using the principles we shall describe, has reported productivity increases of 30 percent, reduction of scrap and rework of 60 percent, and a redesign of a key engine to make it easier to manufacture while simultaneously providing more power with less fuel. Moreover, the same engine is more reliable and needs less owner maintenance. Hewlett-Packard, in a rather different industry, responded to its competitive challenge with a modern quality management program that in some areas reduced defect rates by 90 percent, and in others reduced quality related costs by as much as 50 percent. In each of these American companies and in others, quality is seen as the key competitive challenge and opportunity, and a response along modern quality management principles has yielded enormous results, not only in quality but also in productivity, cost reduction, and employee satisfaction. A bottom line for each has been increased security in its marketplace. The 1986–87 success of Ford Motor Company—outstripping GM in earnings for the first time since 1924—is due in no small part to its use of modern quality management. The successful Taurus/Sable autos have been designed and are produced using the best principles of modern quality management.

Of course, quality management is not just an American/Japanese story, either. In 1980 Jaguar faced a very major crisis. Sales in the United States, usually 50 percent of its market, had dropped to 3,000 cars per year. As John Egan, chairman of Jaguar, put it, "If a manufacturer is to survive, and, more importantly, to prosper, he must make not only the right product but ensure that it achieves a reputation for quality and reliability at least equivalent to its competitors." An urgent quality management program at Jaguar produced impressive improvements in its quality and reliability, and within three years U.S. sales had increased fivefold.

While these stories are persuasive, they do not prove the case for quality scientifically. Isolated success stories like these would never be accepted by the medical community as evidence of the efficacy of a new drug. Although hard and rigorous evidence that meets FDA standards will probably never be available, a remarkable 1983 study of the U.S. and Japanese room air conditioner industries reported by David A. Garvin in the *Harvard Business Review* comes as close as practicable to proving the linkages between quality and productivity and to identifying the quality management practices and attitudes as the determining factor. An abbreviated discussion cannot adequately present the many startling aspects and findings of Garvin's study of seven Japanese and eleven American room air conditioner plants. The plants accounted for 90 percent of each nation's industry. Garvin found that

Japanese plants were superior across the board, whether quality was measured by incoming rejection rates, assembly line defect rates, or service call rates. Japanese plants averaged failure rates that were seventeen to sixty-seven times lower than their U.S. counterparts. Even more impressive, on all measures the poorest Japanese plant had a failure rate less than half that of the best U.S. manufacturer. The roots of superiority are also clear, for every Japanese company traced its success to a system of company-wide quality control.

(We shall shortly describe this system of modern management.) We cannot resist adding that although Garvin does not so state in his article, GE must have been in his U.S. sample, and was soon to abandon room air conditioner manufacturing. GE chose to market room air conditioners manufactured abroad. While it may be in the interest of GE to reposition itself as a financial/marketing firm, one cannot help pondering the impact of these decisions on American workers, on manufacturing managers, and on our economy.

Does modern quality management really impact the bottom line? By now, even Wall Street must be getting the message. In autos, Toyota, the leading Japanese proponent of quality management, is the most profitable corporation in Japan while Ford, the leading U.S. proponent, is running away from GM. American companies that stress quality are bounding back from troubled times—Xerox, Kodak, Harley-Davidson, and Corning Glass are examples.

What Is Quality?

One of the problems in quality management is that "quality" is a concept that is not easily understood. In any field of endeavor in which people struggle for increased understanding and control—in effect, to become more scientific—it is crucial to define basic terms. Consequently, before we describe the modern quality management agenda that U.S. industry should adopt, we need to consider what quality is.

It is natural to think of quality in terms of concepts such as "goodness" or the like. While this is not completely off the mark, there are more helpful ways of thinking about quality. An essential concept is customer satisfaction. A quality item (or service) meets customer needs and expectations and does that *consistently*. Thus Joseph Juran, a leading American thinker about modern quality management, in his definitive *Quality Control Handbook* in 1952 defined "quality as fitness for use." He amplifies this concept by examining the multiplicity of uses and performance characteristics that are typical of most items. Philip B. Crosby, another American prominently associated with the quality movement, puts it even more simply by stating that quality is "meeting requirements." W. Edwards Deming's influential 1950 Tokyo lectures on statistical quality control repeatedly emphasize a focus on the customer and the need for consistency.

Efficient and consistent delivery of a quality product requires a clear and specific definition of "customer," "use," and "requirements." To be specific about what quality is, in our teaching and consulting, we frequently have students and clients go through the exercise of defining quality for such disparate "items" as a hamburger, a hotel stay, a ballpoint pen, and an automobile.

For example, taking a crack at defining quality for the humble hamburger, we might start with concepts such as doneness, juiciness, taste, tenderness, freshness, and aroma. We might add measurable characteristics such as weight, diameter, thickness, color, temperature, and fat content, and then include safety characteristics such as bacterial content and chemical additives. But should we not also recognize the importance of speed of provision, of availability, transportability, and "peripherals" such as the several characteristics of bun quality, dressings, and garnishes? Finally, some might suggest that we not leave out *cost*. This last suggestion might startle the economists among you; yet a modern perception is that cost is merely one aspect of the multidimensional set of characteristics that we call quality. Such a quality definition exercise—regardless of the product or service—quickly identifies the *multidimensional nature of quality,* the difficulty of actually measuring quality, and the diversity of uses and of users, that is, customers. Quality is indeed fitness for use, broadly conceived. Understanding this drives management closer to understanding its customer and its raison d'être.

The multidimensionality of quality creates many opportunities for the enterprise. (Problems are opportunities in disguise.) Since a single product or service is unable to simultaneously achieve highest marks on all dimensions, a key aspect of quality management is appropriate targeting. Do we emphasize performance aspects such as capacity, speed, or strength, or do we emphasize optional features such as diversity of speeds, automatic controls, self-cleaning, or adjustment? What about appearance, durability, reliability, serviceability, and robustness to changes in the user environment? An important first step in quality management—whatever the "product," automobile or copier, hamburger or hotel stay, computer-controlled milling machine or jet liner—is to identify the key components of the quality vector and how they segment in the marketplace.

How do we distinguish the quality of the ubiquitous McDonald's hamburger from the quality of a hamburger served at the Waldorf Astoria? We must contrast the "quality" of a stay at a Holiday Inn in Statesville, North Carolina, with that of a stay at the Hotel George V in Paris as well as the quality of a Bic throwaway ballpoint pen and that of a solid gold Montblanc. To manage for quality we must make important distinctions between "quality of design" and "quality of conformance"; that is, between quality "within class" and quality "across classes."

What, indeed, is the point, when we compare a $29.95 stay in the Holiday Inn to a $299.95 stay in the George V, a 29 cent Bic pen to a $129 Montblanc, a $6,500 Hyundai Excel automobile to a $32,000 BMW "ultimate driving machine"? First, we can notice that when we make such "across class" comparisons the customer bases, the product uses, and concepts of satisfaction and requirements may be quite different—yet, not entirely so. At some level, a pen is a pen, and a hotel is a hotel.

Moreover, care is necessary, for there are undoubtedly persons who contemporaneously own and use a Bic and Montblanc, a Hyundai and a BMW, and have stayed at the Holiday
Inn and the George V. In short, both within class and across
class, quality is important. Indeed, it is quite possible that in
some respects a Bic might be superior to a Montblanc, and a
Holiday Inn superior to the George V. At any rate, one task
of management is to fundamentally upgrade quality and move
across class boundaries, while another is to deal with the nitty-
gritty quality issues that revolve around quality within class.
Quality across class is essentially a matter of product design.
Modern quality management greatly enhances the process of
design to achieve targeted quality. So let us presume that a
product class has been selected, and shift our attention to
being *best-in-class.*

At this point, "fitness-for-use" and "meeting requirements"
become the dominant considerations. Often such definitions
require some care and precision in identifying actual or target
customer populations and assessing actual or potential uses
and requirements. In the typical large corporation with tens of
thousands of employees, few are in close enough touch with
the customer or have the skills or experience to gain a solid
basis on which to judge final quality issues. Yet it is vital that
the organization *as a whole* be able to do so, and having made
the judgments of what constitutes the requirements, the organization must transmit them clearly to all its members and line
them up to act effectively and in concert to produce the quality
required.

Three Key Tasks

There are three interlocking tasks of modern quality management: first, assess customer needs and expectations,
thereby defining fitness for use; second, translate the quality
definition into clear specifications and requirements at each
stage of the production process; and third, create a system
capable of efficiently and consistently meeting those requirements. To put it mildly, all this is much easier said than done.

Quality must be designed with the customer in mind or by the customer. This definition must be multidimensional, multifaceted, and dynamic. The definition will change as customers' needs and preferences change and as the competition changes. When designing the Taurus/Sable autos, the Ford Motor Company engineers identified 428 quality dimensions. Customers were asked to compare Ford designs to those of sixty competitors. For each characteristic (dimension) a "best-in-class" was selected. Then for each of these characteristics (door handle, ignition switch, jack, acceleration) clear competitive targets were established.

The next task is to translate these quality definitions into clear requirements and specifications. For example, in a firm producing coated milk carton stock to be supplied to milk distributors, an important aspect of the customer oriented definition of quality is that the cartons be leak-free. This definition must be translated to a series of requirements to the coating department for polyethylene coat weight, for the absence of pin holes in the coating, and for stiffness in the paperboard. In order to achieve the coating performance requirements, the coating department must meet operating targets or specifications on pressures, temperatures, machine speeds, clearances, and cleanliness. Similarly, the goal of leak-free cartons places on the paper-making operation a series of requirements that the board have a minimum "taber-stiffness" and meet caliper, basis weight, and smoothness specifications. Further back in the process, other requirements will be necessary, for example, on the size and moisture content of the wood chips used to make the paper.

Thus we come to the inescapable conclusion that to meet end-customer quality requirements, the firm must meet a series of internal quality requirements throughout its entire organization. Deming communicated this idea very powerfully and simply in his 1950 Tokyo lectures with the diagram shown here as Figure 2.

The third task is the hardest: creating a system capable of efficiently and consistently meeting these requirements. This system must be built around the spiral of progress in quality,

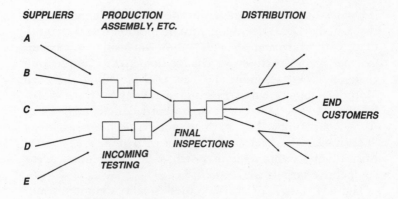

FIGURE 2. Where Is Quality Made? *Adapted from W. E. Deming, Tokyo 1950.*

often called the Juran Spiral (see Figure 3). The quality spiral must start with market research to determine the customers' needs and expectations; to determine the competitors' products, strengths, and weaknesses; and to understand where the competitors are likely to be when your product is ready for the market.

Work in the quality spiral then passes to the design department, where designers translate the customers' needs and expectations into product specifications and requirements and work with suppliers to develop the requirements and specifications for purchased parts and materials. Designers must assure that reliability objectives will be met and that the product is manufacturable at requested cost and quality.

The quality locus then passes to the process designers, who develop production processes that prevent most mistakes, make quality control easy, and provide quick signals when anything goes wrong. They specify process checkpoints and tests to assure that all problems are caught as early as possible. Checkpoints are often on key process variables rather than on the product to prevent defective products from being created.

Quality then passes to the purchasing department to assure that the right materials, components, and subassemblies are

THE SPIRAL OF PROGRESS IN QUALITY.

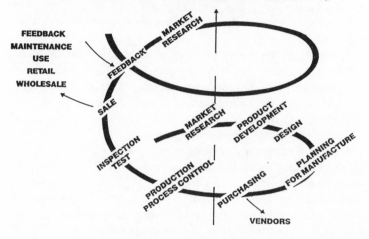

FIGURE 3. The Spiral of Progress in Quality. *Adapted from J. M. Juran Upper Management and Quality, Fourth Edition, Sixth Printing, February 1987.* © *1982 Juran Institute, Inc., 88 Danbury Road, Wilton, CT 06897-4409*

available. Suppliers are made part of the quality team: partners in success, partners in constant improvement.

Only now does quality become the responsibility of the production department. At this point, the traditional quality control methods are applied, on the shop floor. But even here technology is rapidly changing. New methods are needed for automated systems, for robotics, for just-in-time inventory systems, for quality levels measured in the defective parts per million range. Inspections and tests still play major roles during and after manufacturing, where they provide much of the information needed to assure quality, to constantly improve the manufacturing processes, and to constantly improve the designs.

But quality concerns do not stop with the final test in manufacturing. Now quality management must focus on shipping, installation, sales, and service. The order taking process must be accurate and prompt, the right products delivered, the installations correct, and any necessary repairs made quickly and correctly. The product documentation must be right. The bill must be correct.

Throughout this entire process, information on each problem or defect must flow back upstream for quick corrections and changes to prevent future problems. Information on every product or process change, every material or part change or substitution must quickly flow downstream for incorporation in assembly and test operations.

There are many implications of the quality spiral. The challenge in managing quality cuts across all the traditional departmental boundaries in a company. Large amounts of information must be collected, analyzed, understood, and shared. People must be trained not only in their own jobs but in the jobs of the functions immediately preceding and following theirs. Clear definitions of quality and the corresponding requirements and specifications must exist at every step of the spiral. Measurements must be made, analyzed, and used at every step throughout the spiral.

Key Implications of These Viewpoints

The question is this: if we know all of these things, what is keeping America from doing them? What is keeping us from reasserting ourselves as the top competitor in the industrial world?

The Crucial Role of Senior Management

Following hard on the heels of the recognition that quality must be managed throughout the entire corporation and across all functions is the inescapable conclusion that quality is senior management's job. This requires more than just top management's commitment; it requires top management's leadership and active participation. Quality simply cannot be delegated. Senior management alone has the authority and responsibility to set the goals, make the plans, allocate the resources, and make the specific decisions necessary to make this happen throughout the organization. The entire firm will be watching what senior management *does* as well as what it *says* about quality.

Many of America's top managers are poorly equipped to provide this leadership. The lessons of modern quality management are not being taught in America's leading business schools; they are being learned the hard way. These lessons are not being learned by reading management texts; they are being learned by studying top competitors, from joint ventures (e.g., GM and Toyota), and from studying partners (e.g., Hewlett-Packard and Yokagawa Hewlett-Packard; Xerox and Fuji-Xerox).

Our experience convinces us that Japanese management generally has been much better equipped to handle the requirements of the quality revolution than their American counterparts. For example, our leading Japanese competitors have a top management structure that grew up during the postwar years when improving quality and productivity in Japan was all important and became part of the corporate culture. Moreover, they are supported by the world's leading institution of quality education and technology—the Japanese Union of Scientists and Engineers. Management is supported by a competent technical cadre. Manufacturing engineering is one of the most respected fields of study in leading Japanese universities. Most U.S. engineering schools still ignore or pay lip service to it. Top managers in Japanese companies often have come up through the ranks, often working as design and manufacturing engineers, sales representatives, repair and service persons, and in marketing. Moreover, they never seem too old, too busy, or too self-important to study and learn. Senior Japanese management often seems to be more interested in the latest details of U.S. quality management than American managers who typically only have time for the big picture: someone else will take care of the details.

The Crucial Role of Training

Since quality cuts across all parts of the company and must be managed at every management level and by every worker, it is clear that quality is not just the function of the quality department. Quality is everybody's responsibility, and everybody must be capable of doing this job. The consequences of this are enormous: *each* person must be involved, *each* must be trained in basic quality methods, and *each* must clearly understand his or her part and how it affects the product, the service, and the customer. But different jobs have very different training needs. While there are common principles of quality management, there is no simple set of quality methods that universally apply to billing, design, research, manufacturing, sales, repair service, and market research. Companies have to understand these different needs and train the people for each job, but at the same time create a common language, a common set of goals, and a common understanding of the customers' needs. To regain our competitive position, U.S. industry must mount the most massive training program in its history. This training program in quality will be similar but far larger than the massive quality control training programs launched during World War II, our last quality crisis.

In most companies in the United States, the capability to carry out such training does not currently exist. We have yet to see a single firm overestimate the amount of training necessary to do this job, or overinvest in it. Firms are lacking in-house expertise on the basic elements of quality management, statistical methods, and teamwork that must be taught. They lack the facilities, programs, and logistical support.

There are several distinct objectives that this training must meet. First, an awareness must be created throughout the firm of the importance of quality, of the seriousness of the competitive challenge, and of the potential for great improvements. This base knowledge and set of attitudes must be held by everyone and understood at a level that will equip and motivate them for action. The goal, after all, is not that employees know about these ideas, but that they act on them. We are talking about an intensity of knowledge sufficient for basic changes in behavior.

But quality awareness is just the beginning of the training challenge. Specific technical concepts and tools must also be taught. The exact needs vary with employee level and function, but a common set of statistical and problem-solving techniques has emerged that is fundamental to actually doing concrete quality improvement. Our experience in teaching these tools for quality improvement indicates strongly that they are best learned through active involvement and practice. Thus firms face the challenge of augmenting classroom instruction books, manuals, and videos with an apprentice-like program—and there aren't enough "masters" to go around.

Thirdly, in addition to the technical tools of quality improvement, managers must learn a new quality management system. In many firms new organizational structures must be created to implement a quality revolution. Basic skills must be developed in quality planning, quality control, and quality improvement.

And finally, there is a novel training requirement. A very key skill must be learned by management and workers alike—teamwork. The companies most successful at implementing the quality revolution have utilized teamwork to a far greater extent than has been customary in traditional U.S. firms. Teams are absolutely necessary to cut across the organizational boundaries and attack the major chronic quality problems. Thus a psychological, touchy-feely component of training is vital. It may seem bizarre for two "techis" like us to be saying this, but we believe it to be crucial.

The Crucial Role of Statistics in Quality Management

Goods and services are produced in an imperfect and unpredictable world; yet we expect to achieve consistent conformance to multifaceted customer requirements. The systems that create goods and services redound in variation, and this very variation is at the core of most quality problems. If it were not for variation there would not be any quality problems. To see why, return to our milk carton production scenario. Suppose there was no variation in our milk carton production system. That is, suppose that all characteristics of the paperboard, of polyethylene coating, and of the milk carton assembly process were perfectly stable and controlled precisely at targeted values. Thus either we would produce no leakers and have no quality problems—since the customers' needs are met with each carton, or every carton would leak and we would shortly have no quality problems—since we would soon be out of business. Therefore, the essence of quality problems is that we can meet the requirements some of the time—perhaps very often—but not all the time. Using statistics is the art and science of understanding and acting in the face of variation. Only the statistically trained manager or engineer can effectively move us toward our quality goals.

Reduction and control of variability clearly increase the firm's ability to conform to requirements, but they also have another very important effect. They reduce cost! We can see how this happens from our milk carton example. Reduction of the variability in the milk carton coating process will improve our ability to satisfy the customer, because a more even coating, a more consistent polyethylene penetration, and fewer air bubbles all mean better seals and fewer leaks. The cost savings to the company are as dramatic as the quality improvement. First, less variation means fewer rejects, less scrap, and fewer customer complaints and claims—all obvious sources of savings. Less obvious but equally important is that reduction in coating variation will permit the operators to reduce the coat weight safety margins they use to protect them against the swings and variability in the process. When they are able to closely control the amount of polyethylene going onto the stock and the evenness of its spread and penetration, they can put considerably less on! All this happens with no loss of performance. This same theme can be replayed for all parameters of the coating process. For example, by controlling variation of the coating temperatures we can reduce temperature targets. This yields energy savings. Moreover, there is an interaction between coating temperature and coat weight. Tighter control of temperature will permit still more uniform coat weight and lead to further polyethylene savings. Since we are producing a more consistent final product with more consistent materials, we need less inventory to insure against failures. Just-in-time inventories become possible. Moral: *reduction of variation simultaneously increases customer satisfaction and reduces cost.* Consequently, a major theme of modern quality improvement is cost reduction through control of variation. As we sometimes put it to our students and clients, "Variation in all its manifestations is the enemy!"

Let us take a look at how to attack this very tricky and elusive enemy called variation. Effective attack on variation requires some novel attitudes, tools, and behaviors on the part of managers, engineers, designers, and workers. At the basis of the attack is knowledge of the enemy. This is where statistics enters the quality management scene, for statistics is the branch of mathematics that studies variation.

What Must Be Done by Industry

Whether the United States regains international competitiveness depends more on the actions of individual companies than on anything that can be done by the government or by the society at large. The mission of each firm is, quite simply put, to become the high-quality/low-cost producer in the industry or market. For firms that are already facing substantial foreign competition, there is really no choice. They must change or die—or rest content to become, if they are lucky, marketing agents or distributors for foreign producers. For domestic firms that have not yet felt the bite of overseas competition, there is only a little more leeway—they have a bit more time before foreigners enter or before domestic competitors adopt the new quality agenda.

Becoming the high-quality/low-cost producer in any industry requires three actions. Top management must take a leadership role. They must develop a strategic quality plan and define their personal roles. John Egan of Jaguar gives us a model. When he assumed the role as chairman of the failing Jaguar in 1980, he identified 250 quality related tasks that had to be done. He personally assumed the leadership of the top five tasks and assigned seven others to the managing directors. As stated earlier, U.S. sales are now at record levels, and productivity (number of cars produced per worker) has jumped from 1.3 in 1980 to 3.9 in 1986.

The second action must be a massive preparation of the entire company. Management must decide what quality technology—knowledge, skills, and tools—their people need and make sure they get them. The training must include problem-identification/problem-solving skills that provide the foundation for constant quality improvement. This includes statistical tools that run a wide gamut from basic charts and graphs that can be used by every employee from CEO to machine operator, to complex and sophisticated statistical methods such as regression analysis, statistically designed experiments, and reliability prediction models. The firm's quality training program must include interpersonal skills and tools that facilitate and accelerate the process of team formation and team problem solving. This training must include the basics of strategic quality management for all managers throughout the company: quality planning, quality control, and quality improvement.

The third action is to *do* something. Managers must select several bellwether projects and get them done, and participate in the process. The problems selected should be generic, chronic, and tractable. Quality improvement progresses one step at a time. As major problems are solved and the results tracked and publicized, the cost reductions, quality improvements, and market gains will become impressive. These bellwether projects will provide models and motivation for growing numbers of managers to tackle a wide range of chronic problems that have endured for years.

What Must Be Done by Academia

Education has a vital role to play in restoring America's competitiveness. American workers and managers are often poorly prepared for the roles they must play in a world-competitive industry. Many of the basic methods in quality control and assurance are mathematical and statistical. Skill levels in basic mathematics are poor. Skills in statistical methods are usually nonexistent. Workers often have only the very weakest of scientific training. We have found that quality training courses frequently have to start with basic high school math and science to provide the foundation for problem-solving skills and quality improvement methods. Both the Japanese worker and the Japanese manager receive far more training of this type in school and in industry. The Koreans also appear to be well trained in these skills. The West Germans use a strong school system and years of apprenticeships on which they have built a strong work force.

All business schools and engineering schools should start by carefully reviewing their M.B.A. and their B.S. and M.S. engineering degree curricula. They must assure relevance to America's quality and productivity improvement efforts. They must add specific courses and create new teaching materials for them. They need industry's help in this process, for the universities will at the outset be followers, not leaders, in this effort. In some cases, existing courses should be reviewed to identify incorrect material and methods that no longer work.

Universities must begin industry outreach programs. Faculty and students must have contact with the real problems American industry is facing today. Close cooperative working relationships must be established between business leaders and academics. There is a wealth of important research problems in industry that are not being addressed in the universities.

Universities must review their research agendas and support a strong increase in work on quality and productivity topics.

Without destroying their important agendas and missions on long-term and "basic" theoretical research, they should reward at least some research that has immediate practical application. They must reward research that actually gets used. They must also break down their departmental boundaries and barriers and encourage crossdepartmental research teams. Many of the most important problems facing American industry today cannot be solved in specialized and compartmentalized university departments.

Universities must also review their promotion and reward policies. They must decide how they are going to, indeed *if* they are going to, measure the quality of their products: the students, the research, the contributions to society.

What Must Be Done by Government

During World War II the U.S. government, particularly the War Department, played a leading role in making modern quality control methods available throughout U.S. industry. The government created research centers in quality control and formed quality standards writing teams. These methods and standards became a significant part of quality management methodology used throughout the world in the decades following the war.

In the past ten years, the government has played a very negative role in helping America improve its quality position. Government agencies insist on outdated procedures for inspection and quality assurance. Purchasing procedures are often the opposite of good quality management-vendor relations. The government has abandoned its quality standards activities. Government agencies such as the Federal Aviation Administration (FAA), Motor Vehicles Bureaus, Department of Defense (DOD), NASA, and Social Security Administration are more often cited as bad examples of quality management than they are looked to as role models.

The government can provide much needed leadership. Good quality management can reduce costs significantly. Where these methods have been applied (e.g., Wisconsin state government) the results have been impressive. The government can revamp its DOD purchasing and contracting procedures and reward suppliers exceeding the quality and reliability terms of the contracts.

The government can fund basic research in quality and productivity methods. It must continue to support the joint academic-industry research programs in this area to create a strong technology base for U.S. industry to use.

The government can continue to support the Quantitative Literacy Project for our high schools and grade schools. This project is an important first step in bringing a basic understanding of quantitative methods to high school students throughout America. But we need much more. Basic problem-solving skills must be emphasized at all grade levels. Students must learn the principles of the scientific method and develop the skills necessary to plan experiments, collect data, and analyze the results. They must develop the verbal and writing skills necessary to communicate clearly and effectively.

Conclusion

There is no quick fix. We must change the management of America's key industries. We must retrain our engineers. We must improve the education of our future business leaders. We must revamp our secondary school systems and our colleges and universities.

There is good news. Much of this is already happening. There are outstanding leaders in some of America's top companies who are already making sweeping changes throughout their firms. They are creating Quality Institutes within their companies and initiating massive training programs. They are organizing strong quality improvement programs that are already providing spectacular returns. Teams of top managers are traveling to Japan for in-depth studies of new quality management techniques. The National Science Foundation is funding joint academic-industry research programs in quality technology and management.

Congress has just created a national quality award to publicize the quality improvement results of America's quality leaders. Engineering and productivity research centers are springing up in some of America's top universities. New quality and reliability courses, even departments and interdepartmental programs, are springing up in colleges and universities. Business school professors are holding annual conferences to examine their curricula with respect to quantitative methods and quality management. Engineering schools are redefining what is needed, and groups of professors are meeting with industry leaders to examine their courses and programs in quality and reliability.

Many of America's leading companies are sharing their methods, sharing their quality courses with their suppliers and even competitors, and setting ambitious new quality goals for themselves. We are moving fast, but are we moving fast enough? The answer is no. Our competitors in Japan and West Germany are still on the move, some think at ever-increasing rates. Our competitors in Singapore, Korea, Taiwan, and Thailand are also moving fast. Can America compete? Of course, if we want to badly enough. It won't be easy, but it certainly won't be boring.

9

From Complacency to Strategy: Retaining World Class Competitiveness in Services

DOROTHY I. RIDDLE
KRISTOPHER J. BROWN

I n 1982 when the U.S. trade representative raised the issue
of multilateral rules for services trade in the General Agreement on Tariffs and Trade (GATT), the United States was
viewed as the leader worldwide in services. In 1986, only four
years later, *The Economist* ranked the United States sixth in
worldwide services trade—behind the United Kingdom,

DOROTHY I. RIDDLE is a professor in the Department of International Studies at the American Graduate School of International Management in Glendale, Arizona. She also is president of International
Services Institute in Tempe, Arizona. Dr. Riddle has taught in
Greece, India, the People's Republic of China, Taiwan, and the
United States and has held several positions in the health services
sector. She has made numerous presentations and has published
extensively on the global services industry and economic development.

KRISTOPHER J. BROWN is business strategist for the International
Services Institute, where he has organized the compilation of a data
base on service transnational corporations. Mr. Brown has earned
degrees from the Sorbonne, the University of California at Berkeley,
and the American Graduate School of International Management and
has held several positions in the services industry.

Spain, France, Switzerland, and Italy, respectively. By March 1987 the *Institutional Investor* had lowered the credit rating of the United States from first to fourth place—behind Japan, Switzerland, and the Federal Republic of Germany.

What happened in between? Contrary to popular opinion, any decline in U.S. services competitiveness has not been primarily a result of unfair trade tactics on the part of other countries or diminished services quality. The decrease in U.S. services market share can be attributed directly to a normal increase in world competition that, for the most part, was disregarded by U.S. service firms accustomed to dominating world markets. Increased global competitiveness has, in turn, rendered U.S. service firms that are content with mediocre service quality standards vulnerable to loss of market share when pitted against Japanese or European service firms that emphasize superb service quality.

Attention to service quality, then, is not the major issue confronting U.S. service firms—though current service standards are no longer internationally competitive. Rather, there is a complacency about international competitive positioning and a willingness to hide behind protectionist measures that ultimately will erode the international standing of U.S. service corporations. Instead of implementing additional protectionist measures, which will accomplish nothing but the stagnation of world trade, the United States must develop an appropriate domestic service sector policy, train service sector workers imbued with high quality standards, and pursue a path of international cooperation to stimulate world economic growth.

The Role Played by Services

A major difficulty in understanding the economic role played by services stems from the characterization of services in the U.S. media as "postindustrial." In actuality, services are "preindustrial" or "coindustrial" in the sense that manufacturing is dependent on services to function. At least 40 percent—and perhaps as high as 60 percent—of activities in the extractive and manufacturing sectors are in reality service activities, especially in high-technology industries. It is estimated that about 80 percent of the cost of developing a new computer and about 70 percent of developing a new telecommunications switchboard are spent on services and software.

Although services have historically been denigrated as "nonproductive" or discounted as "residual," they in fact form the major component of virtually every economy—not only that of the United States. Without transportation, communications, utilities, and viable financial markets, no economy can function. Countries can survive by importing commodities or manufactured goods, but without the service infrastructure to distribute those goods, they will be inaccessible to customers. A weak services infrastructure can seriously impair the growth and efficiency of activities in both the extractive and manufacturing sectors. Services are the "vital force," if you will, that bind an economy together. A healthy and literate work force, an efficient public sector, and adequate infrastructure are more crucial to economic growth than is the availability of raw materials or the manufacture of goods.

Services and manufacturing are interlinked or merged in such a way that it is inaccurate to describe services as "dependent" on manufacturing any more than manufacturing is dependent on services. Granted, the structure of service delivery depends on the types of equipment available to service firms. For example, banks could not offer self-service banking without automatic teller machines having been invented. On the other hand, the manufacturers of automatic teller machines are dependent on the banks to buy those automatic teller machines. Consumers purchase durable goods not as ends in themselves but in order to streamline or facilitate production of a service in a business or home. It should not be surprising, then, that the primary purchasers of goods are service firms. Service firms purchased more than 80 percent of the $25 billion of computers, office equipment, and communications equipment shipped in the United States in 1982.

Services make possible a more widespread, flexible, and resource-conserving manufacture and distribution system for goods. If service firms are not dynamic and thriving, goods will be more costly and will remain on warehouse shelves. In addition, manufacturing firms are now called on to meet increased consumer demand for a more complex bundle of services to accompany many manufactured goods. Certainly, IBM's success must be attributed not only to the quality of its information systems but to the range and excellence of the services that are associated with the equipment. Many other manufacturing firms have improved operations through forward integration into retail and wholesale distribution and other related services. Not surprisingly, the most rapid growth is exhibited by firms that provide "producer services," i.e., accounting, marketing, transportation, financial, and leasing services to manufacturers (or service firms) that lack the necessary internal resources and expertise.

Competitiveness, whether in manufacturing or in services themselves, is becoming increasingly dependent upon service excellence, not just product design. Changes in both technology and customer expectations have increased the interaction between customers and manufacturers; thus, a "service orientation" permeating the entire organization is becoming more crucial. With the lines blurring between manufactured product and service component, the dependence of manufacturing on quality services is increasing.

Common Myths Regarding Services

In addition to the characterization of services as "postindustrial," both the professional literature on services and the popular press perpetuate several common myths about the nature of services that obscure understanding of the dynamics of the service sector. While most services are "intangible" in the sense that they represent a productive *process,* other characteristics normally associated with services are in fact inaccurate generalizations on dimensions that are relevant to all economic activities.

Services as "Labor Intensive." Many people associate "services" only with those "personal services"—i.e., cleaning, repair, child care—that are typically labor intensive. However, R. E. Kutscher and J. A. Mark reported as early as 1983 in the *Monthly Labor Review* that service industries comprised nearly half of the top 20 percent of the most capital-intensive industries in the United States. One only has to think of the infrastructure services—transportation, communications, utilities—to understand why that should be so. In virtually every country worldwide, the major percentage of gross fixed capital formation is in the service sector—again a reminder that service firms are responsible for purchasing the majority of capital equipment.

One of the major advantages of services is the flexibility with which they may be produced—either with the use of capital equipment or in a labor-intensive fashion. For developing countries, this means that the service sector can serve as a cost-effective means of absorbing and employing excess labor. But for a country such as the United States, a labor-intensive service production style is a matter of choice—a corporate decision based on market niche considerations.

Services as "Perishable." Much has been written about the inability to "store" or "inventory" services, with the classic example being usually that of a plane taking off with empty seats that then cannot be sold. In reality, the empty seats on a plane are not examples of perishable products but rather of poorly utilized production capacity. The plane is merely part of the equipment used to produce the service of transportation. The capacity management issues of matching demand for the flight with the number of seats available are precisely the same as those in best utilizing machinery in a factory production run.

Services as "Simultaneous." One of the most common myths about services is that they must be produced and consumed at the same time, thus making it impossible to trade services at a distance. However, simultaneous production and consumption (known in the public administration literature as "coproduction") is only one of several methods by which services can be produced. Many professional services—e.g., legal, accounting, advertising, maintenance, and repair—are more easily performed *without* the customer present. Few accountants, for example, are eager to have clients looking over their shoulders, and many garages prohibit customers from entering repair bays. New technology in telematics (telecommunications plus informatics or computers) has made many services "transportable" in a manner not formerly possible. Even activities such as health services, where face-to-face interaction between patient and physician was assumed to be essential, can now be delivered from thousands of miles away. For example, Canadian doctors diagnose and prescribe medication for patients in the Caribbean over telematic links that provide the doctor with detailed information about the patient; the communication can even be interactive in nature.

Self-service is an increasingly common production method that provides both customer and producer with more flexibility in the production process. The "decoupling" of production and consumption has gained momentum as machines designed to be operated by customers—from photocopying machines to car washes to stamp dispensers—have become more common. Service firms have been able to both increase customer satisfaction (through increased control over timing and place of delivery) and decrease labor costs by factoring in customers as "unpaid workers."

Services in the U.S. Domestic Economy

In the United States, over 70 percent of gross national product (GNP) has been produced by service industries since 1960, while over 70 percent of the work force is engaged in service occupations. To many, such figures represent a "deindustrialization" of the economy, i.e., a decrease in the importance of the industrial/manufacturing base of the U.S. economy. In actuality, growth in manufacturing and in services has increased at approximately the same rate. The change that has

occurred has been in employment opportunities. Over 80 percent of new jobs have been created by service firms, while
millions of jobs have been rendered obsolete in the manufacturing sector by new technology.

What is not commonly known is the fact that the United
States has *never* had a manufacturing-based economy. The
highest percentage of GNP stemming from manufacturing was
34 percent in 1943 at the height of World War II military
production; usually, the percent of GNP from manufacturing
hovers around 25 percent. Furthermore, the United States is
not the only nation to have achieved the status of a world
economic leader through services. Japan moved from being an
agricultural economy to a service economy at the turn of the
twentieth century, with over 50 percent of GNP from services
by 1960. Indeed, one could credit the strength and integration
of the Japanese services infrastructure as a major factor in
Japan's success in exporting manufactured products.

A major source of inaccuracy regarding the U.S. economy is
the invisibility of services in statistical reporting (or the over-
emphasis on manufacturing and agriculture). In the 1986 *U.S.
Industrial Outlook,* for example, 58 percent of the chapters were
devoted to various manufacturing industries that comprise
just less than 25 percent of the U.S. economy.

While GNP figures list "agriculture" and "manufacturing"
(each of which comprises thousands of different industries),
the service sector is reported in a disaggregated fashion—e.g.,
"construction," "transportation," "wholesale/retail"—further complicated by the fact that "social, community, and personal" services are typically labeled just "services." To the
naive reader, then, the service sector appears to be less than
20 percent of the U.S. economy. The *Christian Science Monitor*
made such an error in a 1985 article wondering why there was
so much attention being focused on services, which comprised
"less than one-third" of the U.S. economy.

Productivity in Services. Probably the most damaging mis-
perception about service industries is the accusation that they
are not productive, or at least not as productive as manufactur-

ing. As a result, the formulation of industrial policy, both in the United States and abroad, has focused primarily on stimulating manufacturing rather than service sector growth. The common assumption has been that any necessary services would develop automatically. It is interesting to note, however, that Japan *has* addressed services from a policy perspective, having decided several years ago to focus on world leadership in services and high-tech industries while moving sunset manufacturing industries (e.g., automobiles) offshore—including to the United States.

One reason services are often considered nonproductive is because of their association with an apparently bureaucratic and sluggish public sector. Private sector enterprises in the United States, however, far outweigh the public sector. Productivity gains are difficult to determine in the public sector due to the practice of recording public sector output at input factor prices instead of using market price equivalents. For example, the value of a public health clinic would be determined by the costs of labor and materials used rather than by actual value added, as would be the case in private sector health services.

Furthermore, since tons of steel are much more easily counted than the output of attorneys or accountants, national account statistics in the United States have grossly underestimated the value of private sector services. Government statisticians have resorted to plugging in workers' earnings as a proxy for the value of their output in 20 percent of private sector service categories—once again making productivity gains statistically impossible to calculate.

The service productivity issue thus remains plagued by measurement problems that have yet to be resolved. At the macroeconomic level, examination of static ratios of a percentage of GNP produced by a given percentage of the work force does result in figures indicating that the service sector is not particularly productive. However, examination of the marginal increase in GNP produced by each new worker in the service sector reveals a considerably higher productivity rate.

But a more serious issue in the productivity debate is one of definition. Virtually all of the measures currently used are based on the quantity of output, not the quality. In manufacturing, quality is assured by discarding defective products. But in services, no screening process exists to weed out "imperfections"; thus all service products count "equally." In other words, if bank teller A serves ten people during a thirty-minute period in a brusque manner, that teller is recorded as being more productive than teller B, who serves five customers with greater interpersonal sensitivity and increased customer satisfaction.

Value Added in Services. Since productivity measures normally used in manufacturing are inappropriate in determining the true worth of services, it may be more suitable to look at comparative figures in value added. In the United States, services account for 70 percent of total value added, as opposed to 6 percent and 24 percent in the extractive and manufacturing sectors, respectively. In the European Communities (E.C.) by 1981 the share of gross value added by manufacturing had shrunk to less than 26 percent, while that of "market" (private sector) services alone had risen to almost 43 percent.

A 1986 issue of *Business Week* deplored the proliferation of the "hollow" corporation, one in which a self-contained production base is deemphasized and virtually every function is contracted out. What the authors of the article failed to realize was that firms providing subcontracted functions, primarily service organizations, were adding the greatest value to the final product in elements that could not be inventoried— namely, convenience, speed, security, and, most importantly, flexibility. In Japan, where services account for over half of GNP, policy makers do not expect to raise productivity levels (as traditionally defined) in the service sector. The Japanese have long realized, thanks to the work of W. Edwards Deming, that added value is created through human elements as opposed to physical processes.

Perhaps one reason for the denigration of the "hollow corporation" stems from the fact that U.S. firms have typically not had satisfactory relationships with suppliers when subcon-

tracting services. If those subcontractors do not deliver quality
services, then how good is the value added? In order to control
quality, U.S. firms had typically elected to provide services
in-house when possible.

Employment in Services. Over three-quarters of U.S. citizens
work in the service sector, and the trend is virtually guaranteed
to continue. The June 1987 issue of *Business Week* reported no
turnaround in the decline of manufacturing employment,
while job growth in services accounted for the majority of new
jobs. Service sector employment opportunities increased by 1
million in just the first half of 1987, and U.S. Labor Department projections claim services will provide 90 percent of all
new jobs by the year 2000.

Some critics claim that the new jobs in services are not really
new, but are rather a result of industrial restructuring toward
the externalization of service functions. For example, when a
manufacturing firm hires an accountant from the outside to
replace an in-house accountant, one job is lost in the manufacturing sector and one is gained in the service sector. But what
of it? Externalization allows manufacturing firms much more
flexibility, lowers fixed costs, and allows externalized service
firms to specialize and gain economies of scale.

Contrary to popular belief, service sector job creation has
not been only in wholesale and retail activities such as fast-
food, but has been also in high-quality professional and high-
technology fields such as finance, insurance, real estate, and
telecommunications. Most service work is not menial and
poorly paid. Rather, services are far more involved with "information" than "personal service." A 1984 U.S. government
report noted that more than 60 percent of U.S. employment
was in some type of information occupation such as education,
computer programing, accounting, or management.

Spectacular service sector job growth in the last two decades
allowed the U.S. economy to absorb the great flood of workers
that entered the market as a result of the baby boom, the
increase in single-family households, and women employed

outside the home. In the fifteen years after 1965, the service sector provided 27 million new jobs—a 37 percent increase. As a result, even with a phenomenal 40 percent growth surge in the labor force between 1965 and 1980, unemployment in the United States rose only 2.5 percent.

A service economy, just as a manufacturing economy, does generate a number of unskilled jobs. These positions, however, are necessary in a society where there are unskilled workers needing such jobs. Over 14 percent of the U.S. work force has only an elementary school education. Those critical of the service economy are quick to point out the multitude of entry level positions in service industries as evidence of the lack of productivity in service economies. However, such positions provide employment not only for unskilled workers but also for the thousands of unemployed youths seeking part-time or summer employment, for new workers needing initial work experience, for parents wishing to work part-time, and for retired persons wanting a change and some additional income.

It is commonly assumed that compensation is poor in services. This assumption is used to support the argument that transferring workers from the manufacturing sector to the service sector will lower overall wages in the United States and lead to a decline in the standard of living. Here again, the error lies in accepting the wage rate of the "services" category as representative of all service industries, instead of taking into account wage rates in finance, construction, transportation, and other service industry categories. In 1982 business services averaged wages of $13,458—above the national average per capita GNP of $13,160—and professional services paid almost twice as well. Many workers who transfer from skilled positions in manufacturing, however, are (for all intents and purposes) unskilled workers in services and cannot expect more than minimal wages unless retrained.

The real problem may be that strong unions in manufacturing have pushed wages for many skilled positions well above the wage level for service professions. One could question the appropriateness of a wage scale in which steel workers earn

more than school teachers. In a service society where competitiveness depends upon a skilled and literate work force, education should have a very high value.

Many service firms are assumed to limit wages to a minimum
level through continual worker turnover. Service industries,
however, have already discovered that it is more economical
to retain and promote trained, quality conscious workers than
it is to continually recruit and train new workers. Burger King,
for example, has college scholarships available to students
who have performed well for the corporation while in high
school and wish to advance in the corporation.

Misconceptions about the desirability of service occupations
have resulted in a mismatch between the jobs currently flood-
ing the labor market and the people available to fill them.
While statistics on high unemployment in the United States
were rampant in the spring of 1986, thirty-one public and
private service corporations set up tables in an Atlanta hotel
in an attempt to fill over 2,000 white collar jobs. Service firms
are desperately in need of employees with new abilities, especially computer and word processing skills. At the present
time, the effects of service labor shortages are most evident in
low-wage, low-skill occupations; but the impact of the labor
shortfall has already spread to more skilled service occupations. For example, a national hospital chain is presently confronted with a three-month delay in finding new computer
programmers and systems analysts for the company.

The shortage of qualified people to fill service jobs may
eventually serve to silence critics who claim service employment is poorly paid, as the shortage is putting upward pressure
on salaries. Higher salaries will make service occupations more
attractive to those workers previously reluctant to make the
transition from employment in manufacturing to employment
in services.

Services in U.S. Trade

The United States has been an exporter of services since the
nineteenth century when it developed a strategic position

transshipping commodities and goods to and from England and Europe. From 1977 to 1982 both merchandise and services exports grew at approximately the same average annual rate—13 percent and 14 percent, respectively. Growth rates dropped considerably after 1982—to 3 percent and 6 percent—but services exports were still growing twice as fast as merchandise exports.

Unfortunately, any services trade data must be viewed with caution. The newer high-growth services are often not captured in the balance of payment statistics, and services traded by subsidiaries of manufacturing conglomerates are typically reported in the merchandise account. In attempting to explain the growing global discrepancy in the service trade account, a 1984 Organization for Economic Cooperation and Development (OECD) study found that the problem was in an underreporting of services exports; for example, a detailed analysis of Norway's service trade accounts showed underreporting of 40 percent.

The U.S. services trade statistics are far from perfect. A 1986 special report by the Office of Technology Assessment estimated that 1983 services exports were actually between $67 to $84 billion—an underreporting of 100 percent. In addition, the report estimated that overseas affiliates of U.S. firms earned revenues of as much as $97 billion in 1983. For 1984 services exports were estimated to be almost half the volume of merchandise exports; and the balance in the services account was estimated at a surplus of $14 billion.

The Role of Service Imports. While service imports from the United States have been common in most countries, service imports into the United States were relatively uncommon until the 1980s. Since 1982 the major growth areas have been in financial services, transportation, and retail trade; however, imports have remained well ahead of exports.

To a great extent, the growth of service imports into the United States in the early 1980s has been simply a result of foreign exports "catching up" to the U.S. level of exports. The current U.S. competitive position in services cannot be consid-

ered unfavorable, as many U.S. service transnational corporations (STNCs) still continue to dominate international markets. For example, even in 1986 when Japanese banks were
flush with assets, Citicorp remained the most profitable bank
worldwide.

In addition to services trade, the effects of foreign investment in the United States must also be taken into account
because the boundaries between trade and investment are
becoming increasingly blurred. Foreign investment is especially critical when speaking of the service sector, since many
service firms must be present in the foreign market to deliver
their service. By 1980 almost half of all foreign direct investment in the United States was in services; and over 85 percent
of all foreign owned establishments in the United States were
service firms.

Average pay to U.S. workers in foreign owned service firms
in 1982 averaged $21,166 annually—half again as much as in
U.S. owned service firms. Although some may fear a negative
impact from foreign direct investment in the U.S. service sector, foreign service firms appear to have helped raise the standard of living in the United States. With the changes in telematic technology, however, foreign service firms will no
longer need to be established in the U.S. market in order to
provide services to U.S. citizens. The benefits of establishment, such as wages and taxes paid, will only continue to
accrue if the U.S. investment environment is attractive to foreigners.

Expansion of U.S. Service Transnationals. U.S. STNCs grew
internationally after World War II in large part by following
U.S. manufacturing transnationals overseas in order to retain
them as clients. Initially, few STNCs had conscious international market development strategies.

But continued growth for U.S. STNCs has now become
linked to the ability to develop local clients in those foreign
markets. Therein lies the difficulty. While U.S. banks can enter
Taiwan, for example, and service the U.S. firms there, they are

not allowed to offer services to the Taiwanese, a policy that elicits cries of protectionism from the U.S. banks. At the same time, U.S. domestic markets for certain services (e.g., insurance) are becoming saturated, making U.S. STNCs more dependent than ever on foreign markets and consequently more sensitive to any apparent nontariff trade barriers.

The major change in the competitive environment of international services has been the increase in foreign competition. Until the early 1980s, U.S. STNCs had virtually no competition abroad. European firms established in foreign markets had generally entered during colonial rule. As colonies gained independence after World War II, such firms either withdrew or were nationalized. Japan did not begin focusing on service exports until the early 1980s, and so U.S. firms encountered little competition.

The Present Competitive Position of U.S. STNCs. Despite a slowing in U.S. services export statistics, U.S. service transnational corporations continued to dominate world markets at the end of 1985. The "Big Eight" accounting firms controlled much of the world market directly or through joint ventures. U.S. advertising firms still controlled the bulk of agency billings worldwide, and U.S. airlines accounted for over two-thirds of the global revenues of the top ten airlines. Although only three U.S. banks were among the top twenty banks worldwide at the end of 1985, their asset levels were higher than average, and Citicorp was number one. Similar examples can be found in many other service industries.

U.S. STNCs not only dominate markets numerically, but they are often viewed as industry leaders. In Asia Citibank is viewed as the premier training ground for bank personnel, and Turkey is establishing a training center for its bankers that will be modeled after the Citibank training program in Athens. Ironically, U.S. service firms sometimes have a more prestigious image abroad than in our domestic market. For example, McDonald's is viewed as having set quality standards in food handling and service provision worldwide.

Understanding the Relative Competitiveness
of U.S. Service Exports

In 1982 the U.S. current account was in surplus—not because of manufacturing strength, but because of a substantial surplus in services trade and investment income. The United States has depended for years on strength in services and on revenues from foreign direct investment for a positive trade balance. It must be pointed out that 31 percent of revenues from foreign investment are actually revenues from U.S. service firms established in other countries. The U.S. position as the largest debtor nation in the world by the end of 1986 stemmed primarily from a rapidly increasing deficit in the merchandise account coupled with a small deficit in services:

	Balances in 1982	Balances in 1985
Merchandise	$ −36.4 billion	$ −124.4 billion
Nonfactor Services	$ 7.4 billion	$ − .5 billion
Investment Income	$ 29.5 billion	$ 25.2 billion

Of the nonfactor services traded, the U.S. had a surplus of at least $5.2 billion by the end of 1985 in the newer "other services"—including professional services, telecommunications, etc.

Traditional Explanations

The traditional explanations given for the decline in the competitive position of U.S. service exports have all been external, i.e., someone else's fault. Some claim that the strong dollar discouraged purchase of U.S. services. Others claim that increased protectionism in foreign markets closed trade doors to U.S. firms. Still others claim that the U.S. market is too "open," thus allowing foreign service firms to invade the U.S. market rather easily. Examining each assertion in turn, we can see that such external explanations are simply not adequate to explain the decline in U.S. services competitiveness.

Strength of the U.S. Dollar. While it is true that the dollar was strong during the early 1980s, trade in services was not affected in the same manner as trade in goods. The majority of U.S. service exports were being sold through subsidiaries in local markets, making the strength of the dollar virtually irrelevant.

Protectionism in Foreign Markets. There is little evidence that foreign protectionism in services rose in the early 1980s. In all economies, service industries have traditionally been regulated by the government in order to ensure a viable economy, access to vital services for all citizens, a degree of quality control, and preservation of cultural integrity. Most developing countries' governments simply do not pay enough attention to services to impose stringent regulations.

U.S. complaints about foreign protectionism have focused in particular on the Canadian and Japanese markets, even though both countries were net importers of services from the United States between 1982 and 1986. Protectionist measures cited by U.S. firms included quotas for foreign banks in Canada and preference for local construction firms in Japan— forms of protection that had been practiced for decades. When the Japanese foreign minister was asked by the U.S. government to deregulate the Japanese banking and telecommunications sectors, he noted that the U.S. government was pressuring Japan to enact changes in months that have taken years to achieve in the United States.

The one market where "protectionism" was predicted to increase was in the E.C., because of its plan to achieve internal integration of its services market by 1992. This plan could entail preferential treatment to firms from E.C. member countries; however, by the end of 1985 there had been no demonstrable decrease in world services exports to E.C. member countries.

Openness of the U.S. Market. The third rationale given for
the decrease in U.S. competitiveness is that the large U.S.
market is an open one (or at least the most open in the world),
and that other countries have taken advantage of that openness to export large quantities of services to the United States.
In reality, the U.S. market is not that open. The small nation
of Singapore, for example, has a more open environment than
does the United States.

Virtually every form of regulation confronted by U.S. firms
in foreign countries also exists in the United States. For example, the Japanese have been complaining for years about the
unfairness of a thirty-year-old treaty covering the rights of
airlines to carry passengers between the two countries. A more
glaring example is the U.S. derogation in the OECD Code of
Invisibles that claims the U.S. shipping industry must be protected as an infant industry. Moreover, in the United States,
most services are regulated at the state, not the federal, level;
therefore, a foreign service firm exporting into the United
States must deal with fifty sets of regulations. Just as in countries criticized by the United States, preference in the United
States is usually given to U.S. firms for government construction and research contracts at all government levels—local,
state, and federal—and government contractors must "buy
American."

Protectionism in the United States

Unfortunately, the United States has chosen to cling to traditional explanations rather than to accept responsibility for
diminished competitiveness in services. Thus while Japan and
many of the developing countries have internationalized their
economies, the United States has ironically responded with
bilateral and protectionist policies that have reduced the degree of internationalization of the U.S. economy. Legislation
that requires the president to retaliate against those countries
that run large trade surpluses with the United States is based
on two mistaken beliefs: (a) that trade deficits are caused primarily by the unfair trade practices of other countries; and (b)

that bilateral trade surpluses of other countries are evidence of their deceit.

All countries must expect to run deficits in some current accounts, but those deficits need to be offset by surpluses in other accounts. Japan, for example, has trade deficits in raw materials and food products. Unfortunately, the United States is running trade deficits in virtually all categories except "other services." Although congressional debates imply that the size of a country's trade surplus with the United States is directly correlated with the degree of protection in its markets, there is in actuality little relationship. The five countries with which the United States had the largest deficits in 1986—Japan ($59 billion), Canada ($23 billion), Taiwan ($16 billion), the Federal Republic of Germany ($16 billion), and the Republic of Korea ($7 billion)—are not necessarily the countries with the most unfair trade practices.

What U.S. policy makers often forget is that the United States ran continuous trade surpluses with the rest of the world during the eighty years up to 1971 while claiming to be the world's most open market. In 1975 the United States had the largest current account surplus ($18 billion) of any OECD country. If the ten countries with which the United States had the largest surpluses had implemented policies similar to those debated in 1987 by the U.S. Congress, the immediate effect would have been a loss of $16 billion in U.S. net exports as its trading partners sought to balance their bilateral accounts. If all the countries with which the United States had surpluses followed suit, the United States would have been left with a current account deficit of $9 million.

Japan has taken a more realistic approach. The Japanese External Trade Organization (JETRO) concedes that Japan cannot continue to increase its share of the world market in terms of GNP and export sales. The Japanese are convinced that economic growth in Japan depends upon the expansion of the world economy as a whole. Already threatened by increased competition from the newly industrializing countries (NICs) and other developing countries, the Japanese believe their ability to stay competitive in international markets is dependent to a great extent on international cooperation. Any trade wars with the United States or other nations that limit Japanese exports would further aggravate the unemployment problems that Japan has begun to experience.

Complacency as the Root Cause of Diminished U.S. Services Competitiveness

The real issue is not primarily the quality of U.S. service exports or even factors in the global trading environment. Our greatest weakness lies in our complacent attitude toward our position as a world leader, and the assumption that our leadership role—particularly in services—will continue with virtually no effort on our part. While most successful U.S. service firms have recognized and responded appropriately to changes in the competitive environment, many U.S. industry leaders and policy makers have assumed rather arrogantly that we will always be "the leader."

Disregard for National Development Needs. Over the years, a number of U.S. STNCs have become accustomed to developing markets as they pleased without regard for the national priorities, cultural values, or development goals of the nations where they were conducting business. When their only clients were U.S. manufacturing transnationals, such an attitude might have been excusable. But when wishing to develop local clientele, such an attitude typically results in local government restrictions being imposed—quite understandably.

All too often, U.S. STNCs have operated as though development needs were unrelated to their activities. For example, U.S. accounting firms have been operating in Taiwan since the establishment of the nationalist regime. Despite the strong political links between the two countries, there has been so little "technology transfer" that in 1985 there was only one Taiwanese accountant for every 38,000 persons (compared with one to every 707 persons in the United States or one to every 625 persons in Singapore). While the U.S. accounting firms could have played an active role in training and development of Taiwanese accountants rather than simply having U.S. accountants provide the services, relatively little has been done.

A more serious consequence of U.S. complacence has been that of limiting exports from developing countries, thereby depriving these countries of badly needed foreign exchange earnings. For example, U.S. advertising firms have established offices in many developing country regions and then "divided up the territory," providing only domestic or limited regional services. Consequently, few services are exported because the subsidiary of a U.S. advertising agency located in, say, Indonesia would not compete against another subsidiary of the same firm located in Thailand.

Disregard for Rights of National Governments. Worse than the assumption of U.S. superiority has been a belief held by many U.S. executives and government officials that U.S. service firms have a *right* to be established in foreign markets. Rather than viewing themselves as guests of a host government, U.S. service firms often consider the market as theirs for the taking. Then when regional groups such as the E.C. or the Association of Southeast Asian Nations (ASEAN) plan to create preferential service trade groups, U.S. STNCs denounce such actions as "unfair." Yet the markets controlled by regional trade groups do not even begin to match the size of the U.S. domestic market.

In 1986 the U.S. government was pressured by domestic insurance firms to threaten retaliatory action against the Republic of Korea unless U.S. insurance firms were allowed to enter the Korean market. As a result of a saturated domestic market, U.S. insurance firms needed to expand internationally and assumed they had a right to enter Korea. The Koreans eventually bowed under pressure and granted permission, thereby appeasing U.S. policy makers. Yet in actuality, Korea could render U.S. insurance operations commercially unfeasible in the country by setting up impossible admission and capital requirements. It might have been wiser to allow Korea's insurance market to expand to the point where the

public demanded greater choice and where Korean firms
would benefit from foreign competition.

Focus on Short-Term Goals. U.S. service transnationals have
also been accused of focusing on short-term profit goals instead of establishing sound long-term working relationships
with both industrialized and developing countries. As Deming
pointed out in *Quality, Productivity, and Competitive Position,*
short-term focus in the United States makes "constancy of
purpose"—an all-important factor in remaining competitive—
virtually impossible. U.S. capital markets standards are an obvious reflection of such a short-term focus; shareholder return
requirements lead to corporate financial goals that divert executive attention away from market needs.

Officials of Japanese banks established in the United States
bluntly describe their U.S. counterparts as greedy. Conversely,
Japanese banks are willing to take losses for ten years in order
to build a business in a foreign country. Their success in the
United States can be attributed in part to their long-range
strategy of offering the U.S. economy a high volume of low-
margin loans. Japanese banks, which now hold 8.4 percent of
all commercial loans in the United States, allow the U.S. government, the U.S. Treasury, and domestic businesses to borrow at much lower rates than usual. They also provided more
than $100 billion in loan guarantees and letters of credit for
U.S. states, cities, and universities in 1986. Marubeni Corporation, one of Japan's largest trading companies, recently
secured a loan of more than $350 million for National Steel at
favorable rates. A National Steel official revealed that a Japanese bank was used because of its willingness to assist the
ailing company while U.S. banks refused.

Of course, not all U.S. firms follow short-sighted policies.
McDonald's, for example, has done exceptionally well overseas because none of the over 200 franchises a year that start
operations abroad expect to turn a profit for at least five or six
years. Where franchises were operating longer than five years,
sales averaged $1.3 million a year.

Keys to Being Competitive in Services

The United States still holds the advantage in many service industries. Numerous U.S. service transnationals such as Mc-Donald's, Arthur Andersen, Citicorp, and Walt Disney Productions already enjoy a high degree of brand awareness and loyalty abroad. The largest service transnationals, unlike many domestic service firms in the industrialized countries and most in the developing countries, are highly diversified and able to use profits earned in one industry or world region to offset or subsidize losses in another. At home, the existence of a large consumer market in the United States facilitates development of specialty service firms whose service products may eventually be exported to foreign markets that desire them.

However, unless the United States acts immediately to reverse complacent attitudes and the domestic neglect of proper incentives for services quality in the face of foreign competition, the United States will lose its competitive position to countries such as the Republic of Ireland, Japan, and Sweden that are implementing programs to promote their service industries. Moreover, many of the developing countries are joining forces to integrate their service capacities, such as the telecommunications networks that link many of the ASEAN nations. The United States must develop a comprehensive plan to develop and promote the service sector, not only to accelerate growth in the service sector itself but to enable the manufacturing sector to capitalize on the strength of U.S. services abroad.

Developing the Necessary Human Resources

Since the quality of a service operation usually depends on the skill level and commitment of its employees, an effort must be undertaken to refocus the nation's education and training programs to emphasize the importance of services. In Japan, where one out of two workers is expected to be employed in the service sector by the year 2000, the Japanese "Outlook for Guidelines for the Economy and Society in the 80s" outlines current efforts to prepare the worker for the structural change to a service and information economy. Policies outlined in the handbook promote government assistance in education, training, and the placement of individuals in service industries.

Changes Needed in General Education. Much of Japan's success can be attributed to its focus on education. The United States boasts that 50 percent of its high school students go on to college, yet only 75 percent complete high school in the first place, compared to 95 percent in Japan. Moreover, U.S. twelfth-graders recently ranked twelfth or below out of twenty countries in geometry, advanced algebra, and calculus. These figures are even more disturbing considering that, in the next twenty years, the pool of eighteen- to nineteen-year-olds will decline by 25 percent, making it increasingly difficult to attract a large number of qualified candidates into institutes of higher education.

Much needs to be done to improve the quality of teaching in the United States. By 1992 more than a million new teachers will be needed in public secondary schools. Presently, it is estimated that 50 percent of all U.S. science and math teachers are not qualified to teach those subjects. It is particularly important that school curricula reflect the types of skills needed in services—information processing, computer expertise, and interpersonal skills—and that qualified teachers with appropriate technological support be available.

Changes Needed in Business Education. While the number of students receiving undergraduate and graduate degrees in business administration increases steadily, virtually none of these students leave their institutions with any practical or conceptual knowledge of services. Business curricula have traditionally ignored the role of services in the domestic (much less the international) economy, focusing instead on the importance of manufacturing. The standard texts in accounting, management, and marketing all assume that students will be working in manufacturing corporations. The unique requirements of services—where most of the students will in fact be employed—are overlooked entirely.

Business school courses, teaching cases, and models for the design of service course material must be developed in services management, marketing, accounting, operation design, quality control, and each of the other functional disciplines. In addition, attention must be paid to the management requirements of smaller business units—e.g., franchises, branch offices, entrepreneurial ventures—not just large corporations. Continuing education for employees in service firms is also crucial and a need that can be met effectively by existing business schools once services content becomes integrated into the curriculum.

Changes Needed in Job Retraining Education. Little has been done in the United States to ease the difficulties that blue collar workers and even management from manufacturing firms have in crossing the manufacturing line to fill service sector jobs. In Japan, for example, redundant personnel in the manufacturing sector are transferred into the service sector rather than laid off. The same approach could be attempted in the United States, accompanied by revised worker training programs and family care services that would facilitate the transition.

Labor laws and unemployment insurance laws must also be revised. Many states revoke unemployment benefits for those who enter a full-time training program or who relocate in search of employment, thereby creating disincentives for unemployed workers to take necessary steps.

Developing a Proactive Perspective

The recent acknowledgment of diminished U.S. competitiveness in the international arena has precipitated a host of defensive and reactive responses. Rather than passively bemoan the decline in U.S. international competitiveness, U.S. service firms need to take a proactive stance in order to remain on the leading edge of innovative service delivery.

Proaction in Market and Product Development. U.S. service transnationals that have fared well abroad have learned never to rush into a market. The United States has a great advantage over the smaller developing countries by having an established presence abroad and access to a large consumer market at home. U.S. service firms can therefore monitor general consumer responses on a large scale more easily than most countries.

The ability to conduct necessary market research does not necessarily guarantee its accomplishment, however. One domestic example of the consequences of neglecting market research was the decision of United Technologies Corporation and AT&T to dissolve ShareTech, a joint venture in the shared telecommunication services field. ShareTech expected to dazzle customers with technology, yet paid little attention to market demands. After massive investments in capital equipment, the company's sales force discovered there was no market for the service.

Thorough market and product research becomes even more crucial when designing services that are congruent with the needs of developing countries. The United States must concentrate on services that fit the needs of culturally and economically diverse nations, rather than simply on those services that performed well in the domestic economy.

Greater attention also should be given to the product life cycle of many services, which are shortened by the rapid rate of technological change and the power of mass communications. While U.S. service transnationals must be careful not to export obsolete services, they also must refrain from exporting services that overestimate the capacities and requirements of developing nations. Many developing countries, for example, have experienced difficulty in growing into highly advanced telecommunications networks that far exceed the communication needs of the country.

Proaction in Innovation. As in any sector, to stay competitive in the service sector the United States must do what it does best: innovate. While the rest of the world is often only capable of copying and applying, transnational corporations from the United States have been the primary innovators in most service industries, from the development of computer software to the conception of complex financial instruments.

Unfortunately, unlike most other countries, much of our nation's research goes toward military products such as the strategic defense initiative, and the extent of spillover benefits into service industries is not clear. Outlays in civilian R&D by private business and government are relatively small and are slipping below our competitors as a percentage of GNP. Japan and our other trade rivals, who do not have comparable defense burdens, target their R&D spending toward product and process development in high potential areas such as superconductivity, which is expected to revolutionize operations in transportation, utilities, and even health care.

Another possible area of research is that of direct marketing techniques such as television, video, and catalog shopping that bypass traditional intermediaries in the retail field. The Japanese are experimenting with a city where all shopping, other than convenience items, is being done through videotext and overnight home delivery. The United States historically has had poor response to videotext services but very good response to direct marketing systems. Perhaps the strengths of each could be combined.

There is also a great need for innovation in terms of the upgrading of services infrastructure in order to compete with the worldwide transportation and communication networks in many developed countries. Concern has been expressed by government officials and business leaders about inadequate airport, railway, road, and shipping facilities in the United States, and much of the communications infrastructure still needs upgrading. The United States will soon face greater competition from the developing countries (e.g., Singapore) that have recently been pouring massive amounts of public and private sector capital into the development of services infrastructure.

While most R&D policies in Japan and Europe focus on the "new technologies" (such as the E.C.'s ESPRIT program for European firms working in the information field), to equate the process of work only with computers, microchips, and lasers is too narrow and ignores the human element that is so crucial to a successful service operation. R&D efforts might best be directed toward the service activities that develop around the equipment.

Unlike manufactured goods, services cannot be copyrighted or patented, thus leaving any domestic or foreign firm free to copy and apply a service delivery system at will. Yet the quality of service operations relies not on equipment and technology, but on the flexibility, skill level, and supervision of employees. One market research firm estimates that it takes only three weeks after a U.S. product is introduced before it is copied, manufactured, and shipped back to the United States. But an innovative, flexible, and well-managed service operation defies easy imitation. Thus one aspect of the research component of U.S. industrial policy needs to focus on the development of employee skill and management techniques for service delivery systems that capitalize on telematic technology.

Proaction in Personnel Development. One of America's greatest export strengths is in the management of personnel in service as well as in manufacturing organizations. The restructuring of industry toward an information and service economy requires a greater mental commitment on the part of all employees to accept responsibility for the entire system rather than for narrow tasks. Such a commitment can only be elicited from employees when they feel the management, whether domestic or foreign, is considering their own needs while accomplishing the goals of the organization.

A study of 101 U.S. companies found that those that were

participatively managed outscored the others on thirteen out of fourteen financial measures. Yet in the United States 75 percent of all participative management programs fail. Failure was most often due to reluctance not on the part of employees, but on the part of management. Managers who feel they are producing acceptable results through traditional management methods are usually not interested in adapting their approach to what the local culture requires.

Transnational companies that have translated domestic methods of management to fit foreign values are usually those that fare the best. Top and middle managers of Japanese auto manufacturers in the United States appealed to U.S. value of equality by eating in the same dining hall with employees and calling them associates. In a radical departure from the traditional adversarial relationships in most U.S. firms, the Japanese consider employee management an issue of social concern rather than an extension of a production process. The Japanese style of management has achieved flexible work teams, attention to quality, and high employee loyalty.

McDonald's success abroad has been attributed to exporting not only food but management skills as well. Their strategy has hinged on the ability to infuse every store with the McDonald's devoted culture and standardized procedures. The company uses a "tight-loose" management style that tightly controls operating procedures but allows a loose approach to individual creativity. In several markets the company enlisted the aid of large partners who had a key role in helping the U.S. management team learn and transplant the organization's values.

Developing Appropriate Government Support

To date, U.S. industrial policy has provided incentives almost entirely for the manufacturing sector. Despite such an incentive bias, service firms have expanded more rapidly than have manufacturing operations. Nevertheless, as long as "industrial policy" is identified entirely with the manufacturing sector, and government officials believe that the United States is a manufacturing-based economy, it will be impossible for U.S. firms to regain a premier role in international services. The slowdown in overall growth in the United States is a direct consequence of having no coordinated plan to develop and support the service sector.

The United States might consider following a path of international cooperation similar to that of Japan, using a strengthened service sector as the major component in the "engine" of world growth. If protectionist measures in the United States precipitated any recessionary trends in Japan—which imports more products and services from the United States than France, Italy, and the Federal Republic of Germany combined—the effects on our domestic economy would be disastrous. Moreover, the Japanese eventually will be surpassed in terms of export sales by another economy. What will be the consequences if the United States chooses to close its markets to each country that becomes an economic threat to U.S. supremacy?

Public Policy Tools Needed. Even though U.S. service companies remain in the vanguard of innovation, we still associate R&D with traditional manufacturing enterprises like steel plants and high tech businesses. More than 80 percent of the benefits of the R&D tax credit accrue to manufacturing. Most product and process improvements in service industries do not qualify. R&D tax credits are needed also for service industries—especially those that may help our trade balance.

The Republic of Ireland has implemented one of the most comprehensive packages of benefits for service industries. Such benefits include the availability of venture capital and tax credit for employing and retraining persons laid off from the manufacturing sector. The U.S. service industries need incentives similar to those for manufacturing, plus unique incentives that address the particular difficulties and potentials of services.

Union Support for an Open Trading System. Rather than recognize the need for structural readjustment, competitively obsolete manufacturing industries have petitioned successfully for government protection from competition. In part, the impetus for protection has come from manufacturing sector unions that have been successful in increasing wages for male workers to a level significantly higher than that in such core industries as education.

We have much to lose from increased protection in our trading system. If trading partners retaliate, many U.S. service transnationals are potentially vulnerable as current industry leaders. In addition, protection is very expensive for both intermediary firms and final consumers. In order to remain competitive, our service firms need the widest range of intermediary services available at the lowest possible prices.

Since labor unions have been major leaders in the move back toward protection, convincing labor leaders of the gains available through a more open system will be crucial. Protectionist measures to date have not only saved far fewer jobs than they were supposed to but also have increased costs so much that the measures may well be eliminating more jobs in the long run than they have saved. Once labor leaders are convinced of this fact, they may be more amenable as they are able to penetrate service industries more effectively.

Services to Support Service Exporters. The Office of Service Industries of the U.S. Department of Commerce has made tremendous progress in documenting and analyzing key U.S. service industries. However, there still remains much more work to be done. Virtually none of the regional or embassy commercial section libraries have materials on services exports or programs for assisting service sector firms. Programs to assist small and medium-size service firms are particularly needed.

While some services trade missions have taken place, again much more needs to be done. Promoting services is strategically different than promoting goods, and expertise is needed in developing service promotion programs.

Conclusion

While selected U.S. service transnationals continue to dominate the international market for services, complacency about
U.S. leadership in services has resulted in an erosion of market
share. The United States had virtually no competition until
after 1980; but since then service firms from the E.C., Japan,
and developing countries have become aggressively more
competitive.

The United States has been particularly vulnerable to competitive pressures because of having no coordinated policy for
service sector incentives, an acceptance of mediocre service
quality, and little training for service sector workers. In order
to retain a world leadership role in service, the United States
must first accept services as an engine of growth, and then
formulate and pursue a pragmatic, comprehensive service sector policy that will enhance the competitive positioning of U.S.
service organizations and the U.S. service economy as a whole.

10

Can American Business Compete? A Perspective from Midrange Growth Companies

ARTHUR LEVITT, JR.
GORDON C. STEWART

W hile there is widespread discussion about America's competitive decline, there is no debate that it has happened. Evidence of our deteriorating international posi-

ARTHUR LEVITT, JR., has been chairman and chief executive officer of the American Stock Exchange since 1978 and is chairman of the American Business Conference. From 1969 to 1978 Mr. Levitt was president and director of Shearson Hayden Stone Inc. (now Shearson Lehman/American Express, Inc.) and was a partner in its predecessor firm from 1962 to 1969. He is a trustee of the Rockefeller Foundation and Williams College. Serving in both republican and democratic administrations, Mr. Levitt was chairman of the 1980 White House Conference on Small Businesses and a member of President Reagan's task force on private sector initiatives.

GORDON C. STEWART is vice president for public affairs at the American Stock Exchange, where he is responsible for developing the positions of the Exchange in such areas as the federal budget, international trade, and competitiveness. With academic degrees in history, political science, and directing, Mr. Stewart has combined political and theatrical interests throughout his career. Prior to 1982, Mr. Stewart was the deputy chief speech writer for President Jimmy Carter and served in the White House from 1978 to 1981. He was the original director of the play *Elephant Man* among others.

tion goes far beyond the alarming trade statistics. It can be found in our savings rates, productivity figures, education levels, and—most persuasively of all—in our standard of living. Real wages in the United States are stagnant. The U.S. investment rate is near the bottom of the industrial world. Private savings are declining. Net national savings fell below 2 percent of GNP in 1986, making huge foreign capital inflows inevitable. According to the Council on Competitiveness, average annual growth in U.S. manufacturing productivity over the last twenty-five years was but a third as high as Japan, and only a little more than half that of West Germany. Americans consumed 4 percent more than they produced in 1986.

By any reasonable measure, the United States is growing poorer vis-à-vis many of its most potent competitors. While this reality can be cloaked in massive deficits and major devaluations, such devices cannot mask forever the fact that there has been and continues to be a full-scale transfer of wealth from the United States to many other parts of the world. Indeed, these disguises only make the specter of the future more disturbing.

Common Reactions to the Competitiveness Crisis

The recitation of dismal American trade developments usually produces several responses. A perfectly reasonable one is to stress the macroeconomic problems that both cause and are caused by our competitive condition. A survey of American Stock Exchange (Amex) companies shows that 90 percent of those with overseas dealings view the general competitiveness of the United States as extremely or moderately important to their own business success, and they see the debt problem as key in either case.

On many occasions, the CEOs of American Stock Exchange listed companies and members of the American Business Conference (ABC)—a Washington-based coalition of 100 high-growth companies—have met with the president and leaders of Congress to urge their view that the federal deficit be addressed convincingly. They have expressed their support for tax increases as part of an overall budget plan.

These executives are concerned that our accumulated debt has doubled since 1982, and could increase half again in the next recession. They fear the consequences of what Lawrence Malkin describes in *The National Debt* as overall U.S. totals

so staggering as to be incomprehensible: 2 trillion dollars owed by the federal government, and rising; 1.5 trillion owed by American corporations; 1.5 trillion owed in mortgages; 500 billion in installment credit; 300 billion owed in uncollectible debts by third world banks; and, for the first time since World War I, more owed to foreigners by everyone in America than they owe us.

Most of the CEOs surveyed recognize a linkage between the federal deficit, a low domestic savings rate, heavy foreign borrowing, an overvalued dollar, and our national competitive decline—whether that is defined by deficits in current accounts, merchandise trade, net exports, or other less tangible measures. Amex-ABC companies tend to agree that credible bipartisan action on the deficit by Congress and the White House could do more for the competitiveness problem than all the caucuses, conferences, and speeches put together. However desirable macroeconomic solutions may be, no one can depend on them to be enacted, or expect to see quick results if they are.

A second, and more alarming, common reaction to the depressing state of America's competitive position, particularly to the $170 billion merchandise trade deficit, is righteous anger at foreign trade practices. There is a strong temptation to concentrate on changing our competitors' ways, since that is far less threatening than changing our own.

The midsized growth companies represented by the American Stock Exchange and American Business Conference do not believe that curbing dumping, clarifying export licensing, protecting intellectual property rights, and insisting on reciprocal market access are bad ideas. Many companies in fact have strong views on these issues. But while they believe that fair access to foreign markets for U.S. exporters is important, they are equally certain that domestic market share protection by government is not the answer to America's competitiveness quandary.

A third response to the American competitiveness problem is not to compete at all. For a variety of reasons, too many American manufacturing and services companies have simply declined to enter foreign markets. Of the top twenty U.S. exports to Japan, eleven are now commodities and raw materials, which less developed countries traditionally sell to more developed ones.

Ironically, while the United States complains about unfairness, others are rushing in to take advantage of a changing climate in Japan that favors upmarket imports. In 1986 the Common Market countries increased their exports to Japan by more than 57 percent. U.S. exports to Japan that year increased by only 12.2 percent.

Competitive Experience
in Some Economic Sectors
Runs Counter to General Trends

Before abandoning the competitive field totally to macro-economics, or being swept away by a tide of anger at our competitors, or writing off the situation as hopeless, it is worth considering that many businesses are actually competing very well right now, regardless of foreign trade barriers. Despite the real and the exaggerated problems, there are U.S. companies that have been winners in foreign as well as domestic markets for some time. A substantial number of them come from what might be called the "midrange growth sector" of the American economy. Strong evidence of such individual successes exists among the listed companies of the American Stock Exchange and the membership of the American Business Conference, both of which have been surveyed specifically on their international activities.

While American Stock Exchange companies vary widely in size, the average sales are about $200 million, with a median of about $50 million. Average market value is $154.3 million, the median $43.3 million.

To qualify for membership, American Business Conference companies must demonstrate an annual growth rate at least three times that of the economy plus inflation. The average annual revenue of ABC companies is $390 million. The median rate for job creation is about 14 percent annually.

The average annual international sales growth since 1980 for American Stock Exchange companies with overseas dealing is over 26 percent. Between 1980 and 1986, American Business Conference firms achieved an average annual growth rate in international sales of over 27 percent.

Together, the American Stock Exchange and American Business Conference companies offer insights into the competitive directions of midrange growth companies from similar but slightly different perspectives. ABC members are about equally divided among Amex, NYSE, NASDaq, and privately held firms. The Amex companies represent a wider sample, and are not as "self-selected" on the basis of annual business growth criteria. Studies of both groups were organized to provide statistics, examples, and conclusions about their experiences in international competition.

A major common finding is that Amex-ABC companies welcome international competition as a way of life for other countries and believe that it must become the real world for American companies as well. A few decades ago, goods made in the Far East were scorned as poorly made by cheap labor. Today, in too many instances, "Made In The USA" has gone from a hallmark of craftsmanship to a question mark of quality. As summarized by the Amex and ABC for The Brookings Institution, "The competitiveness problem is not just a matter of access—it's a matter of acceptance. If other nations do not covet our products, have confidence in our products, or feel comfortable with the way we sell our products, then access to their markets becomes a moot point."

Perhaps the strongest common theme between both sets of companies is that they regard global competitiveness as a major business opportunity, not a discouraging threat. The CEOs, sometimes immigrants themselves, are more likely to view the globe as one worldwide market than as separate, competing, closed nations. They tend not to make strong distinctions between their domestic and overseas operations. For them, competitiveness is not so much an issue of trade, jobs, and exports as it is of technology, investment, and world market share.

The clear conclusion is that penetration of foreign markets has become, and will continue to be, crucial to Amex-ABC companies' overall growth strategies. Essentially they prefer to enter world competition on the offense. Since world market share is more important to them than exports per se, they believe that going after their foreign rivals' markets abroad is often the best way to protect themselves at home. Abraham Krasnoff, CEO of Pall Corporation, an Amex-ABC New York manufacturer of high-tech filtration equipment, says simply, "We attack foreign competitors on their home ground by doing the job better in all aspects."

American Stock Exchange Competitiveness Survey

The American Stock Exchange companies responding who had overseas dealings reported a median annual international sales growth of 10 percent.

Further, the median percentage of total revenues they derived internationally rose from 5 to 10 percent from 1980 through 1986.

Like the ABC companies, the sector mix of Amex companies with overseas dealings is quite broad. They include traditional manufacturers such as Sealed Air in Saddle Brook, New Jersey; sophisticated national security services companies such as BDM in Virginia; high-tech companies such as Adams-Russell in Massachusetts; industrial and consumer product firms such as Hasbro, Brown-Forman, and A.T. Cross—all also members of the American Business Conference.

Annual sales growth of their international business, 1980-1986

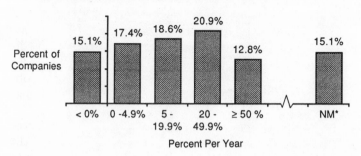

Median percent per year international sales growth, 1980-1986: 10.0%

Not calculable since they had no internationally derived revenues in 1980. These companies are excluded from the median.

In spite of their diversity, the overseas experiences of these midrange growth companies show many common patterns. Their most important foreign markets today are, in order of importance:

1. Europe—especially the United Kingdom, France, and Germany.
2. The Far East—especially Japan, Taiwan, China, Korea, and Hong Kong.
3. Canada.

In terms of future business prospects, they see most promise in the Far East, followed by Europe, with Australia, rather than Canada, third.

Since 1982 about 40 percent of all Amex companies with overseas dealings have moved production facilities offshore to cut costs, and almost 50 percent of ABC companies have moved manufacturing facilities offshore to reduce costs. Ireland, Mexico, Puerto Rico, and Taiwan were the most commonly named sites for new plants. The strong dollar also led companies to shift sources of materials and some production offshore.

Proportion in each industry with overseas dealings

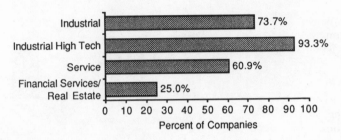

ABC Competitiveness Studies

The international management consulting firm McKinsey & Company is conducting a continuing study of ABC companies to see what clues they offer to business's part of the competitiveness puzzle. One clear finding is that competitiveness is far more than an exercise in labor cost cutting. They cite four factors of greater importance to them:

first, controlling total costs, especially for market access, capital, and taxes;
second, being flexible and willing to take entrepreneurial risks;
third, accepting that cultural bias not readily addressed by government action is the most common barrier to foreign trade; and
fourth, trade barriers as a whole are less an issue for them than ownership of foreign operations.

Whatever America's overall competitive condition may be, the CEOs studied are convinced that individually their companies can be successful abroad. They share a willingness to do what is necessary to compete. They try to translate technology quickly into value-added products and services of the best quality. And they believe they have to hustle, peddle, sell, merchandise, and market with all the energy and optimism they can muster.

Neither the ABC report nor the Amex survey is intended to offer answers for all businesses. There seems to be no catechism for competing internationally—any more than there are ten commandments for business success at home. According to William Lilley III, president of the ABC:

ABC executives are fully aware of the fragility of their international success. None are complacent about maintaining that success. Nor do they believe that their example yields easy, readily transferable lessons for industries suffering decline and job losses. If this survey is used simply to camouflage the grave economic problems confronting the United States, problems of which the lack of competitiveness is both a symptom and a cause, it will prove to be a counterproductive exercise.

General Competitive Strategies of Midrange Growth Companies

One of the major lessons from the experience of successful growth companies is that despite the glitter of some industries and the seeming ordinariness of others, broad sectors of the economy do not necessarily win—companies win. An analysis of ABC companies, which must grow each year to belong, was done by Donald K. Clifford, Jr., and Richard E. Cavanagh for their book, *The Winning Performance.* The ongoing McKinsey & Company study of these companies' overseas efforts is a continuation of that work.

More than 90 percent of the highly profitable midsized growth companies they studied went after special niches where they could offer the greatest value for their customers' special needs. For example, G. Allen Mebane took an unglamorous sector and made his company, Unifi, Inc., the leading producer of texturized polyester yarn. In a market heavy with foreign competition, about one-third of Unifi's sales are to foreign markets, including mainland China.

According to Clifford and Cavanagh, the common strategic elements in successful competition used by ABC companies include:

1. An emphasis on innovation, whether in design of new products or designing new markets for old products, to create value for the customer.
2. Believing that value—not low price alone—is what wins out.
3. Finding, creating, and servicing niches defined by customers' needs leads to growth.
4. Minimizing bureaucracy and unrelated diversification in favor of a highly motivated work force with a clear sense of the company's goals and values pays off in competitive focus.

Examples of successful competitors who have followed these strategies come from all parts of the business spectrum. U.S. companies may not make as many electronic components as some countries, but Sealed Air Corporation makes the plastic bubbles in which those components are shipped here. As CEO Dermot Dunphy describes it, "We compete internationally in the same way as we do in the United States: quality, price, and service."

Michael Jaharis scored a competitive success for Key Pharmaceuticals, an Amex-ABC company, by innovating not with new drugs themselves, but with new ways of delivering them through transdermal patches. Loctite Corporation's anerobic adhesives are more expensive by the ounce than Lafite-Rothschild or Chanel No. 5, but their many uses that CEO Bob Krieble encourages his salespeople to find and publicize result in great value to his customers. As he describes it, "We invented both our technology and our markets."

Customer satisfaction is the obsession of successful competitors. Earle Williams, CEO of BDM International, a highly sophisticated national security testing firm, likes to emphasize the importance of quality and service by using a formula. For fifteen years the company motto has been:

$$CS = RQ_2 \; TC_2$$

Customer (C) Satisfaction (S) = Requisite (R) Quality (Q+) and Quantity (Q) of Work; on Time (T) with Costs (C) Controlled (C+)

How they rate their own performance in international markets

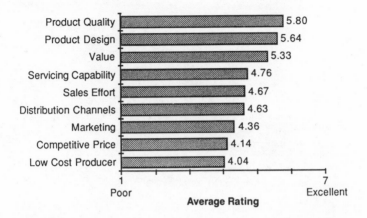

Poor
Average Rating
Excellent

Williams points out that each word has a precise meaning in the formula. "Requisite" and "on Time," for example, are there to prevent the paralysis resulting from perfectionism. While aiming always for customer sales, Williams says, "We compete by offering and emphasizing United States technology as the best in the world."

The emphasis that successful midsized growth competitors place on quality and value also can be seen in the way the Amex companies rated their performance on their own terms, and in relation to their competition.

Growth Strategies Applied to International Competitiveness by Individual Companies

Almost unanimously, the surveyed high-growth CEOs believe that overseas success requires an unswerving commitment to quality, value, innovation, service, and the ability to identify—or create—markets. Roland Boreham, Jr., CEO of Baldor Electric, an Arkansas manufacturer of electric motors, summarizes the elements in his company's successful approach: "We compete by promoting value-added products,

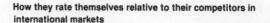

How they rate themselves relative to their competitors in
international markets

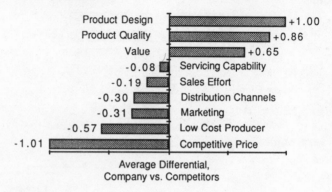

Average Differential,
Company vs. Competitors

niche marketing, better product performance, more product
variety, and by using entrepreneurial salesmen."

How They Begin Overseas Activities

In extending its research to include specific approaches to
overseas growth, McKinsey & Company finds that the successful midsized companies typically "go international" at an early
stage in their development. They like to place early small bets.
Pall Corporation, for example, began to look for international
expansion opportunities in 1960 when it had $7 million in
sales.

They do not take large long shots. Over 75 percent of their
country operations achieved profitability in two years; 64 percent in less than one year.

The push to go international typically originates with the
CEO. URS Corporation, a California engineering and con-
struction firm, penetrated Asia largely as a result of Arthur
Stromberg's own considerable commitment of time and effort.
At the beginning, he spent nearly one-half of his working time
in Asia. Additionally, on his "off-hours" he became head of the
Pacific Basin Economic Council. That position permitted him

to meet important Asian political figures—contacts that helped URS to further establish an Asian presence.

The growth companies tend to proceed on the basis of transferring their major domestic advantages to foreign operations, i.e., technology in the case of Cray Research, a concept in the case of Dunkin' Donuts, or a strong marketing approach for Brown-Forman. Eighty-two percent of the ABC executives surveyed prefer to enter foreign markets unilaterally, rather than pursue cooperative arrangements with indigenous firms. This is a logical extension of their strong sense of individual entrepreneurship.

However, in going international, the companies have shown considerable flexibility in the business arrangements they use to gain footholds in foreign markets, even though eventually they prefer total control of their foreign operations to partnerships or joint ventures. For example, when Grey Advertising began its expansion in Europe, it typically bought into existing advertising agencies. It did not insist upon complete ownership. Only after becoming accustomed to the local culture and winning the confidence of the local employees would it move toward working control and then total ownership.

How They Expand Foreign Operations from Export to Investment

Since "being close to the customer" is an axiom for so many of the Amex-ABC companies, they often share a common progression of their overseas activities—from sales, to customer service, to marketing, then on to investment in production and R&D. They even tend to follow a similar geographic route of international growth—from Canada to Britain to Western Europe to Japan.

Many companies emphasize the importance of linguistic skills for international success. W. L. Lyons Brown, Jr., learned Italian because Brown-Forman was seeking to become the distributor of Bolla Wines in the United States, and Bolla was unwilling to do business in any other language than Italian.

When Cray Research wanted to try to sell several supercomputers in France, its CEO, John Rollwagen, temporarily relocated his office there to improve his French.

To succeed internationally, Amex-ABC firms give great weight to innovative marketing strategies. Sometimes that means knowing when to capitalize upon the peculiarly American qualities of products. Brown-Forman has enjoyed considerable success in Japan with two of its consumer products— Jack Daniels and California Cooler—by exploiting Japanese fascination with American popular culture. CEO Brown stresses the importance of careful, prestigious marketing overseas: "We distinguish our products with image-building advertising and quality design and workmanship."

To a person, Amex-ABC CEOs stress the importance of hiring foreign nationals to run overseas operations. Abraham Krasnoff of Pall Corporation believes that the use of local nationals is absolutely indispensable because "the idiosyncracies of localities are profound." The accounting firm of Arthur Andersen & Company has tapped the "huge opportunities" its senior partner, Robert Philip, Jr., sees in international markets by establishing separate operating units in over forty countries managed exclusively by local personnel trained by the company.

Ninety-two percent of ABC companies' overseas operations are headed by foreigners, and one-third now have foreigners in their own top management. This is consistent with a very direct, personal approach to leadership. Overall, less than 1 percent of their staff is at corporate headquarters. CEO Daniel Greenberg's initial organization for expanding Electro Rent internationally was simple enough; he divided the world in half. He went west; his chief operating officer took responsibility for Europe.

Given their propensity to hire foreigners, these growth company CEOs stress the importance of constant communication between the home office and international offices. They use meetings, telephone calls, and other communications channels both to understand what is going on in the field and, just as important, to insure that all employees share a common sense of mission. Dermot Dunphy of Sealed Air holds numerous meetings that include both his American and international managers. His goal "is to make all my managers indistinguishable from one another except for their accents."

Other CEOs in service industries report that a foreign sales force helps them to identify business opportunities, ease crosscultural communication, and improve marketing strategies. Chairman Larry Horner of Peat, Marwick, Mitchell, & Company puts it simply, "We emphasize client services. Foreign nationals are important to that." Patrick McGovern, chairman of International Data Group, which publishes computer magazines, reports that "our international competitiveness reflects our ability to attract the best people for our overseas operations."

Dividends from Foreign Divisions— Cross-sourcing, New Product Applications, and Links Between International Operations

While globally successful companies—such as Cray Research and Genentech—are purely export oriented in the classical sense of selling the same fully American made product to many countries, most overseas success today involves investment abroad. Whether it is adapting a product to local needs (Dunkin' Donuts even changes its fillers to fit different countries' tastes), or offering a service such as accounting in the local language, closeness to the customer and the two-way benefits of competition reward companies who can operate multinationally.

Many companies benefit from substantial crosslinkages between their international operations. For example, Burndy, a producer of electronics and electrical connectors for a wide range of industrial markets, crossexports over one-half of its international sales because some countries' subsidiaries or affiliates have greater skills or efficiency in certain types of product design or manufacturing technology than others. These manufacturing locations become world suppliers to Burndy customers, no matter where they are. For example,

Burndy's Japanese affiliate frequently sells locally designed and produced products throughout Asia, Europe, and North America; these products are not otherwise available from Burndy facilities in those countries. Crossfertilization is further encouraged by selective transfer of personnel across markets.

Loctite's Japanese subsidiary has pioneered several applications in the electronics industry, which it regularly records on video tape and distributes to other countries. This practice has directly affected the company's responsiveness in that it permits Loctite to serve Japanese electronics companies whenever they establish offshore facilities. Thus, when Sony moved its manufacturing to Singapore, "Our people were right there to help them transfer technology." Sealed Air's bubble mask cushioned masking was initially developed by its English subsidiary to protect the body of Jaguar automobiles during assembly.

A variant of new product applications is the creativity overseas affiliates show in adapting U.S. products to foreign conditions. For Bob Rosenberg of Dunkin' Donuts, it sparked ideas on how to widen his U.S. market reach: "Our route to Penn Station was through Manila." The Philippines licensee had innovated the concept of kiosks served from a central bakery rather than full-service stores with their own on-premise bakery. "It resulted in a fundamental rethinking of our entire business operation—how we did things in the U.S." Today Dunkin' Donuts has scores of kiosk-type stores located in Zayres, major transportation centers, and other high-traffic areas where people shop, work, or play.

Companies with manufacturing facilities overseas benefit at home from foreign management abroad. According to John Gilmartin, president and CEO of Millipore, a Massachusetts maker of high-tech fluid purification products, the harshest critics of his company's products are the managers of his Japanese plant. For them, production of an absolutely superior product is a matter of personal honor. Many CEOs would agree with Jack Lynch, CEO of Adams-Russell Electronics, who observes: "We find our overseas manufacturing personnel, especially the engineers, much more cost-conscious than the U.S."

Crosspollination of techniques and concepts is also a positive factor in encouraging growth companies to compete overseas. J. P. Barger, CEO of Dynatech Corporation, whose products include data communications and medical instruments, observes that "maintenance of our successful domestic markets requires a fully-integrated and successful international presence in order to capture product innovations from abroad." Charles Denny, chairman of ADC Telecommunications in Minneapolis, stresses that "international competition is important as a source of revenue, diversification, and exposure to foreign technology."

Total Costs Are Key Measure of Overseas Operations

Roger Johnson, chairman of Western Digital Corporation, an Amex and ABC company, makes clear that labor and resource costs were not key to locating facilities in Cork, Ireland. He stresses instead the importance of controlling total costs. The main components of Western Digital's total costs are, in descending order of importance:

1. cost of market access/quality assurance
2. cost of capital/taxes
3. cost of customer support
4. cost of labor/manufacturing

Johnson argues that for many high-growth companies the first two costs typically dictate the location of new manufacturing facilities. Unless those costs are favorable, American labor could offer its services free and Western Digital would still move offshore. With a favorable tax rate and a net capital cost of 3 percent in Ireland, he believes it would be bad business not to relocate.

As many high-growth companies see it, the competitiveness debate in Washington assumes a labor-intensive manufacturing sector organized along traditional lines. Amex-ABC com-

panies believe that competitive manufacturing depends today
upon skillful use of capital to acquire appropriate technologies
and to train employees to put those technologies to use. Ac-
cordingly, to maintain the nation's manufacturing base, many
of their CEOs believe government should pursue economic
policies that would lead to a more favorable cost of capital, a
stable rate of monetary exchange, and a tax system that encourages savings and investment.

Nature and Cost of Capital Stressed

The cost of capital has been the subject of careful study by
George N. Hatsopoulos, chairman of Thermo Electron, an
Amex-ABC high-tech instruments and cogeneration company
in Waltham, Massachusetts. He believes, along with many
Amex and ABC CEOs, that the high U.S. cost of capital in
relation to Japan is a more significant problem than labor
costs. In testimony before the House Energy and Commerce
Committee, Hatsopoulos noted, "When you look at the
growth of labor costs in real terms, you find that current wages
in this country are almost identical to those in 1970. By contrast, Japan's real wages have about doubled over the same
period."

ABC's membership supports Hatsopoulos's view that the
cost of capital is a dominant factor where productivity and
quality are concerned. This is not to say that other problems—
such as regulation, education, and management of people—do
not exist, or that many other things cannot also be improved,
such as the reduction of trade barriers in other countries. But
even such trade barriers, as bad as they are, are less restrictive
than they were twenty years ago. The fact that we have more
severe competitive problems now indicates that something
else must have changed. According to Hatsopoulos's study,
the biggest such change is the accumulated long-term effect of
our disadvantage in the cost of capital.

ABC and Amex executives generally agree with his findings
that U.S. tax laws tend to encourage debt over equity as a

means of finance. They also believe that even greater than our costs of "fixed capital" are the costs of "knowledge capital formation"—the additional knowledge firms get through R&D, market development, and understanding the needs of their customers. This knowledge costs money, much the same as fixed capital, and it has a value that accumulates over time.

The high cost of "knowledge capital" is especially important to growth companies because over and over, in both domestic and foreign operations, their strategies involve more emphasis on being the highest quality producer than on being the lowest cost producer. As Ray Stata, a founder of Analog Devices, a maker of integrated circuits, puts it, "A lot of people seek market leadership so they can become the low-cost producers. That's hogwash. The reason to seek market leadership is to attract the top talent and have the resources to clear the brush and trailblaze the new frontiers."

One thing certain about Amex-ABC company attitudes toward capital is that they believe in "patient capital." Even though they tend to show results early, ABC companies cite a willingness to wait five years as an acceptable period before turning a profit in an overseas territory. Amex companies report a range of waiting periods.

Characterization of Success

In summary, these high-growth firms showing success abroad show several common characteristics:

1. Making international expansion an integral component of their firm's future, not a sideline.
2. Understanding that successful export strategies must often be accompanied by investment in a permanent foreign presence.
3. Focusing on the products of human capital—technology, innovation, marketing, and management—rather than trying to compete on the basis of traditional comparative advantages, such as cheap labor and economic scale.

How long it typically takes them to show a profit when they enter a foreign market

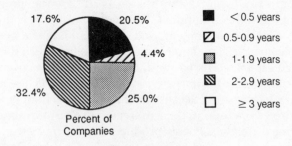

■	< 0.5 years
▨	0.5-0.9 years
▦	1-1.9 years
▧	2-2.9 years
☐	≥ 3 years

17.6%   20.5%   4.4%   32.4%   25.0%

Percent of
Companies

4. Establishing a presence abroad and competing with foreign firms on their turf to defend and enhance their position in the American market.
5. Getting close to the customer, serving growing markets efficiently and effectively, exploiting favorable capital costs, and capturing innovation.
6. Recruiting and utilizing talented foreign nationals who best understand local markets, business practice, and employees allowing companies to become melting pots of talent.

Through all of their strategies and techniques, the basic message is that for these high-growth companies international operations are not a side show—they are at the very center of their businesses.

Midrange Growth Company Views on U.S. Trade Policy

The great emphasis Amex-ABC CEOs place on individual responsibility for success in overseas competition would suggest a highly skeptical stance toward the value of retaliatory protectionism by the United States—and that is what both surveys clearly reveal. The companies raise the general theoretical objections that protectionism only escalates itself and that even if every single barrier to U.S. entry into foreign markets were eliminated, only about $20 billion to $30 billion would be cut from a trade deficit moving toward ten times that.

However, Amex-ABC CEOs also have important specific reasons for fearing trade hostilities. They point out that since their companies are already successful in foreign markets, they are the ones who will be retaliated against by foreign governments in any trade war. No one, they say, is going to punish the United States by keeping out American VCRs.

Further, these CEOs have direct experience with the global interdependence of modern commerce. Abraham Krasnoff of Pall Corporation points out that his hard-won successes in opening Japanese markets are threatened when his customers in the Japanese electronics industry are battered. He expresses the concerns of many about protectionist conflict when he points out that "we all have a stake in a healthy Japanese economy."

The survey of American Stock Exchange companies also pointed up the growing interdependence in terms of their own import needs.

Reactions to Foreign Trade Barriers

While opposed to protectionism, ABC-Amex companies identify a variety of tariff and nontariff trade barriers that impede their ability to enter foreign markets. Some of these barriers can and should be lowered through governmental action, but most of the CEOs believe that current trade laws, vigorously applied, are sufficient for the task. They prefer to focus on opportunities rather than on obstacles.

Cultural preferences formed the most common foreign barrier to trade identified by the ABC study. Under this category are grouped a number of manifestations of cultural chauvinism. These include the reluctance of talented foreign technicians and sales people to join American owned subsidiaries, the tendency of governments to rely upon local suppliers, and the unwillingness of consumers—both individuals and firms—to buy American products and services. Japan and the members of the European Economic Community (EEC) were

Proportion that import various goods and services in significant quantity

Nature of Respondent's Business

	Industrial	Industrial High-Tech	Service	Financial Services/ Real Estate
Raw Materials	29.5%	10.0%	8.7%	6.3%
Manufactured Items	34.4	33.3	17.4	6.3
Services	3.3	0	0	0

the countries most often associated with the cultural preferences barrier. The EEC was singled out for its domestic content requirements.

Tariffs constituted the second most commonly cited trade barrier. Brazil is particularly notorious for its prohibitively high tariffs. Korea and Japan also were faulted on this score.

Discriminatory regulatory standards, a problem associated almost exclusively with Japan, was the third most commonly cited trade barrier. This category encompasses a variety of unpredictable, prejudicial, or unevenly applied regulatory policies. One example is Japan's lengthy patent process. It effectively blocks the introduction of innovative products until local firms have had time to catch up. Other executives cited instances in which their products were rejected by Japanese authorities for seemingly irrelevant reasons such as "improper" packaging.

Additional foreign trade barriers identified were: data flow restrictions, discriminatory tax policies, prohibitions against the repatriation of capital, and technology transfer requirements.

Export Licensing Cited

Not all trade barriers are of foreign origin. ABC companies believe the export licensing system, which is designed to prevent the export of strategically sensitive technology and is administered by the American government, has placed over half of them at an international competitive disadvantage. The process for obtaining an export license was described as un-necessarily cumbersome, and marked by squabbling between the Departments of Commerce and Defense.

The delay can cost sales, since other nations tend to admin-ister their export licensing programs far more efficiently. For example, it takes the U.S. government an average of 145 days to issue an export license for a Cray Research supercomputer. The government of Japan licenses the export of Japanese supercomputers in 30 days.

John Rollwagen, chairman of Cray Research, Inc., notes:

When U.S. high-technology manufacturers lose their market share, they lose precious revenue to continue their research and develop-ment. Without that revenue for R&D, U.S. corporations will lose their preeminent standing and the country will become dependent on for-eign manufacturers for critical technologies.

The Special Case of Japan

By a two-to-one margin, ABC companies identified Japanese companies as their fiercest competitors. By a similar margin, they named the Japanese market as the most resistant to entry. Both observations are part of the same phenomenon: twen-tieth-century Japanese mercantilism. In order to underwrite their international ventures, Japanese firms rely upon their domination of a secure home market.

As ABC executives see it, American penetration of the Japa-nese market is vital to meeting Japan's competitive challenges around the world. At issue is how best to open the Japanese market to American business. While the barrier the CEOs cite overwhelmingly is cultural preference, they believe that over-coming such chauvinism is essentially a function of the will and skill of American managers. They feel that unless American business as a whole makes the necessary investment in quality, service, innovation, and strategic marketing, it will never be-come fully competitive in Japan.

High-growth companies do not argue that the American government has no role to play in opening the Japanese mar-

ket. Some Japanese trade barriers can only be eliminated, or
at least mitigated, through diplomatic pressures. Further, having seen some of the brightest American growth companies of
a few years ago, such as those in the semiconductor industry,
succumb to Japanese targeting, neither Amex nor ABC executives are prepared to have the government abandon the field
of battle.

Nevertheless, the ABC leaders surveyed argue that government can best help American business penetrate the Japanese
market by reducing the federal debt, establishing a sound
monetary and tax policy, and encouraging intelligent regulatory and educational reforms. They believe government must
place the central responsibility for American competitiveness
in Japan and elsewhere upon the shoulders of American business.

The American Stock Exchange companies surveyed also
found Japan to present the most difficult obstacles to entry. In
particular they cited such elements as language, culture, the
tendency to prefer local products, the practice of local companies copying U.S. products, and difficulties with Japanese
banking and financing practices. Technology transfer problems also were listed, as were Japanese government regulations such as difficulty in obtaining patents, delay in approving
medical products, and inflated quality testing requirements.

The next most difficult country the Amex companies cited
was China, where the problems centered more on that country's relative shortage of foreign exchange and lack of direct
experience with high technology. In Germany they found the
chief obstacle to be general cultural preferences for local products.

Possibilities for U.S. Monetary, Trade, and Tax Policy

In terms of public policy, Amex companies agree with their
ABC colleagues that the most important role for government
is in fiscal policy, exchange rates, and broad social concerns.
About half of the Amex executives believe that the federal

deficit, the related high real interest rates, and overvaluation of the dollar are the most important causes of our record trade deficits. Almost 30 percent cited lack of American business competitiveness as the most important cause, and only about 20 percent listed foreign trade barriers.

In terms of the future, fewer than 20 percent of the Amex companies favor further reductions in the dollar. In fact, 70 percent would support an international review of the monetary system to provide for more stable exchange rates.

On the highly sensitive and controversial issue of U.S. responses to foreign trade barriers, the larger Amex sample differs somewhat from the ABC CEOs'. While only 5 percent favor a general increase in U.S. trade barriers, over 75 percent would support an increase against countries that erect barriers against U.S. products and services.

Some interesting sector differentials show up in Amex views of current U.S. trade policy.

Sector differences also appear in answers to what Amex CEOs believe to be the most important barrier to foreign markets for U.S. products and services. Only 8 percent of the high-tech companies cited lack of price competitiveness, while 40 percent of the industrial companies put it first. "Cultural chauvinism" was ranked first by 37 percent of the high-tech companies, followed by poor U.S. marketing at 31 percent. Only 12 percent of the industrial and 14 percent of the service companies placed cultural obstacles first.

The high-technology view of Amex-ABC companies is well summed up by Stephen R. Levy of Bolt Baranek and Newman, a Massachusetts company specializing in R&D products and services that is a member of both organizations. He notes that with a 1986 deficit of $150 billion, our trade balance in manufactured goods is the largest component of the merchandise trade deficit.

Levy warns that while our high-technology exports have been growing in both unit and dollar volume—rising from 30 percent of manufactured goods exports in 1980 to nearly 50 percent in 1986—even with this growth the United States has become a net importer of high-technology goods for the first

How they would like government policy to be structured

	Industrial	Industrial High-Tech	Service	Financial Services/ Real Estate	Total
Favor a Further Reduction in the Dollar	16.9%	24.1%	14.3%	15.4%	19.7%
Favor an Overhaul of the International Monetary System to Provide for More Stable Exchange Rates	70.4	63.3	65.0	84.6	69.3
Believe the Current U.S. Response to Foreign Trade Barriers is:					
Excessive	8.6	3.3	13.0	21.5	9.6
About right	44.8	26.7	26.1	28.5	35.2
Too weak	46.6	70.0	60.9	50.0	55.2

Nature of Respondent's Business

time. Clearly, says Levy, U.S. high-technology industries may have been victimized by our overall industrial competitiveness problem as much as older manufacturing sectors.

On the national fiscal level, ABC and Amex CEOs share a concern about the widening gap between the nation's total spending and total savings. They are particularly troubled that the growing difference between what we spend and what we produce creates an international indebtedness of over $500 billion, leading to $1 trillion by the early 1990s. Along with the enormous federal budget deficit increasingly financed by borrowing abroad, these developments greatly trouble Amex-ABC companies.

To help with the fiscal problem and the low personal savings rate, there is growing support for some kind of consumption tax that would raise revenue and attempt to increase the national savings rate from 2.2 percent of GNP to about 8 percent. As George Hatsopoulos testified before Congress, since the turn of the century the United States has generally paid for its investments in industry with national savings. But very recently this has changed, and by 1986 we paid for only about 40 percent through savings, even though industrial investment was a smaller percentage of GNP. To lower the deficit and increase savings, many ABC and Amex leaders believe that a consumption tax will provide the necessary carrot and stick, much as allowing the price of oil to rise did for managing energy consumption.

Competitiveness Beyond Economics

Even new macroeconomic approaches will not be sufficient, the successful international competitors of the Amex and ABC believe, if deepening social problems are not addressed as well. They fear economic progress will be inadequate and even impossible if fragmentation among business and labor, rich and poor, black, Hispanic, and white continues, or worsens.

The gap between the educational haves and have-nots seems to be getting wider. "What kind of a competitor can a society be," one Amex-ABC CEO asked, "whose people can't fill out a job application, read simple operating instructions, or mark a ballot? If the opportunities of our society cannot be spread more evenly, then the poor, the uneducated and the illiterate will become a greater drag on our national ability to compete." The future depends on those now in high school; yet the national dropout rate of American high school students is 25 percent—and rising. Today, about 23 million people in America are functionally illiterate.

The areas that most concern Amex-ABC companies are technical and linguistic education. A recent survey of math skills showed that U.S. students ranked fourteenth of the fifteen countries studied. Forty percent of thirteen-year-olds are reading below the skill level of their age. About 700,000 high school graduates cannot read their diplomas.

Amex-ABC CEOs believe that industries and countries are not the only ones who compete. Societies compete as well. And competition between societies is measured not only in the workplace, but in education, ethics and values, and in attitudes and motivation.

These CEOs feel strongly that the kind of society that lives up to its promise of equal freedom for individuals to grow will realize the fullest economic potential of its people as a whole. In their view, that is the hallmark of a competitive society and why the present competitive challenge may be the greatest America has ever faced. While pressing for economic and social policy improvements tomorrow, Amex-ABC CEOs are determined to show that American companies can compete with the best in the world as it is today.

Final Report of the Seventy-fourth American Assembly

At the close of their discussions, the participants in the Seventy-fourth American Assembly, on *Running Out of Time: Reversing America's Declining Competitiveness,* at Arden House, Harriman, New York, November 19–22, 1987, reviewed as a group the following statement. This statement represents general agreement; however, no one was asked to sign it. Furthermore, it should be understood that not everyone agreed with all of it.

Preamble

America's economy is growing more slowly than it used to, more slowly than we need it to, and more slowly than our competitors' economies. We are consuming far more than we produce and earn—and we are having growing difficulty paying the bills. Our prosperity is threatened, as is our capacity to provide world leadership and to achieve a more just and competitive society.

The evidence is unmistakable. We have the largest budget deficit, trade deficit, and foreign debt in our history. Individual debt, corporate debt, and government debt are all perilously

high, while our savings rate is among the lowest in the industrial world.

We cannot long continue on this path without profound
consequences. Economically, we risk a continued slide of the
dollar, higher real interest rates, accelerating inflation, still
slower growth, and prolonged recession at home and abroad.
Socially, we are staring at the possibility of even deeper domestic inequities than those we have allowed to fester in recent
years. Insufficient attention to the problems of the growing
American underclass will erode the capacity of the United
States to be a more competitive international society. Politically, we may well suffer increased polarization and paralysis.
Globally, as economic competition grows in importance relative to military confrontation, we face a possibly irreversible
U.S. decline, with an attendant erosion of our ability to protect
vital national interests. This would be accompanied by growing threats to Western values, influence, and prosperity, and
to democratic interests throughout the world.

In short, we are gambling recklessly with our destiny. That
we are not alone in this judgment is evidenced by the October
19th stock market crash, the ensuing turmoil in the world's
financial markets, and the broad urging by world leaders that
the United States put its house in order.

Because of these deeply troubling realities, the American
Assembly examined the governmental, private sector, and individual and societal dimensions of America's declining competitiveness. We also examined the complex connections
among these different sectors because of their importance in
getting America back on track.

Our sense of urgency results from the fading opportunities
to make the necessary changes before grave, perhaps irreparable, consequences are upon us. We recognize that the immediate future holds painful changes for us. We do not know
whether those changes will be constructive or destructive,
whether we manage the change and spread the burdens or let
random forces control us, or whether we emerge stronger or
weaker for the long-term challenges ahead.

Building on the nation's formidable strengths, this Assembly report offers a vision of what we must do, including concrete first steps to control an uncertain future and move the United States toward sustained competitiveness at home and abroad.

By this we mean that the average annual growth of the U.S. economy and of each American's standard of living must be both as fast as practical and at least as rapid as the other major industrial economies. Only then can we hope to achieve our economic, political, social, and geopolitical aims.

Our economic troubles, it should be emphasized, were primarily made in America, and the solutions must primarily be made in America as well. We should begin by enhancing the will and capacity of individuals and businesses to compete more successfully, bringing our trade and current account back into balance, and restoring our economic vitality. But the need to accomplish the foregoing does not stop at individual firms and other institutions or at our own borders. International cooperation to achieve faster and more balanced world trade and growth are also essential to improve the prospects for increasing our global competitiveness as well as producing potential gains for all nations.

I. Public Sector

Macroeconomic policies must be used to fundamentally alter our national behavior of consuming more than we produce, shifting the emphasis from "buy now, pay later" to "pay now."

In the near term, this will require difficult steps to further reduce our national budget deficit. Reductions in both domestic spending and defense outlays and increases in taxes beyond the measures adopted in November 1987 are essential to economic health and enhanced competitiveness.

On the revenue side, because of our excessive consumption relative to production, a phased-in national sales or value-added tax—with protections against regressivity—is one valuable anti-deficit weapon. A phased-in gasoline tax and suspension of the next round of individual tax reductions is another.

It should be noted, however, that a significant minority dissented from this recommendation. We should fully tax Social Security benefits to the middle and upper classes. Finally, we recommend gradually tightening the limit on home mortgage interest deductions for the middle- and upper-income taxpayers—a subsidy we can no longer afford on either economic or equity grounds. We recommend eliminating interest deductions for the part of first home mortgages above $1 million, as a means of equitably and very gradually phasing out the home mortgage deductions. We also recommend eliminating all second home mortgage interest deductions.

On the spending side, equally dramatic actions are required, again with questions of both economics and fairness at the fore. We should, for example, reduce veterans' benefits and agriculture subsidies to those who do not need them—those in the middle and upper classes who can live comfortably without them.

Cutting unnecessary defense spending must begin with reducing ineffective and inefficient weapons systems, installations, and bureaucracies. The president's steps toward arms reduction with the Soviet Union may lead to additional accords that could open the way for further restraint in defense spending. This should be coupled with greater sharing in defense responsibilities by other industrial nations.

The billions of dollars provided by all of these steps must be sufficient to meet two critical goals. First, they must reduce our annual budget deficit. Second, they should then be used to enhance our competitive position at home and abroad primarily through increased spending for civilian research and development, both basic and applied, and for retraining and education.

To further enhance the competitiveness of our private sector it would be important to accomplish this while keeping total government spending as a portion of gross national product below recent historically high levels.

With a sounder fiscal approach, monetary policy will have a greater chance of guarding against recession. On the monetary front, moreover, we suggest not relying on a declining dollar to improve our trade balance, particularly because it may weaken our will to make other changes that are critical to our longer-term position.

In any case, a reduced budget deficit by itself can be expected to have immensely beneficial effects on America's trade balance. Reducing the budget deficit also might ease protectionist pressures, which we strongly oppose, especially because foreign competition has been a major factor in improving U.S. manufacturing productivity and thus competitiveness.

Affirmative steps are needed to restore U.S. trade, not negative ones that threaten to diminish all of our futures. We need new and creative international economic statesmanship and cooperation. We need more balanced global trade and growth. (Surplus nations, especially Germany and Japan in the near term, must assume more responsibility for these two goals by stimulating faster economic growth and importing more from the United States and other trade deficit nations.) We need special steps to help less developed nations that are struggling with immense debt burdens to resume faster growth, increase their distribution of benefits, and reestablish some of our important export markets.

There are times when the U.S. government should act forcefully to protect the legitimate trading rights of U.S. industries. However, in the global marketplace, as at home, we must remember that we are all in the same boat, that protectionist actions in one nation risk being answered by protectionist actions in other nations, threatening mutually assured economic destruction. That is why the leadership of the United States is so critical in achieving a more efficient, effective, and comprehensive world trading system through the successful conclusion of the Uruguay Round.

Together, all these measures not only will expand world trade for everyone but help Americans recapture a larger share of our own growing markets.

Beyond these broad budgetary and trade stances, various federal policies have indirect but profound effects on American industry, workers, and other institutions. This has long been known and accepted. What is not known is how these sometimes conflicting policies specifically affect our global competitiveness.

We therefore urge that the President's Council of Economic Advisers or the legislature's Congressional Budget Office be required to issue reports examining these existing policies and their competitive effects.

For similar reasons—as well as the need to keep the competitiveness issue on the front burner for both government officials and the nation at large—we also urge the adoption of competitiveness impact statements for all new laws, rules, and regulations adopted in Washington.

Finally, we come to the additional issue of whether and when the national government should continue to intervene explicitly in the economy in ways that help or harm specific sectors, industries, or companies. Although some strong sentiments against such practices were expressed by a good number of participants, a small majority believes that this would be appropriate for three discrete purposes related directly to economic competitiveness:

1. In cases where national security is at stake. This could mean both positive cases, as when a particular industry is deemed critical to national security, or negative ones, as when the unrestricted export of certain strategically sensitive products is deemed similarly dangerous. In the latter case, however, U.S. export control policies have been too arbitrary and have led to a declining confidence abroad in the security of contracts with U.S. companies as well as unnecessary lost export sales. Reform is necessary to improve U.S. competitiveness.

2. In cases where the evidence is unmistakable that other governments are creating significant unfair advantages for a particular industry. It should be emphasized that, even then, taxpayer aid, in whatever form, must be geared to the removal of the foreign unfair trade practice.

3. In instances where short-term government assistance would help restore a significant U.S. company or industry suffering from or threatened with serious import injury. But

this should be done only on the condition that there is a quid pro quo requiring increased capital or human investment and sufficient gains in productivity by the company or industry itself. Also, remedies should be implemented in order to minimize trade distortions and to allow the collection of revenues that might be used to finance much needed investments. Thus, tariffs or auctioned quotas should be preferred to foreign export restraints.

The reason usually given for lack of progress is political difficulty. We believe that while individual elements are indeed controversial, there exists strong political support for an overall solution. Those leaders who offer a coordinated, equitable attack on the forces that threaten our standard of living will be rewarded by the electorate. Similarly, those who only point to political obstacles to justify their inaction will be defeated.

II. Private Sector

Once leaders in the world, American companies have lost command of markets to international competitors. Though macroeconomic factors like the exchange rate and trade policies have harmed our ability to compete, a strong case was made that these problems were chiefly the result of ineffective management practices as well as a cause of other problems. There are businesses and markets in which U.S. companies no longer compete at all. Those who try to compete find that working harder is not enough, that fundamental changes are necessary.

While the entrepreneurial sector has fortunately provided our economy with its unique dynamism, the spirit of risk-taking and the ability to innovate and to anticipate the customer's wants and needs have too often been submerged by our focus on short-term goals. American management has neglected the opportunity to mobilize the knowledge of its own work force. We noted a growing bias against unions in some quarters. These have caused many companies to turn out low-quality products at high cost, when their companies were doing precisely the opposite, leaving many American managers wondering why customers began to distrust the label, "Made in the U.S.A.," or why they cannot even buy certain products with such labels.

We call for union and worker commitment to industrial competitiveness; management commitment to more cooperative, less adversarial collective bargaining relationships; and employment security for its work force. We also agreed that increased employment security requires a more mobile and flexible work force, and we urge greater public and private efforts to help workers move from redundant jobs to needed employment.

In addition, there has been an orgy of financial manipulations, which has led to speculation and takeover attempts. Wall Street has taken management's eye off the ball. The excesses of the system have contributed ineluctably to the stock market collapse.

The crash has at least shocked the system back to reality and focused the attention of U.S. business again. There is a growing realization that the broader problems of the economy will have to be solved at the level of the business firm. It is therefore fortunate that signs of light are discernible in some quarters of American business. We heard of major firms that have gone back to their fundamentals. "What is our purpose?" they have asked, and answered that it was to bring the highest quality products and services to the customer at the lowest possible cost, and thereby create jobs and improve the living standards of all Americans.

We considered a giant company that listened once again to suggestions from its work force on product development and was able to recapture markets once thought lost forever to competitors from Japan. We also heard of numerous smaller firms that have succeeded, through innovation and quality, in exploiting profitable niches around the world.

An increasing number of American firms are now bringing back home the lessons of industrial masters such as W. Edwards Deming and Joseph Juran, who taught Japanese industry long ago when U.S. companies would not listen. Those lessons are deceptively simple. And after hearing from experts for three days, we have collected some basic principles of what makes a firm competitive, the first of which is quality—an emphasis on making the product or service right the first time. Together, all these principles are:

Quality. This does not mean quality merely to specifications but quality that improves constantly, quality that is characterized by constant innovations that create a loyal customer. It means achieving this attitude from top to bottom, from the board room to the factory floor.

Low-cost. This is not instead of quality but as a result of quality. It may seem cheaper to shove as many products or services out as fast as possible, but if quality is ignored, the cost in rework, scrap, supervision, and, most of all, disappointed customers will be more expensive than any business can bear.

Customer-driven. The customer is part of the process. The business exists not merely to satisfy the customers' needs today but to anticipate their needs of tomorrow.

Employee involvement. The successful business no longer sees employees as a *cost* of production but as a *resource* for production. Although job uncertainty will never be eliminated, it must be recognized that long-term commitment of and to workers is at least as important as machinery or technology. Employee involvement in efforts to improve productivity and quality is vital, and they must also be able to share in the gains.

Continuous improvement. This means never being satisfied, not only with the products or services, but with the way the organization makes the goods, distributes, sells, and services them. Innovation is required in all of these activities. It means changing our attitude from America's traditional "If it ain't broke, don't fix it" to "If it ain't perfect, don't leave it." There are a number of American firms taking leadership in implementing these innovations, and there is a critical need to accelerate this process.

We also note that since business firms exist in an environment heavily influenced by government policies, government should be mindful that its policies not frustrate but foster efforts of American business to be globally competitive.

III. The Individual and Society

Education, we believe, is the single most critical element in enhancing the individual's contribution to our society's long-term competitiveness; increasing the educational attainment of all Americans is in the direct self-interest of each American. There is widespread dissatisfaction with our schools at the elementary and secondary levels, and concern for both the quality of U.S. technical education and the very relevance to a modern, globally competitive economy of its graduate curricula in business and management. Therefore, continuously improving education must become a first priority for competitiveness.

We face a particularly acute problem—threatening this and future generations—in failing to ensure that all our students are literate and mathematically able before leaving school. Emerging from that, we have a related problem in equipping our college students for an internationally interdependent world.

We see the need for action on many fronts, with the understanding that some steps will take more than a few years to show results. We must:

—Do a better job of teaching math, science, and language. (There was an intense, balanced, and unresolved debate about also developing communications skill in our common language.)

—Significantly upgrade teacher training, with emphasis on preparing teachers and students to understand and initiate change.

—Encourage innovation and experimentation.

—Correct inadequacies of the education system's response to the needs of the inner cities, where attendance and ability to educate are unresolved problems.

In higher education, training in engineering, science, and

technology must be expanded and improved. Of special relevance to competitiveness is the need to restore the link between engineering education and the production system, between the campus and the factory floor.

In a changing world, our schools of business must adapt their curricula to contemporary conditions and the future challenges of management. Many aspects of existing business school curricula encourage business practices that weaken rather than strengthen the ability of U.S. firms to compete effectively at home and abroad. We must place increased emphasis on teaching students to work in and eventually to manage organizations consistent with the basic requirements for global competitiveness. Business schools must internationalize the entire course of study, including comparative business practices and foreign languages and the analyses of other countries and cultures. We should also renew emphasis on the teaching of production and operations.

Business has taken many initiatives to train and retrain workers and staff in recent years. Those efforts should be strengthened and become more widespread. In addition, government and business must assume greater responsibility for revising and implementing effective training programs.

Related to that, vocational and technical training at the high school level must be reexamined and, wherever necessary, modified and upgraded in light of changing technology and job markets.

Education is a national priority. We recommend that in all matters governing elementary and secondary schools, primary and continuous responsibility must remain at the state and local levels. The federal government, too, has a vital responsibility to assist financially in ways that supplement state and local efforts, especially in our inner city school districts.

In all of our recommendations, we also recognize that the preparation of the individual young person for adulthood and citizenship is a shared responsibility of the family, the schools, and the society as a whole. The schools must focus on and be judged by how well they teach, not by whether they can solve all other problems with which their community weighs them down. Also beyond the schools, we find a widening disparity in standards of living for important segments of society to be increasingly troubling. A society with growing inequality will find it difficult to maintain its competitive place in the world.

On the equally important subject of values, we discern a marked deterioration in traditional values essential to competitiveness. A lack of both individual and institutional leadership has eroded respect for community and nationhood. We conclude that values of integrity, social justice, and moral leadership are not only necessary in themselves, but lead directly to competitive advantage. Our standard of living and our standard of values are inseparable.

In the end, it is not simply companies, or even countries, which compete—it is entire societies. We believe that a society that advances the opportunities of each of its people will best advance the prospects for all of its people.

Participants
The Seventy-fourth American Assembly

HARVEY E. BALE, JR.
International Public Policy
Manager
Hewlett-Packard Company
Washington, D.C.

CLAUDE BARFIELD
Director
Science & Technology Policy
Studies
American Enterprise Institute
for Public Policy Studies
Washington, D.C.

*Discussion Leader
**Rapporteur
†Delivered Formal Address
††Panel Member

††JACK N. BEHRMAN
Luther Hodges Distinguished
Professor
Associate Dean
Graduate School of Business
Administration
University of North
Carolina
Chapel Hill, North Carolina

ELIZABETH L. BEWLEY
Harriman Scholar
Graduate School of
Business
Columbia University
New York, New York

RONALD BLACKWELL
Economist
Amalgamated Clothing &
Textile Workers' Union
New York, New York

DAVID H. BLAKE
Dean
Graduate School of
Management
Rutgers, The State University
of New Jersey
Newark, New Jersey

††MARK A. BLOOMFIELD
President
American Council for Capital
Formation
Washington, D.C.

WILLIAM H. BOWMAN
Founder and Director
Spinnaker Software
Cambridge, Massachusetts

KRISTOPHER J. BROWN
Associate
International Services Institute,
Inc.
Tempe, Arizona

RICHARD V.L. COOPER
Partner
Coopers & Lybrand
Washington, D.C.

†W. EDWARDS DEMING
Washington, D.C.

LLOYD DOBYNS
Freelance Journalist
Raleigh, North Carolina

JOSEPH DUFFEY
Chancellor
University of Massachusetts
Amherst, Massachusetts

JOHN T. EBY
Director
Public Policy Issues
Corporate Strategy Staff
Ford Motor Company
Dearborn, Michigan

**NOEL EPSTEIN
Publisher
*The Washington Post National
Weekly Edition*
Washington, D.C.

GEZA FEKETEKUTY
Counselor to the U.S. Trade
Representative
Office of the U.S. Trade
Representative
Washington, D.C.

**JAMES FLANIGAN
Business Columnist
The Los Angeles Times
Los Angeles, California

RICHARD N. GARDNER
Henry L. Moses Professor of
Law and International
Organization
School of Law
Columbia University
New York, New York

DAVID B. GLEICHER
President
David B. Gleicher Associates,
Inc.
Duxbury, Massachusetts

A. BLANTON GODFREY
Chairman & Chief Executive
Officer
Juran Institute
Wilton, Connecticut

VICTOR GOTBAUM
Special Advisor
District Council 37
AFSCMG
AFL-CIO
New York, New York

††JEFFREY B. HEBIG
Harriman Scholar
Graduate School of Business
Columbia University
New York, New York

MAREK P. HESSEL
Associate Professor of
Management Systems
Graduate School of Business
Administration
Fordham University
New York, New York

TIMOTHY HYLAND
Harriman Scholar
Graduate School of Business
Columbia University
New York, New York

RALPH R. JOHNSON
Deputy Assistant Secretary for
Trade & Commercial Affairs
U.S. Department of State
Washington, D.C.

*PETER T. JONES
Director
Consortium on
Competitiveness and
Cooperation
Graduate School of Business
University of California
Berkeley, California

KENNETH R. KAY
Executive Director
CORETECH
Washington, D.C.

WILLIAM H. KOLBERG
President
National Alliance of Business
Washington, D.C.

ROBERT D. KYLE
Legislative Counsel for
International Trade and
Competitiveness
Office of Senator Max Baucus
Washington, D.C.

RICHARD D. LAMM
O'Connor & Hannan
University of Denver
Denver, Colorado

ROGER E. LEVIEN
Vice President, Corporate
Strategy Office
Xerox Corporation
Stamford, Connecticut

MALCOLM LOVELL, JR.
Distinguished Visiting Professor
George Washington University
Washington, D.C.

ALAN H. MAGAZINE
President
Council on Competitiveness
Washington, D.C.

MARTA MOONEY
Associate Professor
Graduate School of Business
Administration
Fordham University
New York, New York

JAMES P. MOORE, JR.
Principal Deputy Assistant
Secretary for International
Economic Policy
U.S. Department of Commerce
Washington, D.C.

MILTON MORRIS
Director of Research
Joint Center for Political
Studies, Inc.
Washington, D.C.

REGINALD NEWELL
Director of Research
International Association of
Machinists & Aerospace
Workers
Washington, D.C.

KAZUO NOMURA
Counsel
The Boston Consulting Group
New York, New York

EDWARD H. NORTHROP
Chairman
Xicom, Inc.
Tuxedo, New York

JOYCE N. ORSINI
Vice President and Director of
Research
Savings Banks Association of
New York State
New York, New York

JAMES O'TOOLE
Editor
New Management
Graduate School of Business
University of Southern
California
Los Angeles, California

HUGH PATRICK
Robert D. Calkins Professor of
International Business
Director, Center on Japanese
Economy and Business
Graduate School of Business
Columbia University
New York, New York

EDWARD B. POLLAK
President
Olin Hunt Specialty Products
Inc.
West Paterson, New Jersey

KEVIN F.F. QUIGLEY
Legislative Director
Office of Senator John Heinz
Washington, D.C.

THOMAS REDBURN
Economics Writer
The Los Angeles Times
Washington, D.C.

RICHARD R. RIVERS
Partner
Akin, Gump, Strauss, Hauer &
Feld
Washington, D.C.

ROBERT M. ROSENZWEIG
President
Association of American
Universities
Washington, D.C.

HERBERT SALZMAN
Vice Chairman and Partner
Bradford Associates
New York, New York

EDWARD G. SANDERS
President
IPAC, Inc. (International
Planning and Analysis Center)
Washington, D.C.

††HERTA LANDE SEIDMAN
Managing Director
Tradenet Corporation
New York, New York

HARVEY L. SHULMAN
Chairman
Ramsay Fabrics Company
New York, New York

GORDON C. STEWART
Vice President, Public Affairs
American Stock Exchange
New York, New York

JAMES A.F. STONER
Professor
Graduate School of Business
Administration
Fordham University
New York, New York

DAVID H. SWINTON
Dean
School of Business
Jackson State University
Jackson, Mississippi

FRANK SWOBODA
National Correspondent
The Washington Post
Washington, D.C.

†YOSHIHIRO TSURUMI
Professor
Baruch College
City University of New York
New York, New York

JOHN E. ULLMANN
Professor of Management and
Quantitative Methods
Hofstra University
Hempstead, New York

*LOET A. VELMANS
Former Chairman
Hill & Knowlton Inc.
New York, New York

†PAUL A. VOLCKER
Former Chairman
Board of Governors
Federal Reserve System
New York, New York

CHARLES WANKEL
Assistant Professor
Department of Management
University of New Haven
West Haven, Connecticut

*JOHN O. WHITNEY
Professor
Graduate School of Business
Columbia University
New York, New York

B.J. WIDICK
Ann Arbor, Michigan

**JACK WILLOUGHBY
Staff Writer
Forbes
New York, New York

ERNEST J. WILSON III
Associate Professor
Institute of Public Policy
Studies
University of Michigan
Ann Arbor, Michigan

MILAN ZELENY
Professor
Graduate School of Business
Administration
Fordham University
New York, New York

Seventy-fourth Assembly Director

MARTIN K. STARR
Director
Center for Operations
Graduate School of Business
Columbia University
New York, New York

JUDITH L. DUMAS
Program Manager

Press Representatives

KAREN W. ARENSON
Editor
Sunday Business Section
The New York Times
New York, New York

ELISABETTA DI CAGNO
Editor-in-Chief
Hermes
Columbia Business School
Columbia University
New York, New York

ANDREA GABOR
U.S. News & World Report
New York, New York

PHILLIP L. ZWEIG
Senior Editor
Financial World
New York, New York

Further Readings

Abernathy, W. J., K. B. Clark, and A. M. Kantrow, *Industrial Renaissance.* New York: Basic Books, 1983.

Altshuler, A., *The Future of the Automobile.* Cambridge: M.I.T. Press, 1984.

Basche, J., *Eliminating Barriers to International Trade and Investment in Services,* Research Bulletin No. 200. New York: The Conference Board, 1986.

Beckhard, R., and R. T. Harris, *Organizational Transitions: Managing Complex Change.* Reading, MA: Addison-Wesley, 1977.

Bhagwati, J. N., and D. A. Irwin, "The Return of Reciprocitarians— U.S. Trade Policy Today," *The World Economy,* Vol. 10, No. 2. June 1987.

Blanchard, K., and S. Johnson, *The One Minute Manager.* New York: Morrow, 1982.

Blanchard, K., and R. Lorber, *Putting the One Minute Manager to Work.* New York: Morrow, 1984.

Blanchard, K., P. Zigarmi, and D. Zigarmi, *Leadership and the One Minute Manager: Increasing Effectiveness through Situational Leadership.* New York: Morrow, 1985.

Bowles, S. et al., *Beyond the Wasteland.* New York: Basic Books, 1983.

Brander, J., "Export Subsidies and International Market Share Rivalry," *Journal of International Economics,* 1985.

Choate, P., and J. K. Linger, *The High Flex Society*. New York: Knopf, 1986.

Clifford, D. K., Jr., and R. E. Cavanaugh, *The Winning Performance: How America's High-Growth Midsize Companies Succeed*. New York: Bantam Books, 1985.

Cohen, S., and J. Zysman, *Manufacturing Matters: The Myth of the Post-Industrial Society*. New York: Basic Books, 1987.

Cohen, S., *Uneasy Partnership: Competition and Conflict in U.S.-Japanese Trade Relations*. Cambridge: Ballinger Books, 1985.

Crosby, P. B., *Quality Without Tears*. New York: McGraw-Hill, 1984.

Deming, W. E., *Out of the Crisis*. Cambridge: M.I.T. Center for Advanced Engineering Study, 1986.

―――, *Quality, Productivity, and Competitive Position*. Cambridge: M.I.T. Center for Advanced Engineering Study, 1982.

Drucker, P., *Managing in Turbulent Times*. London: Pan Books, 1981.

Dyer, D., M. S. Salter, and A. M. Webber, *Changing Alliances*. Boston: Harvard Business School Press, 1987.

Foster, R., *Innovation*. New York: Summit Books, 1986.

Fuller, F. T., "Eliminating Complexity from Work: Improving Productivity by Enhancing Quality," *National Productivity Review*. Autumn 1985.

Garfield, C., *Peak Performers: The New Heroes of American Business*. New York: Morrow, 1986.

Garvin, D. A., *Managing Quality*. New York: The Free Press, 1987.

Gilbert, K. R., "Machine Tools," in *A History of Technology*, V.4, eds. C. Singer et al. New York: Oxford University Press, 1958.

Goldratt, E. M., and J. Cox, *The Goal: A Process of Ongoing Improvement*, rev. ed. New York: North River Press, 1986.

Halberstam, D., *The Reckoning*. New York: Morrow, 1986.

Hayes, R. H. and S. C. Wheelwright, *Restoring Our Competitive Edge*. New York: John Wiley and Sons, 1984.

Helpman, E., and P. Krugman, *Market Structure and Foreign Trade*. Cambridge: M.I.T. Press, 1985.

Hickel, J. K., *The Chrysler Bailout Bust*. Washington, DC: Heritage Foundation, 1983.

Holden, C., "New Toyota-GM Plant is U.S. Model for Japanese Management," *Science*, Vol. 233. July 18, 1986.

Hong, B. Y., *Inflation Under Cost Pass-Along Management*. New York: Praeger, 1979.

Imai, M., *Kaizen: The Key to Japan's Competitive Success*. New York: Random House Business Division, 1986.

Jacobson, G., and J. Hillkirk, *Xerox, American Samurai*. New York: Mac-Millan Publishing Company, 1986.

Johnson, C., *MITI and the Japanese Miracle*. Palo Alto: Stanford University Press, 1983.

Juran, J. M., *Upper Management and Quality*. Wilton, CT: Juran Institute, 1982.

_____, *Managerial Breakthrough*. New York: McGraw-Hill, 1964.

_____, ed. *Quality Control Handbook*. New York: McGraw-Hill, 1979.

Kantrow, A. M., ed. *Survival Strategies for American Industry*. New York: John Wiley & Sons, 1983.

Krugman, P., ed. *Strategic Trade Policy and the New International Economics*. Cambridge: M.I.T. Press, 1986.

_____, "The U.S. Response to Foreign Industrial Targetting," *Brookings Papers on Economic Activity*, 1985.

Lawrence, R., *Can America Compete?* Washington: Brookings Institution, 1984.

Leontief, W., and F. Duchin, *Automation, the Changing Pattern of U.S. Exports and Imports and Their Implications for Employment*. New York: Institute for Economic Analysis, 1985.

Magaziner, I., and R. Reich, *Minding America's Business*. New York: Vintage Books, 1982.

Mills, P., *Managing Service Industries*. Cambridge: Ballinger, 1986.

Mooney, M., "Process Management Technology," *National Productivity Review*. Autumn 1986.

Morishama, M. *Why Has Japan Succeeded?* New York: Cambridge University Press, 1984.

Piore, M. J., and C. E. Sable, *The Second Industrial Divide*. New York: Basic Books, 1984.

Reich, R. B., *The Next American Frontier*. New York: Times Books, 1983.

Reich, R. B., and J. D. Donahue, *New Deals: The Chrysler Revival and the American System*. New York: Times Books, 1985.

Riddle, D., *Service-Led Growth: The Role of the Service Sector in World Development*. New York: Praeger, 1986.

Schonberger, R. J., *World Class Manufacturing Casebook*. New York: The Free Press, 1987.

Scott, B. R., and G. C. Lodge, *U.S. Competitiveness in the World Economy*. Boston: Harvard Business School Press, 1985.

Segal, S., *Metropolitan College Mental Health Association*, Vol. 6, No. 3. April 1979.

Servan-Schreiber, J. J., *The American Challenge*. New York: Atheneum Publishers, 1968.

Starr, M. K., and N. E. Bloom, "The Performance of Japanese-Owned Firms in America." New York: Columbia University Graduate School of Business, Center for Operations, Feb. 1985.

Starr, M. K., and P. A. Hall, "The Performance of Japanese-Owned Firms in America: 1982–1985." New York: Columbia University Graduate School of Business, Center for Operations, Feb. 1987.

Thurow, L., ed., *The Management Challenge: Japanese Views.* Cambridge: M.I.T. Press, 1985.

———, *The Zero-Sum Solution: Building a World Class American Economy.* New York: Simon and Schuster, 1985.

Ullmann, J. E., ed., *The Improvement of Productivity.* New York: Praeger, 1980.

———, *The Prospects of American Industrial Recovery.* Westport, Ct.: Quorum Books, 1985.

U.S. Congress Joint Economic Committee, "The U.S.Trade Position in High Technology: 1980–1986." Report. 99th Congress, Second Session, October 1986.

Vogel, E., *Comeback.* New York: Simon and Schuster, 1985.

Vogel, E., and G. C. Lodge, eds., *Ideology and National Competitiveness.* Boston: Harvard Business School Press, 1987.

Wadsworth, H. M., K. S. Stephens, and A. B. Godfrey, *Modern Methods for Quality Control and Improvement.* New York: John Wiley & Sons, 1986.

Yamamura, K., ed., *Policy and Trade Issues of the Japanese Economy.* University of Washington Press, 1982.

Yankelovich, D. et al., *Work and Human Values: An International Report on Jobs in the 1980's and 1990's.* New York: Aspen Institute, 1983.

Yates, B., *The Decline and Fall of the American Automobile Industry.* New York: Empire Books, 1983.

Zeleny, M., "Bat'a System of Management: Managerial Excellence Found," *Human Systems Management.* Vol. 7, No. 3, 1987.

———, "Management Support Systems: Towards Integrated Knowledge Management," *Human Systems Management.* Vol. 7, No. 1, 1987.

———, "The Grand Reversal: On the corso and ricorso of human way of life," in *Physics/To Inhabit the Earth,* eds. M. Ceruti and E. Laszlo. Feltrinelli, Milano, 1987.

Zysman, J., and L. Tyson, eds., *American Industry in International Competition.* Ithaca: Cornell University Press, 1984.

Index

italicized page numbers refer to figures and tables

Abegglen, James, 80
Adams, Franklin P., 52
Adams-Russell Electronics,
    286–87
ADC Telecommunications, 287
agricultural implements and
    construction machinery
    companies, 181
aircraft industry, 181
airplane accidents, litigation of,
    17
Amalgamated Clothing and
    Textile Workers Union,
    200
American Business Conference
    (ABC) companies, *see*
    midrange growth
    companies
American Motors, 164
American Stock Exchange
    companies, *see* midrange
    growth companies
Analog Devices, 289
analysis-paralysis, 190
Andersen, Arthur, & Company,
    284

Andrews, Frederick, 198, 199
antitrust laws, 45
anxiety reduction as
    consideration in career
    choice, 46
appropriability, 116
Argentina, 84
assimilation of immigrants,
    37–38
AT&T, 264
Atlantic Monthly, 96
Au Bon Pain, 153–54
Austin, Nancy A., 193, 203
Australia, 22
Automated Data Processing,
    Inc., 156
automobile industry, 67
    Big Three successes in
        1980s, 164–66
    change needed in, 162–63
    Chrysler bailout, 163–64
    collective bargaining system,
        168–69
    exports to Latin America, 181
    import restrictions on foreign
        cars, 163, 175–77, 215